Praise for the *What Do I Teach Readers Tomorrow?* Series

We know of no resource that promotes responsive teaching as well as these books do. Goldberg and Houser liken teaching to improv, and then describe how teachers can learn to be fully in the moment of instructional decision making by focusing on a handful of things. From the detailed lessons to boxes titled "Decide to teach this tomorrow if your students . . ." these authors anticipate the content teachers want and the questions they raise. These thoughtful books *show* teachers how to make children's reading needs central to instructional planning.

—KIM YARIS AND JAN BURKINS
Authors of *Who's Doing the Work?*

I love this series! Goldberg and Houser succeed at something difficult: freeze-framing their intentional decisions about teaching readers in a way that we can all "see"—and then do—in our own classrooms. They provide a decision-making model that helps teachers feel confident in letting their own observations of students' written and spoken responses to text guide them. They distill the ever-present what-do-I-teach-next question into three choices, and these choices all center on furthering students' ways of thinking as they read fiction and nonfiction. Through classroom videos and notebook entries, we learn the authors' intuitive process. They don't just leave us pondering, but scaffold our ability to be responsive teachers by providing lesson ideas that work for every kind of tomorrow—every reading next step. For fiction, they share lessons on character and theme; for nonfiction, on synthesizing information and understanding perspectives. The bonus is this: when we study and reflect on the authors' decision-making process, we enhance and improve our own. These books should become seminal works.

—LAURA ROBB
Author of *Read, Talk, Write*

Making decisions about reading in our classroom is not easy, even though we make hundreds every day. Often, we don't give much thought to *how* we decide what we do, but with these books, we are taken on a guided tour of what it means to make super-intuitive decisions about what our readers need next. Each chapter addresses decisions about key aspects of building a literature-rich environment and a community of readers, including reading notebooks, teaching students how to synthesize ideas, and understanding perspective. The chapters on great nonfiction and fiction texts and on helping readers learn how to select involving books are favorites, as they give me a more focused method upon which to rely. The books are practical, friendly, and chock-full of ideas and lessons that can be readily implemented.

—GRACE WHITE
Supervisor of Curriculum, Wykoff School District, NJ

These books exemplify the intersection of excellent scholarship and practical application for teachers in the field. They beautifully illustrate those essential metacognitive processes in a progression, and this helps teachers see how instructional decisions become instructional moves that translate into high cognitive demand learning experiences for students. This series is an invaluable teaching tool for those who want to implement authentic Balanced Literacy experiences for their students.

—DR. AKIDA KISSANE LONG
Principal, Florence Griffith Joyner Elementary,
Los Angeles Unified School District, CA

Goldberg and Houser offer an insider's view of intentional decision making in action by making us front-row observers of their thinking process. We stand beside them as they *show* us student-centered reading instruction at its best, listening in on book conversations, gazing over their shoulders to analyze writing in reading notebooks. This step-by-step journey yields explanations of *why, what,* and *how* that we can use to plan next lessons for our readers. The *What Do I Teach Readers Tomorrow?* series is a testament to our professional responsibility to keep students as our compass, their right-now needs and wishes as readers as the destination, and engaging books as the vehicle that takes us there.

— DR. MARY HOWARD
Author of *Good to Great Teaching: Focusing on the Literacy Work That Matters*

This series is a must-have for every elementary language arts teacher! Goldberg and Houser have created a comprehensive support for teachers who want to provide their students with rigorous, thinking-centered experiences in reading and writing. Having these books is like having ongoing coaching and guidance from these two outstanding literacy experts at your fingertips.

—JERRY HARRIS
Director, The Cotsen Foundation, The Art of Teaching

I love the we-are-right-there-with-you tone. It's so clear these authors have been there, and remain right in the trenches. And I love the teacher checklists and quizzes—just the right light touch to use in professional development time. But perhaps most of all, I admire that Houser and Goldberg have taken a complex process—daily instructional decision making—and broken it into doable steps for teachers to try. Deciding what each reader in your room is ready for next will never be something a teacher gets good at overnight, but with these outstanding resources, educators are armed with the right questions to ask themselves, a progression of strategies that enhance the readers' relationship with the text, and the theory and research from in and out of the literacy field that will help them build a community of readers.

—JOYCE FRIEDMAN
Demonstration Teacher, UCLA Lab School, Los Angeles, CA

It is rare for me to read a professional book that is based on the authority of classroom practice, that honors teachers as reflective decision makers and meaning makers, that acknowledges the complexity of teaching, that professionalizes teaching, and that extends the capacity of teachers to develop their own conscious competence in ways that honor their unique situations and students. In this series that addresses how to have the most meaningful impact on fiction and nonfiction readers, Goldberg and Houser provide powerful tools for making intentional instructional decisions for themselves and for the good of the current needs of those specific and unique human beings that populate their current classrooms. This is just such a rare set of books and I recommend that every sentient teacher immediately read them! They will help you develop, then transfer, extend, and adapt deep threshold knowledge about teaching. They will help you outgrow yourself, and help your students to outgrow themselves.

—JEFFREY D. WILHELM
Distinguished Professor, Boise State University
Co-Author of *Diving Deep Into Nonfiction*

To all the finish lines we crossed together.

YOUR MOMENT-TO-MOMENT DECISION-MAKING GUIDE

WHAT DO I TEACH READERS TOMORROW?

GRADES 3–8

GRAVITY GOLDBERG
RENEE HOUSER

Foreword by Russell J. Quaglia

fiction

http://resources.corwin.com/GoldbergHouser-Fiction

CL CORWIN LITERACY

CORWIN
A SAGE Publishing Company

FOR INFORMATION:

Corwin

A SAGE Company

2455 Teller Road

Thousand Oaks, California 91320

(800) 233-9936

www.corwin.com

SAGE Publications Ltd.

1 Oliver's Yard

55 City Road

London EC1Y 1SP

United Kingdom

SAGE Publications India Pvt. Ltd.

B 1/I 1 Mohan Cooperative Industrial Area

Mathura Road, New Delhi 110 044

India

SAGE Publications Asia-Pacific Pte. Ltd.

3 Church Street

#10-04 Samsung Hub

Singapore 049483

Senior Program Director and Publisher: Lisa Luedeke

Senior Acquisitions Editor: Wendy Murray

Editorial Development Manager: Julie Nemer

Editorial Assistant: Nicole Shade

Production Editor: Melanie Birdsall

Copy Editor: Melinda Masson

Typesetter: C&M Digitals (P) Ltd.

Proofreader: Sally Jaskold

Indexer: Sheila Bodell

Cover Designer: Rose Storey

Interior Designer: Anupama Krishnan

Marketing Manager: Rebecca Eaton

Copyright © 2017 by Gravity Goldberg and Renee Houser

Heart clipart for Lesson 6 in Chapter 5 courtesy of clipart.com

Printed in the United States of America

ISBN 978-1-5063-5123-0

This book is printed on acid-free paper.

SUSTAINABLE FORESTRY INITIATIVE
Certified Chain of Custody
Promoting Sustainable Forestry
www.sfiprogram.org
SFI-01268
SFI label applies to text stock

17 18 19 20 21 10 9 8 7 6 5 4 3 2 1

CONTENTS

Chapter 5: Decisions About Understanding Characters   152
Teach Readers to Empathize With Others

© Andrew Levine

For great videos, a viewing guide for professional development,
and other resources, visit the companion website at
http://resources.corwin.com/GoldbergHouser-Fiction

LIST OF VIDEOS

Note From the Publisher: The authors have provided video and web content throughout the book that is available to you through QR codes. To read a QR code, you must have a smartphone or tablet with a camera. We recommend that you download a QR code reader app that is made specifically for your phone or tablet brand.

Videos and viewing guide may also be accessed at
http://resources.corwin.com/GoldbergHouser-Fiction

FOREWORD

Adlee epitomizes what it means to be an engaging and effective reading teacher. She does not stand at the front of her classroom during reading instruction. (In fact, there is little standing still at all in Adlee's day.) Rather, she sits with a group of students, engaged in meaningful conversations about reading with them. Other students are in groups spread out around the classroom, simultaneously participating in discussions about their books. Adlee seamlessly weaves in and out of the various groups, listening at times, posing questions at other times, and connecting with students all the time. This is not a unique occurrence; it is the norm for all of her classes.

Adlee is an extremely dedicated, hardworking, and prepared teacher. There is no doubt she enters her classroom with a solid plan about how to proceed with each class. Part of that plan is knowing she will connect with each young person in the room and will need to be ready to adjust her instructional strategies on a moment's notice in order to meet the needs and interests of her students.

As a reading teacher, Adlee is keenly aware of the multitude of mandates placed upon her by the district and state. She also recognizes the importance of having individual goals for the children in her class. She accommodates all of this with an underlying commitment to connecting with her students, letting them know *every day* that each of them matters. Adlee makes an effort to understand her students, their ideas, and their perspectives. This is Adlee's norm—a way of approaching teaching that, if all educators committed to it, would yield astonishing growth in learners.

In *What Do I Teach Readers Tomorrow?* Gravity Goldberg and Renee Houser raise this principle of connecting with students that Adlee exemplifies to a whole new level. When I was first presented with this resource to review, I immediately thought, "Sounds like an interesting book about reading instruction." As I began reading, I quickly learned that the content is far more influential. It contains effective techniques for teaching and learning that may be applied in *every* subject in a way that supports *every* student. This book, and its companion volume, is about valuing student voice in a way that enriches the self-worth of each and every student, meaningfully engages all students in the learning process, and ensures that students understand the purpose in their learning.

While this book will certainly enhance the life of all teachers who teach reading, it will more broadly describe for them the essential components of being a great educator. Gravity and Renee demonstrate that in order to ensure reading is relevant for students, the teacher must provide students with a meaningful and active voice in the learning process. Our research at the Quaglia Institute supports this practice. We have learned that when students have a voice in their learning, they are seven times more likely to be motivated to learn. When students are motivated to learn, their self-worth increases, they are more meaningfully engaged in their learning, and, most importantly, they gain a sense of purpose—they know who they are and how their learning impacts them.

Too many young minds are held hostage by the graphics on a computer screen. Students' imaginations are being presented to them, rather than being developed with them. Fortunately, to the contrary, this book demonstrates that there is nothing more powerful or engaging than children using their own minds, their own imaginations and intellects, and their own interests as they engage with fiction and nonfiction texts. Gravity and Renee show us that when we base instructional decisions on the verbal and written data that emanate from this dynamic and engaging learning environment, meaningful growth in reading and learning ensues. The authors provide ideas, strategies, and guidance for teachers that will allow them to offer new and exciting ways to engage (or re-engage!) learners in reading and writing. They do so by combining incredibly powerful forces that impact student learning: the students' voice, interests, and sense of personal responsibility.

The very best reading instructors connect intuitively with their students. This book helps us cultivate this intuition, and apply it strategically. The authors show us how to communicate, connect, and collaborate with students. This must be an intentional process—one where teachers make a conscious effort to legitimately listen to their students, know them, and bring out the very best in them. This book, including well-documented research and innovative techniques, illustrates how connecting with students and creating an engaging environment relies on collaboration in the classroom. Gravity and Renee challenge us to be the best educators we can be by letting students know they matter and involving them in the learning process. The authors make it clear that in order to move forward effectively, in order to inspire readers, teachers must be driven not by *testing and accountability* outside the classroom, but rather by *trust and responsibility* of students within the classroom.

This resonates with me as an educator and on a personal note as well, as I recently became a grandfather. This new role brings with it a new perspective. As I gaze into my granddaughter's beautiful eyes, I find myself wondering about the future—in particular, her future—quite a bit. I wonder what learning will be like for her. Will she love to learn? Will she enjoy reading? What kind of teachers will she have? Will she be engaged in the classroom? My fingers are crossed that she will have teachers who employ the practices presented in this book. I have already made the typical grandparent promises to my newborn granddaughter—that I will always love her with all of my heart, that I will encourage her to try new things, and that I will always support her. There is one promise I did not anticipate making that I have now added to the list: I will buy this book for every reading teacher she has! Thank you, Gravity and Renee, for making an immediate impact on today's teachers and students . . . with special appreciation from this grandfather.

—**DR. RUSSELL J. QUAGLIA**
Quaglia Institute for School Voice and Aspirations
Portland, Maine

ACKNOWLEDGMENTS

As athletes as well as educators, we truly believe in the power of teams. Each member has a special role and is integral in the process and success. We'd like to thank all of you who are members of our teams for your contributions and support.

Thank you to our students from Edward Everett School and PS 126, where our classrooms were true lab sites. Our students taught us the importance of keeping them at the center of our curriculum and our decision making. Thank you to our colleagues for all of our hallway check-ins, which became the glue that kept us together.

As consultants, we are so grateful for the many teachers who opened their classrooms to us as we rolled up our sleeves and tried out the ideas in this book. A special thanks to the classrooms that hosted our research lessons, video shoots, and photograph sessions: Amy Berfield, Kahlia Benjamin, and Julia Pledl from New Heights Charter School; Lori Yoshizaki from Woodcrest Elementary School; Pam Koutrakos from Hillside School; Gail Cordello and Ronnie Powers from Sicomac School; Anthony DiCarlo, Inas Morsi-Hogans, Annlenore Zalenski, Deirdre Dillon, Laylee Longi, and Nicole Mussolini from Trinity Elementary; Laura Sarsten, Ali Auteri, Alexis Eckert, Diane Mardy, Martha Walsh, Amy Fells, Karin Frassetto, Katie Gwynne, and Katie Kanning from Ho-Ho-Kus School; and Carla Alvarez, Katie McGrath, Nicole Tomasella, Aimee Carroll, Nicole Rodriguez, Courtney Rejent, and Lena Guroian from West Brook School.

Thank you to the amazing team at Corwin Literacy. Wendy Murray, our editor, is the whole package—talented, creative, a visionary, and kind. She shaped our thinking and this book in ways that make it much wiser. Thank you to Lisa Luedeke for supporting our work and believing in us. Thank you to Melanie Birdsall, Julie Nemer, Nicole Shade, and Rebecca Eaton for all your hard work on this book; your help is immeasurable. Judy Wallis, Rosanne Kurstedt, and Nancy Allison offered expertise and feedback throughout the writing process. Thank you to the team who helped create the companion videos in this book: Kevin Carlson, Julie Slattery, Sarah Downing, and Donna Du. We were lucky to have Andrew Levine and Daryl Getman beautifully capture the photographs and connect with kids along the way. Rose Storey's cover and Anupama Krishnan's interior design are in a word: exquisite.

We are extraordinarily lucky to be part of all-star teams at Growing Educators and Gravity Goldberg LLC who are smart and thoughtful and embody the ideas we share in this book. Our colleagues supported this journey both by listening to early ideas and offering feedback and by trying out lessons in several classrooms on both coasts.

My (Renee) team at Growing Educators reminds me of the importance of continually outgrowing our best practices. I'm grateful for the dedication, patience, and courage of my partner, Jessica, who convinced me to move across the country to support teachers in Los Angeles and around the country in their decision-making process. Erin Donelson, who read early versions of this manuscript and gave us insightful ideas for revisions, inspires me through her unwavering optimism, innovative work with educators, and eagerness to say "yes."

I (Gravity) am the luckiest person because my work is complemented by the extraordinary women I get to work with. Julie McAuley is a dedicated powerhouse who is able to organize, collaborate, think many steps ahead, and make even what seems like tedious work a lot of fun. Patty McGee is a deeply passionate educator whose head and heart equally inspire the work we do in schools. Danielle Larsen served as a sounding board and cheerleader, always reminding me what teachers want and need.

Our work is in large part influenced by our mentors, who are numerous. Thank you to Lucy Calkins, Kathleen Tolan, Laurie Pessah, Mary Ehrenworth, Kathy Collins, Ellin Keene, Richard Allington, Carl Anderson, Katherine and Randy Bomer, Dorothy Barnhouse, and Vicki Vinton, who influenced our thinking from near and far away. We'd also like to thank new friends and exceptional educators Mary Howard, Kari Yates, Jan Burkins, and Kim Yaris, who always keep kids at the center of their teaching and writing. Thank you to our Twitter friends and professional learning network who are too numerous to mention by name here, but connect with us about learning, reading, and admiring students.

Much love and gratitude to our parents, who continue to support us both on the field and off. Thank you for driving us hours and hours to watch us play sports, buying all the books we read as kids, and acting as both cheerleaders and role models. We thank you for teaching us the importance of hard work, determination, and the power of long-lasting friendships.

To say we are busy is quite the understatement. While writing this book, we worked full-time, trained and raced in triathlons (Gravity), had a baby (Renee), and even maintained our friendships. We also presented at conferences and traveled the country teaching. None of this would have been possible without a lot of support. John and Brook embody what it means to be true partners. They ordered take-out and cooked dinner too many times to count; they understood when we spent hours glued to our computers at nights and on weekends; they reminded us when we needed to take a break, and listened when we needed someone to assure us we could and should do this. We are so lucky to have you to continuously cheer us on and remind us of the importance of embracing each new day with its challenges and its celebrations.

We met in 2004 as new staff developers at the Teachers College Reading and Writing Project, and our friendship began over a long and lovely drive across the state of Washington. Since then, we have collaborated on presentations, competed in triathlons, soothed broken hearts, and celebrated marriages and babies. In many ways, this book was first conceived on long runs in Central Park in New York City, where we could easily pass the time of a twenty-mile run all the while "writing in the air."

Renee, your strong will, conviction, and confidence are unstoppable and also balanced by your easygoing way and lightness. This combination makes you a wonderful collaborator and friend. All those moments drinking chai lattes, swimming, biking, running and racing, dreaming, and laughing together make me fill up on gratitude. Thank you for believing me whenever I say, "It's just around the corner." We've crossed many milestones together, and this book is another one I am proud to say we did together.

Gravity, you have made the process of writing my first book more enjoyable than I ever could have imagined. Publishing with one of my best friends is a career highlight for me, but I'm even more excited by how our friendship has grown stronger yet through the process. Our work is to help students grow, but through this collaboration you've helped *me* grow both as a writer and as a person; for this I am eternally grateful. I look forward to many more years of asking "Are we there yet?" as we study, race, and write together.

A QUICK-START GUIDE FOR EASY ACCESS

© Andrew Levine

As we set out to write this book, we had one main goal in mind—to help teachers feel confident and intentional in their decision-making process. As former teachers and now literacy consultants, we know firsthand how many decisions a teacher makes in the day. Each part of this book is designed to help you save time and have more of an impact with each choice you make when teaching students to read fiction well. So, here's the "why" of each chapter so you will understand how we decided to frame things as we did, and can more easily dip in and out of sections with speed and ease.

You know how you ask students to look at a novel's cover and make some inferences? Well, the first thing we want you to do is see that we asked the designer to make the visuals fun, because working with readers is fun. From cover to cover, use the visuals to feel energized, like you are a superhero with amazing powers of seeing readers.

Thin-slicing, the book's metaphor. Yep, think about julienning carrots like a master chef does. That's the decision-making speed of a teacher, all right. You'll read more about it starting on page 4. Look for this icon whenever you want to zoom in on when we are especially doing our decision making.

Chapter 1: Each Classroom Moment Is an Instructional Decision. We explain the theory and practice of decision making when it comes to that essential question, "What do I teach readers tomorrow?" This chapter helps us understand why it is essential to get to know our students' thinking well enough to plan our next teaching steps based on what they need. No matter what reading program or model you use, it is never as effective as basing our instruction on the needs of the students in front of us. In this chapter, we explain

- A decision-making process that streamlines planning while maintaining integrity based on the concept of "thin-slicing"
- Common decision-making styles and habits we might want to shift to be our most effective selves
- Why it is essential to let our students be our guides

Chapter 2: Decisions About Book Selection: Characteristics That Matter Most for Teaching Fiction Readers. In this chapter, we show book covers and summaries of fifteen of our current favorite fiction texts. We also explain the characteristics and qualities to look for when choosing fiction texts, and offer examples of lessons you can use them with. This chapter is make or break in the sense that all the work of the later chapters will be far easier if you fill your classrooms with high-quality literature. That one move alone offers up richer teaching possibilities and more ambitious decisions to make, because in essence we are asking our students to get into the minds of the smartest authors to ponder the very content, inferences, and inquiries they have. In this chapter, you will find

- A list of high-quality and engaging fiction texts
- Characteristics to look for in fiction texts
- Lesson ideas that connect to each text

Chapter 3: Decisions About Reading Notebooks: Teach Readers to Develop Thinking About Fiction. OK, you now have all the students' favorites and Newbery and Caldecott winners since 1975 in book bins. *Check* ☑. Your students read them. *Check* ☑. Now, we focus on the first step of the intentional decision-making process. The first step is to get reading notebooks up and running in your classroom, because these dog-eared, backpacking, traveling little books contain probably the richest artifacts of your readers' thinking. We show you how to use reading notebooks as the main "archaeological dig" location for uncovering the findings about readers so you can then make more informed instructional choices. When students maintain their own reading notebooks, they get in the habit of using writing as a tool for thinking more deeply about their fiction texts. We focus on the what, why, and how of using writing to collect, develop, and revisit thinking with others. We include

- Teaching ideas for helping students see the benefits and choose to write about their fiction reading

- Lessons for helping students collect thinking in notebook entries

- Why we can let go of a few common practices that might not be serving us or our students and what we can focus our attention on that does work

Chapter 4: Decisions About Discussion: Teach Readers to Push Their Thinking About Fiction. On to Step 2! In this chapter, we show you the second way to find information for your intentional decision-making process: what students say about their reading and themselves as readers. We show you how to use student conversations about fiction reading as a frequent forum for "listening for the learning." We share how to teach students to use conversations as a way of deepening their understanding. We include

- Key lessons for teaching students how to develop conversations that stay on topic and help with understanding

- What to look for in student conversations

- How to create classroom environments where students are willing and able to have text-based conversations about their thinking

Notice we don't have you running in twenty directions trying to assess your readers, just these two places: reading notebooks and reading conversations.

Chapter 5: Decisions About Understanding Characters: Teach Readers to Empathize With Others. In this chapter and the next, we focus on just two facets of teaching fiction and making instructional decisions about how readers are progressing with them—understanding characters and interpreting themes. Yep, two, not two hundred. Because frankly, we get overwhelmed with hundreds of choices like you do. And more to the point, we believe that virtually every reading skill is naturally embedded in understanding characters and interpreting themes.

Step 3 involves identifying the current types of thinking students are doing, and we've included easy-to-use clipboard notes that show you what to look for. Step 4 occurs when you decide what to teach next from three main options—yes, only three options. We show you how to help students understand characters within and across fiction texts. This section is full of assessment and instructional ideas that will help you get clear on what exactly understanding characters entails so you can teach it to your students. We offer an array of practical tools and resources for quickly looking at students' notebook entries and listening to their conversations so you can thin-slice and name the type of thinking they are using. Then we show you how to quickly decide what to teach next. We teach you how to

- Clearly explain thinking about characters to students with concrete activities and examples

- Show students how to create notebook entries that help them understand characters

- Identify the three types of character thinking in your students' work (Right-Now Thinking, Over-Time Thinking, and Refining Thinking)

- Thin-slice student entries and conversations in order to decide what to teach next

- Recognize the three main teaching choices you can make

- Apply our framework for making quick yet effective instructional decisions

Chapter 6: Decisions About Interpreting Themes: Teach Readers to Discover Life Lessons. This chapter also focuses on Steps 3 and 4 of the intentional decision-making process. We show you how to help students interpret themes. We define what we mean by themes and how our understanding of a book is formed around them. Since this is often a complicated concept to teach students, we offer several key lessons to teach with notebook and conversation examples so you can get started right away with your students. After describing the key lessons, we show you the three most common types of thinking about themes—frames, patterns, and lessons learned—and how to identify what your students are doing. In this chapter, we teach you to

- Define and introduce interpreting themes to students

- Show students notebook entries that can help with interpreting themes

- Identify the three most common ways to think about themes (frames, patterns, and lessons learned) in student entries and conversations
- Apply the thin-slicing and decision-making framework to decide what to teach students next about themes in fiction reading

Chapter 7: Becoming Confident and Intentional Decision Makers. In the final chapter, we offer guidance in becoming confident in your teaching decisions. We help you self-assess what your current decision-making model is and help you choose what to do next.

In the **Appendices**, we offer some of the resources listed throughout the book in an easy-to-reference place. Some of these resources include

- Lists of our favorite fiction texts
- Clipboard notes you can use with your students

RESOURCES AT THE READY

We included a few recurring features in this book to help with your decision-making process. These features include:

- Teacher Tip Boxes: to get a bit more guidance
- Intentional Moment and Your Turn Boxes: to help you reflect on your current practices
- Self-Reflection Questionnaires: to help you build on strengths and set goals
- Clipboard Notes: assessment tools you can use right away
- Video Link Boxes: to step into the classrooms with us and see the lessons in action

While you can absolutely read this book in the order in which we wrote it, you can also focus on one part at a time. If you know right away you want to work on your students' conversations, you can begin with Chapter 4; or if you know your students need more help with characters, you can begin with Chapter 5. No matter where you start, we hope you leave each reading session with an answer to the question "What do I teach tomorrow?" We have so many examples of student notebook entries and conversations, and more lessons that just did not fit in this book, so we invite you to visit our website gravityandrenee .com to find updated and expanded resources.

© Andrew Levine

Each Classroom Moment Is an Instructional Decision

1

"THE POWER OF KNOWING, IN THAT FIRST TWO SECONDS, IS NOT A GIFT GIVEN MAGICALLY TO A FORTUNATE FEW. IT IS AN ABILITY THAT WE CAN ALL CULTIVATE FOR OURSELVES."

(Malcolm Gladwell)

Justin paused at the front of the classroom and observed his students reading. Each student held a fiction book and was opening the pages and beginning to read. Some students had sticky notes out and were marking places, some students were rereading key parts, and some were revisiting the ideas they had already written down in notebook entries about the characters. Like most classrooms, some of Justin's students were on grade level, many were a few levels behind, and a handful were well above or well below grade-level expectations. Students were reading series books, fantasy, and realistic fiction picture books, and some were reading the same books as their partners. While all of these students made choices about what and how to read, Justin took about ten seconds to scan his classroom, and then he stood up and began making decisions about what to teach each student next. There was no script or magic manual that told Justin whom to focus on in his daily small group work and conferences or what to teach them next. In each moment, Justin paused very briefly, took in the information he was gathering about his students, and made an intentional decision.

Like you, Justin makes literally hundreds of important decisions every day that flow from his mind into some kind of instructional action, fast and fluid as quicksilver. And if you are reading this book, we can probably infer you are wondering, "Am I making the *right* decisions?"

Malcolm Gladwell wrote the following description about improvisation in his best-selling book *Blink: The Power of Thinking Without Thinking*, but when we read it, we thought he was writing about being a teacher: "It involves people making very sophisticated decisions on the spur of the moment, without the benefit of any kind of script or plot. That's what makes it so compelling and—to be frank—terrifying" (Gladwell, 2005, p. 113). While Gladwell popularized the term, *thin-slicing* was first cited in 1993 by Nalini Ambady and Robert Rosenthal in the *Journal of Personality and Social Psychology*, so it's a concept with some legs.

As teachers, we are asked to make sophisticated decisions in every moment of the day. Larry Ferlazzo (2014) cited researchers Hilda Borko and Richard Shavelson's (1990) findings that teachers make 0.7 decisions per minute during interactive teaching. Other research estimates as many as 2,000 decisions a day, a great number of them unplanned exchanges with students. The upshot for readers? We wrote this book because we want you to make those intuitive, improvisational exchanges count, and rooted in a foundation of what you think most supports readers. First, let's turn to what Gladwell found in his research about these moment-to-moment choices and what we as teachers can learn from improvisers in the various fields he studied. We'll learn more about how Justin was able to make such quick and powerful decisions about each of his students.

Acting Without a Script: Embracing Our Role as Improvisers

Teaching isn't compared to Second City comedy very often, but think about it—it's actually very similar. Improv comedy shows such as *Whose Line Is It Anyway?* on TV and numerous other live performances involve a group of actors working together without a script. There are no lines to memorize or stage directions to get your cues. It works like this: The first actor says a line, and then another actor has to decide who will go next and what to do and say. Since the parts are not preplanned, the actor has to react in the moment to what was just said and done, and help build the scene from there. Likewise, a student asks the teacher, "What does this word mean?" and she must decide what to say right there and then. Comedians are not the only improvisers, though; so are athletes. Many professions rely on a degree of improvisation. Think about the way in which emergency room surgeons must make a split-second decision as to how to treat a patient. Consider fine artists, who are not given directions for how to create their pieces of art, yet render meaningful images. And finally, picture the way a basketball

© Andrew Levine

Actively listening to our readers' and studying their writing about reading is a sophisticated form of improv. This book teaches you how to develop this learned intuition.

player navigates the court, making split-second decisions. According to an article in *Slate* magazine, "Improvisational comedy workshops have become a staple at business schools, and in the corporate world in general," and entrepreneurs are calling improvisation a "must-have" skill (Stevenson, 2014). As teachers, we are improvisers who act without a script, based on our moment-to-moment ideas about our students. We know you opened this book hungry to learn whether there is a good order to teach fiction structures and features, or how to plan the next day's lesson based on today's—but hang in there with this side-door entrance of ours, because it's a powerful way to rethink your teaching self so that you can more easily redirect your fiction teaching.

How Spontaneity Is Born

What Gladwell found in his research about what makes improvisers so successful has to do with breaking down some of our common beliefs about our decision-making practices. One of his claims is that spontaneity is not random, like many of us believe, but instead involves training, rules, and rehearsal. Those basketball players who look so fluid and spontaneous on the court can only do so because "everyone first engages in hours of highly repetitive and structured practice" (Gladwell, 2005, p. 114). Jazz musicians share similar experiences about their process. While the actual performance is improvised, it only works when each musician has first spent time learning to play well, keeps a consistent cadence, and listens attentively to others. Then the group of musicians can predict and quickly react to what each other will play to create an entertaining musical experience. One foundation for improv seems to be time spent practicing so you can make the rapid decisions in the moment. When Justin was able to walk over to a student, sit down, and decide what to teach next, he made it look easy, but it was based on countless hours of looking at student work, studying his own reading practices, and listening closely to what and how students discussed their books.

Another element of becoming a successful improviser is to know the "rules" of your field. In improv comedy, there is one main rule—always say "yes" and follow the lead of the person who came before you. In teaching students to read fiction, we have some rules or tenets we suggest you use when you are making instructional decisions, too; for example, only teach one skill at a time so students are not overwhelmed and have time to focus.

What all of these improvisers have in common is a focus on answering the question, "What next?" without the luxury of time to sit back and ponder the answer. "What chord should I play next?" "What move should I use to get around the opposing team's player next?" "What skill should I teach this reader next?" Luckily, we don't necessarily need as much time as we think we do when making our decisions.

© Daryl Getman, DAG Photography

When we listen to what students say about their thinking and really look closely, we can thin-slice and make quick yet powerful decisions about what to teach based on the readers right in front of us.

How "Thin-Slicing" Helps Us Make Decisions

As we said, one of the most memorable parts of Gladwell's 2005 book *Blink* is the concept of thin-slicing, which "refers to the ability of our unconscious to find patterns in situations and behavior based on a very narrow slice of experience" (p. 23). Thin-slicing entails getting a very small amount of information and being able to use it to make a sound judgment and decision. Thin-slicing stems from what cognitive psychologist Gerd Gigerenzer calls being "fast and frugal" with our decision making. The part of our brains that can use small amounts of information to draw a conclusion is called the adaptive unconscious. It involves not overthinking and using our conscious effort to analyze information, but also using our "gut instincts" and our intuition about something in those first few seconds of being presented with information. Gladwell explains that adaptive unconscious is not the same as Sigmund Freud's view of the unconscious and instead is seen as "a kind of giant computer that quickly and quietly processes a lot of the data we need in order to keep functioning as human beings" (p. 11).

Some examples of thin-slicing include art experts being able to know a forgery in the first few seconds of examination, tennis coaches being able to know whether the player will fault on a serve in the half a second before it is even struck, and a salesperson reading someone's emotions and future decisions based on three seconds of observation (Gladwell, 2005). It is knowing something in just a few seconds—in the blink of an eye—without consciously stopping to consider all the facts. We are all able to use thin-slicing as a decision-making tool once we have sufficient experience in that area. Gladwell (2005) explains that "when we leap to a decision or have a hunch, our unconscious is . . . sifting through the situation in front of us, throwing out all that is irrelevant while we zero in on what really matters" (p. 34). We need lots of experiences to use thin-slicing, and we need to develop our filter to know what to sift out and what to zero in on.

Think about the last time a student came back from the library and you had only five seconds to observe him, and somehow you "just knew" he had trouble and was disappointed he did not get the book he really wanted. We often "just know" something about our students based on thin slices of information. Renowned authors and researchers John Hattie and Gregory Yates (2014) explain thin-slicing as "the system that enables you to look at complex situations, to perceive them as an expert, and to respond with speed, accuracy, and nuanced sensitivity. . . . As a professional teacher, you have the ability to look at a classroom situation and read it quickly, within microseconds" (p. 297). They go on to explain how this ability allows teachers to rely on feedback cues from students to inform what strategy they teach next.

There are many examples we likely have all experienced with thin-slicing as reading teachers. You graze a review on Goodreads.com of a new young adult novel; twenty-four hours later, you hand the book to the student you had in mind; and forty-eight hours later, he comes to you, literally with tears in his eyes—it was that good. Or you are in the midst of a whole class read aloud, and students seem quiet, and their comments are way off. You know to change gears, so you say to them, "You know what? Let's try something different," and you start reading aloud another book, and the energy in the room comes alive. In each of these everyday teaching decisions, you are thin-slicing.

Answering the "What Next?" Question

In teaching, we often need to teach a grade level for at least a full year—those 180 days—to feel we've developed an instinct for the grade's needs. This book will help expedite the process. In this book, we help you distill the most vital aspects of teaching fiction so you can begin to thin-slice the work of your students and make very intentional moment-to-moment decisions about what to teach next.

Highly effective decision makers are not those who process the most information or spend the most time deliberating, but those who have perfected the art of thin-slicing, filtering the very few factors that matter from an overwhelming number of variables (Gladwell, 2005). When the two of us were developing the concept for this book, *Blink* was in our mind's eye, because clearly, teachers in a room with twenty to thirty students each day are engaged in high-volume, high-impact decision making. We asked ourselves, "So just how *do* the most expert teachers of reading make decisions, both ahead of teaching and in the heat of the learning moment? How can we slow down this thin-slicing process so we truly understand it, and can in turn share it with teachers—and with you, in this book?" There is such a temptation for the "quick fix." If only we could just hand you a universal chart of one hundred common fiction teachable moments, and you could pick and choose, but no matter how many ideas we could offer, they are not geared for *your students*.

You can flip and reflip through a five-hundred-page teacher's guide or scope and sequence, and the answer that is best for your students, right now, won't be in the fine print. Even with all the pressures on teachers from above and outside school, teachers recognize that they have to be empowered to be decision makers who choose what their particular students need next. If a lesson does not go well, then what? If a lesson does go well, then what? It is this "Then what?" question that this book seeks to answer. How do we decide where to go next with students? The short answer is we build upon what they are already doing by extending or adding to what the reader tends to do. The long answer is what this book teaches.

Do More With Less: Building on What a Reader Tends to Do

Let's get back to *Blink*, and how people who are effective decision makers filter information from a vast amount of variables. Gladwell (2005) explains that we tend to think we need lots of information to make a decision, but in fact, "you need to know very little to find an underlying signature of a complex phenomenon" (p. 136). Reading fiction is one of those complex phenomena. For both the short and the long answer of what to teach tomorrow, the key move is to filter out the dozens of strategies, moves, alluring scopes and sequences, groupings, and teacher modules and develop that intuitive sense of what the reader is most ready to build on. And while that something is going to be largely organic to you and your students, in this book we share what we think is a wonderfully small set of practices that we've found yield the richest windows into what to teach next. That's why you will see we intensely focus on the art of understanding characters and themes in later chapters, which we will explain in more detail later.

The Four Steps in Intentional Decision Making

While every decision we make as reading teachers is unique, the parts of our process follow a few predictable steps, and as you will see, they all involve a focus on the *thinking* involved in reading, rather than a focus on neat and tidy character traits or literary techniques like metaphor and flashback, which, while valuable, can lead us astray. These steps will allow you to thin-slice reading decisions.

STEPS IN THE DECISION-MAKING PROCESS

1. Look at the notebook entries and name what the reader can already do.

2. Listen to conversations and name what the readers can already do.

3. Identify the type of thinking each reader is mostly doing.

4. Decide what type of thinking to teach next.

By looking, listening, identifying, and then choosing, we are being more intentional in what we decide to teach next. When we use this four-step process, we can thin-slice and make moment-to-moment decisions about what to teach next.

Fisher, Frey, and Hattie's book, *Visible Learning for Literacy* (2016), describes a "three-phase model" for literacy instruction. The three phases include **surface learning, deep learning,** and **transfer.** Surface learning is the essential first step when learning something new and includes exposure and developing a more basic understanding. Fisher and colleagues argue that surface learning tends to be criticized for not being rigorous enough, but in order to develop depth or transfer, we first need to develop surface understanding. Deep learning involves taking action, thinking metacognitively, and consolidating ideas. Transfer involves choosing when and how to use information in a new situation from where it was previously learned. The three instructional choices explained in this book align with each of these three phases, and in Chapters 5 and 6, we show you how to assess which of these three choices is right for your students. Another way to consider the "What do I teach tomorrow?" question is by thinking about which phase of learning each student is in. The following chart shows the alignment between the *Visible Learning for Literacy* phases and the *What Do I Teach Readers Tomorrow?* instructional choices.

THE "THREE-PHASE MODEL" FROM *VISIBLE LEARNING FOR LITERACY* (2016)	OUR THREE INSTRUCTIONAL CHOICES (2017)	TEACHING AND LEARNING EXAMPLES
	Description: The teacher decides on a learning intention based on what the student(s) need next.	
Surface	Name and reinforce a type of thinking.	• Show students how to begin to see patterns in what characters choose. • Introduce students to the concept of themes.
Deep	Show a different type of thinking.	• Share a guiding question that will help students remain attuned to purpose. • Show students how to revisit a notebook entry and write more about an original idea.
Transfer	Coach readers to apply a currently used type of thinking in other sections or books.	• Show students how to use a strategy in a new text. • Notice when students choose to apply thinking from one text to another.

Intentional Teaching: Decision Making With Students at the Center

In their book *Teacher Voice: Amplifying Success* (2016), Russ Quaglia and Lisa Lande explain why teacher voice is so important: "When teachers have a voice, they are three times more likely to value setting goals and to work hard to reach those goals. When teachers have a voice in decision making, they are four times more likely to believe they can make a difference" (p. 2). Intentional teaching cannot happen if teachers do not feel their voices and insights matter.

Take a look at the chart that follows and notice the differences between teachers viewed as curriculum implementers and intentional decision makers. We can clearly see that being an intentional decision maker puts the emphasis on the students who are in your classroom every day.

TEACHERS AS CURRICULUM IMPLEMENTERS	TEACHERS AS INTENTIONAL DECISION MAKERS
Look first to a manual or guide for what to teach next	Look first to students for what to teach next
Make classroom decisions guided by those who are distant and removed from the students	Make classroom decisions based on the happenings of the classroom and those who work within it
Put their trust in "experts" who may have never met their students	Put their trust in themselves, their colleagues, and their students
Complete tasks and meet mandates	Study students and embody curiosity

There are several possible reasons why we as teachers might feel more like implementers than intentional decision makers, some of which are out of our hands. Some of these reasons are based on district mandates or leadership choices, but many are based on our own style of decision making. But, there are many ways we can reconsider our focus and work to keep our particular students at the center of the discussion.

In her book *Good to Great Teaching*, Mary Howard (2012) highlights the work of teachers who are intentional decision makers, explaining the two main characteristics that make teachers not just good, but great: "First they create full days of reading, writing, and talking with substance valued over 'stuff.' Second, they believe that success is the right of every learner and guarantee that right as they acknowledge and celebrate whatever their students may bring to the literacy table" (p. 68). In other words, being an intentional decision maker makes us great teachers. And by responding to what students "bring to the table," we become responsive teachers; we intake rather than merely implement curriculum; this is a really critical distinction.

INTENTIONAL MOMENT

What types of decisions do you end up focusing on during the day, the week, the unit?

When do you feel like the teacher as "implementer," and when do you feel like the teacher as "decision maker"? How does each feel, and what impact does it have on your teaching?

WHAT TYPE OF DECISION MAKER ARE YOU?

Check all that apply.

When I make reading instructional decisions, I tend to

☐ Look at my curriculum and see what is suggested next

☐ Turn to a teacher manual or guide

☐ Look back at notes about my students and look at patterns for what they need next

☐ Examine students' work and think about what they are doing that I can build upon

After making reading instructional decisions, I tend to feel

☐ Anxious and worried. *Will this really help?*

☐ Like I am second-guessing myself and in need of some colleague support

☐ Confident my students are getting just what they need next

☐ Exhausted from all the time it took to decide what students need next

The part of my reading instructional decision-making process that works for me is . . .

If I could change one thing about my decision-making process, it would be . . .

One goal I have for my decision-making process is . . .

In the next section, we reflect on how some of these decision-making styles might be limiting our choices and moving us away from being intentional with our students' needs front and center.

Decision-Making Styles

Before we can get to the specific ways of guiding fiction readers day by day, let's examine three common decision-making styles we see in ourselves, and in teachers with whom we work. It is helpful to first look at where we are and then consider where we want to go next. Admittedly, these styles are broad-sweep generalizations, but we think they are instructive.

The Forager

One common decision-making style is the forager, where we tirelessly figure out the what-to-teach-tomorrow question by finding resources on our shelves or online that seem to suit. We may confer with other teachers, read professional books, go on Pinterest, and so on, but the point is, in a sense, this decision-making style means outsourcing our own expertise, not necessarily believing in our ability to know what the next best move is for our students.

One example is a fifth-grade teacher, Barbara, who was told the class needed to participate in book clubs, and she was not sure where to start. She read other teachers' ideas online, was handed a packet of literary element graphic organizers, and then spent hours of her own time making an intricate plan. Once she actually began teaching the lessons she planned out, she realized many of her students had big gaps of missing strategies, and many did not now how to have conversations about fiction books. She assumed they would know how to form ideas and back them up with supporting details, and how to write about their thinking. But they did not know how, and thus Barbara was left having to research again, spend many more hours of her time planning, and restart her teaching. She felt burnt out just a week into this unit of study.

There are limitations to the forager style. The amount of work this style requires is really unsustainable, and all the effort put in doesn't necessarily match specific students in the class. Penny Kittle often says in her workshops, "All the lesson topics you ever need are sitting right in front of you. Your students." We can keep this in mind the next time we believe we need to forage online. Embrace your role as an intentional decision maker instead. Let your students be the guide.

The Online Shopper

For those of us who like online shopping, we might like looking at what is new at our favorite online stores and then placing the order. "I have not tried this dress on, but it is on sale, and I think it will go well with the shoes I bought last week." Many stores market to us by suggesting what we might like to buy next, based on our past purchases. As teachers, our decisions might be based on a menu not unlike the drop-down or scrolling screens of online stores. This decision-making style looks like one day's lesson on figuring out complex vocabulary and the next day's lesson on using section headings.

Many of us online shopper types organize our teaching around a menu of reading strategies. We know these strategies are part of a reader's process, but we do not necessarily consider how they work together to help a reader make meaning. Many of our students can perform a strategy "on demand" for us, but when we dig a bit deeper to see how the strategy helps the reader, we often realize it doesn't. Peter Johnston once explained it to Gravity as the difference between teaching strategies and teaching students to *be strategic*—knowing when, how, and why we would choose a strategy. This is just like when we order a pair of shoes and a dress and we like them both, but we really haven't considered if they actually go together or if we have any events coming up to wear them to.

When we use the online shopper style of decision making, we are ordering off a menu of options, and there are a few reasons this might not be working for your students:

Reason 1: Students cannot find a place to apply the strategy.

Reason 2: Students do not use strategies that were previously taught.

Reason 3: Students already "did it" and "are done" with that strategy.

Reason 4: Students feel they must prove they used a strategy (often with worksheets).

Teaching from a menu of strategies can lead students away from making meaning and deeply understanding their books. But, this does not mean we do not teach strategies at all. We teach strategies connected to a larger intention and show students when and why they would choose to use them in an effort to better understand their books—we teach them to be strategic. Dorothy Barnhouse and Vicki Vinton (2012) explain a similar concern: "We feared that insight and understanding risked becoming little more than incidental by-products of wholesale strategy practice, not the explicitly intended goal for every child in the room" (p. 25). Like Barnhouse and Vinton and all the teachers we work with, we want more than strategy practice; we want understanding. Instead of making decisions like online shoppers off a menu, we can begin to look to our students and what they show us they need next.

Autopilot

A third decision-making style is the autopilot that occurs when we do what we have always done and are creatures of habit. When we teach in the same ways day after day, it can become a habit. Habits are not choices, and by nature we tend to lack awareness of what we are doing when we are involved in them. As a result, we become stagnant and forget about the other dimensions and possibilities that exist. Autopilot style means delivering reading minilessons in the same order year after year or checking reading logs so quickly that all we are seeing is book titles and numbers.

For many of the teachers we work with, one major habit involves drawing from the same small pool of strategies we know well and teaching the strategies at the same time of year or over and over again. One teacher, Anne, explained that she always starts the year with an overview of retelling and summarizing, and she has a binder of the ten lessons she teaches. When we discussed this with her and asked why, she thought for a moment and said, "Well, it is what I know. How else would I begin?" The start of the year for this teacher was a cue that began the habit loop. She then chose her routine (binder of lessons) and began teaching until she got the reward (finishing the ten lessons and seeing some students be able to retell and summarize). The autopilot style, as we see with Anne, leaves a teacher going through the paces of delivery of instruction, but the habit loop still leaves a teacher asking, "What do I teach tomorrow?"

Once we know we have choices to make and we do not need to redo our habit loop over and over, we can begin to become intentional decision makers. If you approach your planning and teaching as choice making, you can break out of the autopilot style and habits.

Three Common Teaching Habits

Having spent many hours looking at our teaching habits and the habits of our colleagues, and asking other teachers to reflect and share, there seem to be three main types of habits we fall into that can hinder our ability to create a strong, dynamic trajectory of learning. That is, they literally slow the pace of student learning, lessen the impact of our instruction, and no doubt keep us and our students from feeling energized by the content. These habits include re-teaching habits, telling habits, and rushing habits. Each has its own cues, routines, rewards, and unfortunately some consequences we likely don't want to reinforce.

Chart of Common Teaching Habits

RE-TEACHING HABIT	TELLING HABIT	RUSHING HABIT
The Cue: The teacher sees students struggle or seem confused directly after a lesson.	*The Cue:* The teacher sees students needing more direction and help or not using a possibly helpful strategy.	*The Cue:* The teacher feels overwhelmed with so many students to work with and so much to "cover."
The Routine: The teacher begins to reteach the lesson to a small group or one-on-one in the same way he taught it the first time.	*The Routine:* The teacher tells students the steps of what to do or gives an assignment rather than modeling how and why she is using the strategy as a reader.	*The Routine:* The teacher picks the first thing he notices a student needs and teaches that without considering what the student would benefit most from learning.
The Reward: Students begin to use the strategy with the teacher's coaching, and the teacher feels a bit more at ease that they at least attempted what he taught.	*The Reward:* The teacher feels like she did her job by telling students what to do. The teacher might feel satisfaction when checking off the box with that day's standard or lesson objective.	*The Reward:* The teacher is able to meet with many students and feel satisfaction that he can check off many students' names on his conferring notes.
Why this habit might not be helpful: • Teachers rob themselves of the opportunity to choose a varied strategy to teach that may match individual readers best. • Students learn that struggle is not OK, and the teacher will swoop in and help them if they encounter it. This creates a fixed mindset and dependency.	*Why this habit might not be helpful:* • Students need to see the strategies being used in action with a clear purpose for why they would use them. Without this, they might be confused about how or why they would do this. • The teacher ends up having to reteach (see column to the left) and wasting time because students did not understand what was told to them.	*Why this habit might not be helpful:* • The students learn something that might not be that important in that moment or might not match what they really need next. • The teacher often ends up correcting instead of modeling and teaching. Rather than being intentional, the teacher is focused on being time efficient.

Re-teaching. When we find ourselves teaching a whole class lesson and then sitting one-on-one or in small groups with students and teaching what we just taught again, we might be stuck in a re-teaching habit. We think of this habit as the "let's try this again and again and again" routine. We notice this habit tends to create dependency in students because they learn to expect we will re-teach everything in a small group for them, and they may begin to tune out the whole class lesson. Look for this habit's cue in your classroom. For many, it begins when they see a few students struggle after a lesson, and the struggle sends the message to begin the routine of re-teaching.

Telling. Another habit we might find ourselves in is the telling habit, which we think of as the "do as I say, not as I do" routine. When this happens, we end up telling students what to do but not actually picking up our own books and notebooks and modeling what we are doing. This might seem like teaching, but telling is really not a form of instruction that "sticks." We might end up in this habit because we have not had the time to plan our own demonstration or we feel the need to direct students' moves as they have struggled with independence in the past. This often leads to confusion on the part of students and wasted time because we end up back in the re-teaching habit when they are struggling without the modeling.

Rushing. A third habit is rushing. We think of this as the "I will teach the first thing I notice" routine. This often looks like correcting students with the first challenge they encounter. For example, if we are reading with a student who gets stuck on a complex and topic-specific vocabulary term, we might end up teaching that right away instead of waiting to see if something else comes up that might be more important to teach in this moment. When we rush our teaching, it is often unclear and unfocused, and doesn't necessarily lead to lasting learning.

The key to breaking all of these habit loops is to look closely at our students, get to know them as readers, and make choices based on what they show us they need next. The "What next?" question from teachers that inspired this book might really mean, "Now that we are able to make reading instructional decisions, we want a framework to help us get clearer on our intention and narrow down these choices. We want more than a menu or list." Best-selling author of *Rising Strong* (2015) and researcher Brene Brown explains, "New information won't transform our lives if it simply lands at our feet" (p. 53). Handing teachers volumes of data and information that "land at their feet" is not transformative in the teaching process without knowing how to make intentional decisions with specific students in mind. The following chart shows common experiences with different decision-making models and how we end up feeling with each. In the remainder of this book, we help you feel more clear, focused, and driven when making instructional decisions.

DECISIONS BASED OFF A MENU	DECISIONS BASED OFF AN INTENTION
May feel like a game of "pin the tail on the donkey"	May feel like being an elite athlete
May make us feel	May make us feel
• Disoriented	• Clear
• Dizzy	• Focused
• Lost	• Driven
Success is achieved more by chance and luck than by strategy.	Success is mostly driven by being strategic and working toward goals.

INTENTIONAL MOMENT

Look at your reading instructional habits for fiction readers and consider

- What is my purpose for this (lesson, form, text choice, etc.)?
- Have I exposed students to different kinds of fictional texts?
- Is this helpful for most of my students? How do I know? How do I assess its impact?
- Does the time this takes match its level of importance?
- What would happen if I made a different choice?
- Does it create energy in me and fiction readers, or does it seem neutral?
- Does it get to the heart of what I intend for my students to appreciate about fiction?

Let Students Be Your Guide

One of the things getting in the way of reading progress in this country is that our assessment and instruction don't recognize how profoundly idiosyncratic the experience of reading is. Not only is the process of reading idiosyncratic, but as an extension, what we take away from any reading experience is as well. When we read, we all have what seems like authentic and natural ways of responding, paying attention, and thinking about a text. And of course there is research on cognition that offers us a steady schema of reading, with metacognitive strategies, but think about it: Do you remember all these things being explicitly taught

© Daryl Getman, DAG Photography

When we let students guide the conversations about their books, they also guide us in the decision-making process.

in school? Or is the truth more an elixir of school instruction and reading on your own at home, in college, and beyond?

Know Students Well. Cognitive psychologist Benjamin Bergen, author of *Louder Than Words* (2012), studies how our bodies process language and make meaning. He explains that since "meaning is based on experience with the world . . . then it may vary from individual to individual" (p. 16). It is a process that has been proven to be both dynamic and constructive. Our previous experiences impact how we construct meaning. This is no longer a theory of learning language but a principle studied with brain imaging in multiple research experiments. We know that every student reads and makes meaning in slightly different ways. Hattie's (2012) research found that knowing students well has a huge impact on learning. Fisher and Frey (2009) explain that knowing what students bring with them to reading and what they do or do not do as they read is the "missing piece of the comprehension puzzle" (p. 1).

Unpack Intentions. There is always an intention in mind as we read, but we are not always aware of this intention. Consider David, a fourth grader, who read in the same way every day, no matter the text. He would open up his chapter book and begin reading for the plot, focusing on figuring out what would happen next. David asked himself the question, "What is going to happen next?" over and over. It was not until David began talking to his reading partner, Katie, about her books that he realized there were other elements to pay attention to. Katie was a reader who tended to think about why the character was making the choices he did. She tended to ask herself the question, "Why did the character do that?" As

Katie and David had discussions about their books, they began to realize there were multiple ways to read and that their ways of reading were guided by what they were exposed to. They might not have consciously chosen their reading intentions, but they still had them. A large part of our job as decision makers is to uncover a student's reading intentions and use them to choose what to teach next. In this book, we offer many moves and lessons to help you do just that.

Fisher and colleagues (2016) explain two essentials for making literacy learning more visible for students and teachers. First, we must ensure that students know *what* they are learning, *why* they are learning it, and *how* they will know when they have learned it. Second, teachers must constantly reflect on their impact on student learning and not just what was taught. In other words, "the teacher does not hold any instructional strategy in higher esteem than his or her students' learning" (Fisher et al., 2016, p. 41).

Exposure. While conversations with other readers offer exposure to other ways of reading, these are more subtle learning opportunities. We can also teach explicitly and strategically and be less subtle. There are accidental exposures that we have to other ways of reading, such as in student-to-student conversations. These are hugely beneficial. We can also use intentional exposures to other ways of reading by deciding to show students other intentions they can try on. In his 2009 article "The Right to Think," history teacher Baynard Woods explains that "thinking is not automatic, inspired or random, but learned" (p. 16). Therefore, he argues we must demonstrate how we go about thinking about texts so students learn that "meaning is made" and not magic.

ACCIDENTAL EXPOSURE	INTENTIONAL EXPOSURE
Talking to a friend or partner	Modeling by a teacher or peer
Showing or telling what we do but not necessarily naming or choosing it	Choosing when and why to show it

The Power of Why. Simon Sinek's TED Talk and book, *Start With Why* (2009), explain why some organizations have a much larger impact than others. His concept includes what he calls the "Golden Circle," which is a series of three circles that look like a bull's-eye and three words written within each circle. The center circle states the word *why*, and the two outer circles state *how* and *what* in that order. Sinek's theory is that when organizations start with why or with intention, they are so clear on their mission and vision that every other decision about how and what connects back to the center. As instructional decision makers, we can start every day with the simple question "Why?" before teaching a lesson.

explore this idea

Lesson Planning. John Hattie (2012) uses Winne and Hadwin's (2008) four-stage model of student motivation as an important part of lesson planning. The first stage, called "see the gap," is when students see a gap between what they currently know and what they *intend* to learn. This is why students need to have a clear intention in mind before they make choices as readers. The second step entails "goal setting" with the intention in mind. The third stage is called "strategies" and includes the student choosing strategies that will help with the goal. The final stage is called "close the gap" and is focused on self-reflection on the extent to which the intention has been met. Hattie claims that knowing the stage of motivation helps teachers have a clearer and more visible look at why students are making choices and how they are approaching the learning experience. Sinek is right. Lesson planning is all about the *why*.

check this out

Flexibility. One of the many key findings from Fisher, Frey, and Hattie's research (2016) is how ineffective fixed ability grouping is. Instead, what this research says does work is flexible grouping where the instruction matches the needs of the students. Some of the most impactful practices teachers can take on include providing formative evaluation (effect size of 0.9), microteaching (effect size of 0.88), and spaced versus massed practice (effect size of 0.71). All three of these practices require us to be flexible and in the moment with our teaching decisions so we can decide what to teach tomorrow based on where our students are today.

GETTING STARTED: AN ACTION PLAN

As you reflect on the ways you make instructional decisions about what to teach next, consider the three styles. Do you tend to be a forager, an online shopper, or on autopilot? Know that many of our decision-making styles are just habits that we all fall into and have the power to break. In the following list, we offer a few ideas for getting started with more intentional decision making that keeps your students at the center.

BECOMING INTENTIONAL DECISION MAKERS

☐ Embrace the improviser role. Go find a local improv group or watch an episode of *Whose Line Is It Anyway?* online.

☐ Notice where and when you already use thin-slicing in your life. With your children? While cooking? While playing a sport?

☐ Pay more attention to your intuition and the feelings of knowing something without all the facts. How does it feel in your body?

☐ Take the **Self-Reflection Questionnaire** on page 10. What patterns do you notice? Use the habit chart on page 14 to guide your reflection.

To read a QR code, you must have a smartphone or tablet with a camera. We recommend that you download a QR code reader app that is made specifically for your phone or tablet brand.

Videos and viewing guide may also be accessed at
http://resources.corwin.com/GoldbergHouser-Fiction

 Reflecting on Teacher Decision-Making Practices: The Goal

Video 1.1

 Teacher Decision Making: A Team Meeting

Video 1.2

 Teacher Decision Making: What to Do Next

Video 1.3

Decisions About Book Selection

2

"THERE ARE STORIES WE HEAR THAT WE REMEMBER FOREVER. THERE ARE STORIES WE TELL OURSELVES THAT WE KNOW ARE NOT TRUE. THERE ARE STORIES WE WISH WE DID NOT REMEMBER. THERE ARE STORIES THAT BRING US CLOSER TO OTHERS AND STORIES THAT DRIVE US APART. IS THERE ANY GREATER HUMAN INVENTION THAN THE ALL-POWERFUL STORY?"

(Katie Cunningham)

Classroom communities are built when we gather around texts that are engaging, interesting, and perhaps even challenging as we test our current beliefs with new ideas. "The best classroom management plan is a well-matched book." Those were the words my principal used to encourage me in my first days of teaching. She was right. We love to read books aloud to students, sharing why we love them and how we read them. Author and educator Judy Wallis recommends, "Never teach reading without a text in your hands," and we completely agree.

In this chapter, we present a short list of our current fiction favorites. It's important to keep in mind that this is not a list of texts you *must* have to teach fiction to students in your classrooms. This is because we don't teach books; rather, we teach students. Essentially, we look at books as the vehicle that drives our teaching. This means we *use* books to teach students. Therefore, the books that we present here are excellent to add to your teaching library, but it's also likely that these qualities can be found in your current list of favorite books you use to teach fiction. Burkins and Yaris (2016) suggest, "Make it your mission to find excellent, highly engaging texts that communicate substantive ideas and give students a lot to think about. The book is everything" (p. 50).

One of the partner questions to "What do I teach tomorrow?" is the "What text do I use to teach this?" question. Teachers often wonder if there is a magic list of books that will help them be as effective as possible, and the answer is yes and no. While there is not one set of books that will work for every class or teaching focus, there are qualities we look for when deciding what to read aloud. While this chapter focuses on some of our favorite fiction texts, we are using these texts to illustrate how we go about making choices. Our aim in this chapter is to show you how you can go about choosing some favorites to use with your students. Feel free to use the books we highlight in this chapter and also to go find and curate your own fiction list. Of course, we also chose these texts because they pair with the lessons we highlight in the rest of the book. We also compiled a list of the texts we feature in this chapter along with a list of pairings in Appendix B.

Making a Choice to Read Aloud a Fiction Text

This chapter is organized according to four types of fiction books—picture books, short story collections, novels, and graphic novels. We believe that all grade-level spans can benefit from using a variety of types of texts. The way you use each type of book will inevitably look different in elementary classrooms than it does in middle school classrooms, but we have found all types impact student engagement and thinking. For example, in middle school, we might introduce a complex concept using a picture book or wordless book and then transition to a short story or novel. In elementary school, the picture book or wordless book could be the teaching text throughout the entire unit of study. We encourage you to consider which type of text you tend to rely on in your current teaching practices and imagine creating a balance of several types of texts you use to teach.

Thin-Slicing Fiction Texts

As we created the write-up for each book, we thought of it like a Zagat guide, but instead of rating restaurants, we rated books. Our rating system, described below, is another form of thin-slicing. When we pick up a book, read a few pages, and flip through looking closely, we have a few criteria in mind. When we thin-slice texts, we consider

- **Appeal:** How appealing and interesting will this book be for students? Do the characters, settings, and plot draw young readers in?

- **Opportunities to Develop Empathy:** Does the text offer characters and conflicts that allow readers to connect with characters and put themselves in the shoes of others? Does this book help readers develop their social imagination and a deep empathy toward others?

- **Representation:** Does this book represent the experiences of the students in my class? Can my students find positive examples and models of characters who are like them? Does this book portray characters who are very different from my students in ways that challenge stereotypes?

- **Accessibility to Readers:** Do the text structure and author's choices consider the ways readers make meaning? How does the text move within time (sequential, flash forward and back, etc.)? Are there enough supports (visuals, backstory, explanations, etc.) so that students can understand the characters and themes?

Even if we love a book, we also consider how we can use it with our class of students. Besides our rating system, we consider how it matches our instructional focus. While all fiction texts require us to study character and understand

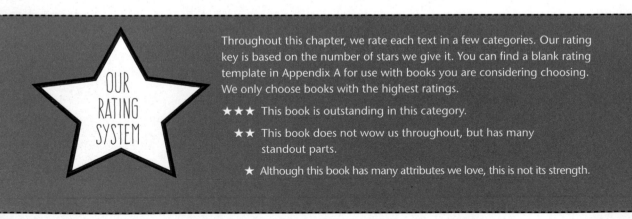

Throughout this chapter, we rate each text in a few categories. Our rating key is based on the number of stars we give it. You can find a blank rating template in Appendix A for use with books you are considering choosing. We only choose books with the highest ratings.

★★★ This book is outstanding in this category.

★★ This book does not wow us throughout, but has many standout parts.

★ Although this book has many attributes we love, this is not its strength.

themes, each text has unique attributes. When explaining why we chose each text, we also include a connection to using it to teach character and theme. While our goal is always to enjoy and learn from a fiction read aloud experience, we also want to be able to refer back to the text over and over again in our lessons to model and give examples.

Picture Books and Wordless Books

Picture books and wordless books are great for all students. These books are an excellent choice for readers who will benefit from learning a new concept in a book with less printed text so that they can focus on accessing meaning through images. Students at various stages of English language acquisition and proficiency benefit from instruction immersed in the verbal and visual language experiences that these books offer. Students who are developing their reading and are considered below grade level or hard to engage in complex texts benefit from teaching with highly engaging picture books and wordless books.

You can teach complex concepts such as mood, tone, symbolism, and foreshadowing through illustrations before teaching them using longer complex texts. Picture books often serve as a catalyst for engaging conversations because readers are synthesizing both the images and the words. In wordless books, readers are creating the story based on a close study of the images. We're teaching students to interpret the images to create the world of the characters and their stories. To help students in their interpretation process, we rely on storytelling strategies to help lift the story from the page. Our friend and storyteller Antonio Sacre reminds us that one of the many benefits to asking readers to storytell the text is that storytelling can make sense and find meaning where there might not seem to be any. When students learn to tell a story based on pictures, they develop a sense of how stories tend to go. Characters are introduced, struggle and face conflict, then take some steps and usually find some lesson and bigger learning. If we want students to think deeply about characters and themes in more complex books like novels, it can help to first develop these skills using wordless books.

In this chapter, you will learn

- What to look for when deciding which fiction texts to use when teaching
- For each fiction text highlighted, we include
  - Title, author, and text type
  - Why we chose this book
  - Rating
  - Excerpts from inside the text with callouts that show sample opportunities to *think aloud* our process of understanding texts during read aloud instruction
- Ideas for creating paired texts and text sets

  In Appendix B, we created a chart of books you might want to pair with these read alouds. We chose them because they align with the content or they have similar features and themes. Some of these paired texts could be used as additional read alouds or for independent reading by students.
- Tips for reading fiction aloud

  The chapter ends with a list of key suggestions for engaging students when reading fiction aloud.

CHARACTERISTICS	OUR RATING
Appeal	★ ★ ★
Opportunities to Develop Empathy	★ ★ ★
Representation	★ ★
Accessibility to Readers	★ ★ ★

Teaching Text: *Journey* by Aaron Becker

This is one of our choices because ... this wordless picture book appeals to readers of all ages with its gorgeous illustrations and imaginative world. It might seem quite unusual to recommend a wordless picture book to upper elementary and middle school classrooms, but there is so much to be learned and enjoyed from reading the pictures and discussing our thinking about the characters and themes. In this book, a young girl's family has no time to play with her, so she draws a door on her bedroom wall, and fantastically it leads to a magical world. You can see by the image on the cover she goes on adventures and ends up connecting with people that her real-world life was not offering. When you "read" this book aloud, it requires you to show each page's pictures and tell the story from the pictures. Students can discuss their own interpretations of what the character is saying and feeling because the story is not written out for them by the author. Enjoy using your imagination and inviting students to do the same.

Thinking about setting changes and how they impact characters: *The setting has changed. She moved from her room to a forest. I wonder what will happen in this new place?*

CHARACTERISTICS	OUR RATING
Appeal	★ ★ ★
Opportunities to Develop Empathy	★ ★ ★
Representation	★ ★ ★
Accessibility to Readers	★ ★ ★

Teaching Text: *Naked Mole Rat Gets Dressed*
Written and Illustrated by Mo Willems

This is one of our choices because ... we can appreciate a mole rat with great style and an even better wardrobe. Mo Willems's cover illustration says it all: This story is going to be three parts silly and one part wise. The spotlight on the naked mole rat hints of a theme about daring to be different. Here we meet Wilbur, an unassuming mole rat who likes to get dressed despite his fellow naked mole rats. It doesn't seem to bother Wilbur; check him out on the cover searching through his closet for his favorite pair of khakis and long-sleeved button-down shirt. Wilbur's attention to his wardrobe stirs up tension with a few mole rats who bring Wilbur's clothing-wearing habits to the wise Grand-pah who is challenged to consider ideas he's never had to think about in the past. *Why not?* The future is bright for Wilbur and the entire mole rat community. This picture book is excellent for all ages of students due to its supportive structure. Readers learn to empathize with Wilbur and study his quirks. In this short text, there are many opportunities to think about themes around relevant topics such as fitting in, individuality, and the role of government in our communities.

But he had no idea
what to wear.

In the end, Wilbur decided to play it safe.

Thinking about character identity: *This part makes me think about how important clothing is to Wilbur's identity. I'm wondering how he will handle the challenge his community members have brought to his identity.*

by MAC BARNETT   ILLUSTRATED BY JON KLASSEN

CHARACTERISTICS	OUR RATING
Appeal	★★★
Opportunities to Develop Empathy	★★★
Representation	★★
Accessibility to Readers	★★★

Teaching Text: *Extra Yarn*
Written by Mac Barnett and
Illustrated by Jon Klassen

This is one of our choices because ... it's a simple story that reminds us of the powerful idea that we can make a positive impact in our communities. Jon Klassen's cover design, with the title crafted out of yarn, a young girl knitting away, and creatures perched here and there, hints at a colorful plot. We meet young Annabelle who discovers a magical box of yarn. She knits herself a sweater and soon discovers that she has a lot of extra yarn. So Annabelle knits for the entire community until an archduke from a faraway land has something different in mind. Combined with the strategically illustrated pages by Klassen, this well-crafted story is one that will ignite class conversations about the impact each person can make and how to share your unique gifts with others.

Things began to change
in that little town.

Author's craft helps us interpret themes: *Hmm, both the illustrations and the words on this page show us change is happening. The town is different—brighter—and the people are different—happy. This makes me think the author wants us to think about changing on the outside and inside.*

BOOK LOOK

Teaching Text: *Let's Go, Hugo!*
Written and Illustrated
by Angela Dominguez

This is one of our choices because... (cue the *Rocky* soundtrack—"gettin' strong now!") it's about overcoming fears, and we all have them! In this story, we meet Hugo, a bird living in Paris who is afraid to fly. Hugo decides to live on the ground where he is perfectly content until he meets another bird who wants to go on adventures with him around the city. Hugo has to confront his fear and confess to his new friend that he needs help. Dominguez's cover illustration is so charming, and invites readers to notice the expression of anxiety on the bird's face and that dapper scarf that is also a bit of a security blanket. Readers of all ages will love this protagonist! Reading *Let's Go, Hugo!* gives readers a chance to fully understand a story by synthesizing both the images and the text. It's also a great text for teaching students that books often have more than one theme.

CHARACTERISTICS	OUR RATING
Appeal	★★★
Opportunities to Develop Empathy	★★★
Representation	★★★
Accessibility to Readers	★★★

Short Story Collections

Short story collections are underutilized teaching powerhouses and a boon to the classroom library. A benefit of reading short stories is the payoff of finishing the story quickly. For readers who are developing the executive function parts of their brain (the parts that see how everything fits together), they feel a sense of accomplishment when completing an entire story in a short amount of time. Readers building their stamina often make gains when reading short stories because they are able to follow the characters through the entire plot of several stories in the amount of time it might ordinarily take them to finish one longer novel.

Collections written by an individual author, such as *First French Kiss and Other Traumas* by Adam Bagdasarian (2003), have benefits similar to those of reading a book series; for example, you get to follow the same characters across the various short stories, and you become familiar with the author's craft and style. As readers, we build a relationship with the characters as they venture through various journeys. Other collections of short stories are about a topic or subject, and each one is written by various authors. For example, *13: Thirteen Stories That Capture the Agony and Ecstasy of Being Thirteen* collected by James Howe (2006) and *Baseball in April* by Gary Soto (1990) both contain stories about the exciting challenges of adolescence. In Howe's collection, the stories are written by several authors, and therefore we meet new characters in each story. In Soto's collection, the stories are all written by Soto; however, each short story introduces us to new characters with new journeys. In these collections, readers have the opportunity to experience a variety of authors and their craft, which adds diversity to their reading plans. These options of reading selections help readers to identify the kinds of stories they like to read.

Teachers often select one short story from a collection to read aloud to the class as an introduction to a genre or concept. Many students gravitate to the other stories that have not been read aloud in the same collection because they now have interest and some experience to draw upon. You'll notice an increase in student engagement and stamina when you incorporate short stories into your teaching texts and into the independent reading plans of students.

Teaching Text: *Days With Frog and Toad* by Arnold Lobel

This is one of our choices because ... it's timeless! The collections of Frog and Toad have a *Seinfeld*-esque quality—everything in life can be connected to them. The stories of Frog and Toad are episodic in every book; therefore, they serve as a collection of supportive short stories. These stories support a close study of characters and character relationships, and there is a predictable pattern in the story structure. Almost all stories begin at either Frog's or Toad's house before the characters venture on a journey. Their adventures are very relatable to our everyday lives of reading, riding bikes, and having picnics in the park. In the end, after a simple problem–solution plot, the themes and lessons of the stories are often revealed through either Frog or Toad declaring it to the other, or Lobel concludes the story with a hint of bigger themes and ideas.

For readers who are ready to study texts with more complexity, we find that teaching complex ideas in simple texts such as *Days With Frog and Toad* provides a strong and successful scaffold. For example, students studying symbolism will have no problem decoding and understanding the simple plot line of a typical Frog and Toad story; however, when readers choose to frame texts (see more in Chapter 6), they might interpret a story such as "Alone" by studying its symbolic elements such as the island representing individuality being important to serving all friendships. Regardless of the knowledge base of students when they kick off their study of fiction texts, we highly recommend adding the Frog and Toad series to both your teaching texts and your students' independent reading repertoire.

CHARACTERISTICS	OUR RATING
Appeal	★★★
Opportunities to Develop Empathy	★★★
Representation	★★★
Accessibility to Readers	★★★

A turtle swam by.

Toad climbed on the turtle's back.

"Turtle," said Toad,

"carry me to the island.

Frog is there.

He wants to be alone."

58

"If Frog wants to be alone,"

said the turtle,

"why don't you leave him alone?"

"Maybe you are right," said Toad.

"Maybe Frog does not

want to see me.

Maybe he does not want me

to be his friend anymore."

"Yes, maybe," said the turtle

as he swam to the island.

59

CHARACTERISTICS	OUR RATING
Appeal	★★
Opportunities to Develop Empathy	★★★
Representation	★★
Accessibility to Readers	★★★

Teaching Text: *Houndsley and Catina* by James Howe

This is one of our choices because ... we can relate to the quirky friendship between the two characters, Houndsley and Catina. James Howe is a beloved author who knows how to tell stories that are easily understandable and relatable for students who are ready for chapter books but not quite ready for full-fledged novels just yet. The cover art, with its soft blues and greens and two friends encircled in that canopy of trees, is the perfect setup for a story about the safety net of friendship. This book provides a bridge from picture books to novels, and its short length and supportive illustrations help readers understand character development. Even though the text is not too advanced, the themes apply to students from across the grade levels. Since this book is the first in a series, it is helpful to read this first book aloud to students. Many students may end up reading the rest of the books in the series on their own. In this first book, Houndsley has to decide what to do when his friend Catina writes a seventy-four-chapter memoir and wants feedback on it. You can even make connections to writing and how to give feedback to peers.

"Yes," Catina said. "First I will find something I like to do. Then I will do it and do it and do it until I am very good at it. And then I might be famous."

"I know something you are good at already," said Houndsley, "although you will never be famous for it."

"What?"

"Being my friend."

Catina began to purr. "Being your friend is better than being famous," she said.

35

BOOK LOOK

Teaching Text: *First French Kiss and Other Traumas* by Adam Bagdasarian

This is one of our choices because ... we can look back at all these rite-of-passage growing pains with a sigh of relief and say, "Glad I'll never go through that again!" *First French Kiss and Other Traumas* by Adam Bagdasarian is a page turner. Your students will not likely admit it, but they'll empathize with the characters in each new story as they learn more about Adam and his adolescent dramas. The title and cover image are spot-on in their appeal to tweens and young teens, who yearn for grown-up experience but want to retreat, too! The lipstick red makes "and other traumas" get noticed, and signals to readers these stories will have a dose of humor, too. Some of the themes and examples in this book are more geared toward mature readers, so make sure to read them ahead of time and consider whether this book is appropriate for your class.

CHARACTERISTICS	OUR RATING
Appeal	★ ★ ★
Opportunities to Develop Empathy	★ ★ ★
Representation	★ ★ ★
Accessibility to Readers	★ ★

Thinking about character: *This is interesting. Adam appears to be calm, cool, and collected on the outside and nervous on the inside. I wonder if this is a pattern with Adam.*

"I hear you want to fight me," he said.

"That's right," I said.

"I'll meet you after school."

"I'll be there," I said. Then he walked away, and I discovered two interesting things about myself. The first was that the idea of fighting terrified me, and the second was that in moments of extreme fear my body produced ice-cold sweat.

Someone said something to me, and I smiled and nodded. Someone said something else to me, and I smiled and nodded at that too. Perhaps they were giving me advice.

Novels

Novels are part of our teaching text sets because we believe in the benefit of building long-term relationships with characters in books we read (which is not a bad practice in life either). By reading novels, we are teaching students to develop their literacy stamina. As texts evolve in their complexity and sophistication, readers develop in their sophistication. Readers will gain stamina for staying with a text longer, and they'll also encounter the need for ambiguity stamina. What we mean by ambiguity is the notion that true understanding comes together in the *end* of the text in more sophisticated novels. In other words, readers suspend complete understanding as they journey alongside characters because they know the author has created a plot that will twist and turn with many opportunities to interpret themes from studying the complexity of characters along the way. Sheridan Blau (2003) in his article "Performative Literacy: The Habits of Mind of Highly Literate Readers" identifies seven traits associated with competent readers. One of the traits is "the willingness to suspend closure—to entertain problems rather than avoid them." Blau goes on to say these readers are willing to embrace the disorientation of not seeing clearly, of being temporarily lost as a way to probe and ask questions rather than rush to find an answer. Due to the longer length of chapter books, we have plenty of time to vacillate in our thinking and develop this habit of mind.

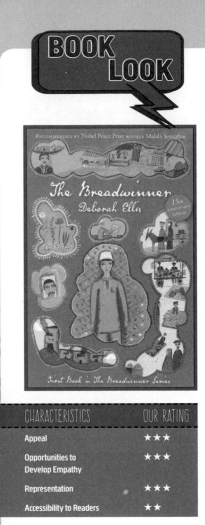

Teaching Text: *The Breadwinner*
by Deborah Ellis

This is one of our choices because ... anytime we have the opportunity to learn about powerful women in different cultures, we're in! Award-winning author Deborah Ellis traveled to Afghanistan before she wrote this trilogy in order to accurately represent the characters. Even though it is a fiction story, it is based on true events. The novel takes place during a time when the Taliban took over and forced the people living in Kabul to live under very strict and harsh laws such as not letting women and girls go to work or school. In this book, the main character, Parvana, a young girl, is forced to take care of her family after her father is taken away. Here's the twist: Parvana, you can see on the cover, chooses to dress in disguise as a boy so that she can get work and earn an income to support her family. Even though the family goes through so many challenges, this book teaches valuable lessons about family, responsibility, and doing whatever it takes to survive.

CHARACTERISTICS	OUR RATING
Appeal	★★★
Opportunities to Develop Empathy	★★★
Representation	★★★
Accessibility to Readers	★★

Thinking about themes: *Wow! This scene is powerful. I can picture the father telling his daughters the story of Malali. He wants his daughters to understand the strength of Afghan women.*

"Suddenly a tiny girl, younger than Nooria, burst out from one of the village houses. She ran to the front of the battle and turned to face the Afghan troops. She ripped the veil off her head, and with the hot sun streaming down on her face and her bare head, she called the troops.

"'We can win this battle!' she cried. 'Don't give up hope! Pick yourselves up! Let's go!' Waving her veil in the air like a battle flag, she led the troops into a final rush at the British. The British had no chance. The Afghans won the battle.

"The lesson here, my daughters," he looked from one to the other, "is that Afghanistan has always been the home of the bravest women in the world. You are all brave women. You are all inheritors of the courage of Malali."

Teaching Text: *Pax*
Written by Sara Pennypacker and Illustrated by Jon Klassen

This is one of our choices because . . . in this novel we meet a young boy, Peter, who rescued a fox and has kept him as his pet for several years. Pax is Peter's best friend and has been there for him through all the challenges of Peter's life. After Peter's mom's death, his father joins the military and forces Peter to return Pax to the wild. The rest of the book takes us on the journeys of both Pax and Peter as they seek to unite with one another. This novel sucks you in and pulls on your heartstrings from the start. Jon Klassen's illustrations are infrequent but powerful. The cover illustration is one readers further appreciate after they have read the novel, because Pax looks so wistful as he gazes at the town. Before reading, ask students, "Is this fox going toward something, or reflecting on what's behind?" Because some of the chapters are written from different characters' perspectives, it offers readers opportunities to really understand characters, their relationships, conflicts, and the themes we can interpret from them.

CHARACTERISTICS	OUR RATING
Appeal	★★★
Opportunities to Develop Empathy	★★★
Representation	★★★
Accessibility to Readers	★★★

Peter recognized that kind of concentration—sometimes his eyes would actually go dry because he forgot to blink, so focused was he on every move of every player—and knew it paid off. Like the kid in the red T-shirt below him, Peter owned his territory on a ball field. He loved that territory right down to the cut-grass, dry-dust smell of it. But what he loved more was the fence behind it. The fence that told him exactly what was his responsibility and what wasn't. A ball fell inside that fence, he'd better field it. A ball soared over it, and it wasn't his to worry about anymore. Nice and clear.

Peter often wished that responsibility had such bright tall fences around it off the ball field, too.

Thinking about themes: *Peter's description of the fence is interesting. I think it means more than literally a fence. I think he's wishing for life in general to be more defined, like a fence defines the field.*

Teaching Text: *Rules* by Cynthia Lord

This is one of our choices because ... we get the chance to meet David and his sister Catherine who in some ways have an average brother and sister relationship and in other ways are faced with real differences.

In this book, the sister, Catherine, has created a list of "rules" for her younger brother David to follow because David has autism. Her rules are an attempt to maintain her perception of a *normal* life. The story takes an interesting turn when she meets Jason at the clinic where David receives weekly therapy. Jason has physical disabilities that require him to communicate through a special icon system on his wheelchair. This new friendship forces Catherine to redefine and reflect about her sense of "normal," and be ready—it may challenge you to do the same. The cover design is one to linger on and discuss—it is deceptively simple, with the bossy rubber duck blaring rules at the submissive goldfish—but there is something about the downward tilt of the duck's underside that speaks to one of the book's themes that in life there are no clear-cut borders.

CHARACTERISTICS	OUR RATING
Appeal	★ ★ ★
Opportunities to Develop Empathy	★ ★ ★
Representation	★ ★ ★
Accessibility to Readers	★ ★ ★

Thinking about character: *Whoa! This scene just got intense. I think Catherine's drawing is innocent; however, Jason's mom and Jason see it differently. I wonder what this might mean about their relationship.*

Hair's my favorite thing to draw, but I only rough it in. Otherwise, I may not have time to finish before Jason's speech therapist comes out to get him.

"What?" Jason's mother asks.

I'll draw his eyes downcast, looking at his book. That way they'll be mostly lids. And it won't matter that I don't know what color they are.

"Girl don't? What girl?"

Everything falls quiet. I glance up.

Mrs. Morehouse is staring at me. "Are you drawing my son?"

My pencil freezes midstroke.

"Just because he can't talk," she says, "don't assume he doesn't mind."

Everyone looks at me. My fingers move over my sketchbook, finding the corner. "I'm sorry," I whisper, turning the page. It takes all my strength, every ounce, not to cry.

"A drink?" I hear Mrs. Morehouse say. "All right. Wait here."

Mom reaches over, but I scoot down the couch, out of reach.

Teaching Text: *The Tiger Rising*
by Kate DiCamillo

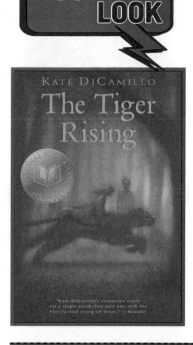

This is one of our choices because ... it's a classic. Kate DiCamillo's writing lures us into the story while we navigate an unexpected friendship between newcomers in town, Rob Horton and Sistine Bailey, who both contend with multiple layers of loss. When we read *The Tiger Rising*, the text calls on us to study the relationships between characters, setting, and events of the plot as they twist and turn and reveal ideas about Rob, Sistine, and our own lives. *The Tiger Rising* gives us the chance to reflect on trust, honesty, friendship, and redemption. The cover illustration is dreamlike and evocative, signaling that this is a story draped with themes; the gauzy light makes us think of the Spanish moss in Florida where the novel is set. And there is Sistine and the tiger, coming into the life of a boy who is "standing still" with grief.

CHARACTERISTICS	OUR RATING
Appeal	★★★
Opportunities to Develop Empathy	★★★
Representation	★★★
Accessibility to Readers	★★

Willie May opened her eyes and looked over the top of her glasses at Rob's legs.

"Mmmm," she said after a minute. "How long you had that?"

"About six months," said Rob.

"I can tell you how to cure that," said Willie May, pointing with her cigarette at his legs. "I can tell you right now. Don't need to go to no doctor."

"Huh?" said Rob. He stopped chewing his gum and held his breath. What if Willie May healed him and then he had to go back to school?

"Sadness," said Willie May, closing her eyes and nodding her head. "You keeping all that sadness down low, in your legs. You not letting it get up to your heart, where it belongs. You got to let that sadness rise on up."

"Oh," said Rob. He let his breath out. He was relieved. Willie May was wrong. She couldn't cure him.

"The principal thinks it's contagious," he said.

"Man ain't got no sense," Willie May said.

"He's got lots of certificates," Rob offered. "They're all framed and hung up on his wall."

> **Thinking about themes:** *Willie May is wise. At first it seems as though she is talking about the rash on Rob's legs, but I think she's really talking about Rob allowing himself to grieve his mom's death. Sometimes when we suppress emotions, it delays our healing process.*

BOOK LOOK

Teaching Text: *Out of My Mind*
by Sharon Draper

This is one of our choices because . . . it takes us into the world of a young girl with cerebral palsy who has a photographic memory, and yet because she cannot speak, no one knows just how smart she is. Talk about a fish out of water—we feel outraged for her when her teachers bore her with babyish activities, and we cheer for her when she gets a device that helps her communicate. Wouldn't you be out of your mind? Melody in fact is *in* her mind; she has an incredibly sharp mind. The novel sheds a light on a disability that many students have little knowledge of, and at the same time the themes and conflicts are relatable to all students—fitting in, making friends, and building self-confidence. This book offers opportunities to develop ideas about multiple characters and to interpret many life lessons. Students can compare how Melody, the main character, has such vastly different experiences in the different settings of home, her neighbor's house, and school. This book will open up discussions about disability and acceptance and pushes against stereotypes of students who are nonverbal. The spare, iconic cover art communicates Melody's wish to escape the confines of other people's typecasting of her—and her vulnerability. Readers might enjoy comparing this cover with that of *Rules* before and after they have read these books.

CHARACTERISTICS	OUR RATING
Appeal	★★★
Opportunities to Develop Empathy	★★★
Representation	★★★
Accessibility to Readers	★★

> **Thinking about character:** *In this scene, we learn about Melody through her thoughts. I can't imagine what it's like to understand and not be able to speak!*

From the time I was really little—maybe just a few months old—words were like sweet, liquid gifts, and I drank them like lemonade. I could almost taste them. They made my jumbled thoughts and feelings have substance. My parents have always blanketed me with conversation. They chattered and babbled. They verbalized and vocalized. My father sang to me. My mother whispered her strength into my ear.

Every word my parents spoke to me or about me I absorbed and kept and remembered. All of them.

I have no idea how I untangled the complicated process of words and thought, but it happened quickly and naturally. By the time I was two, all my memories had words, and all my words had meanings.

But only in my head.

I have never spoken one single word. I am almost eleven years old.

Teaching Text: *Milkweed* by Jerry Spinelli

This is one of our choices because . . . it takes place during the Holocaust in Warsaw, Poland, and follows a young boy who is orphaned and forced to take care of himself. With many tears and cheers, we follow him as he meets friends, loses friends, and learns how to steal to get food, sneak into abandoned shelters, and navigate his city as the Nazis take over. This book is unlike many other children's novels that take place during World War II in that the main character begins wanting to be a Nazi, is ignorant to what is really happening in the world, and suffers a major loss of innocence as he later realizes he would never want to be a Nazi. His story of survival offers so much in terms of interpreting character relationships and themes. While this book might be a bit complex for younger students, its themes and Spinelli's writing style make it compelling for upper elementary and middle school students. The cover illustration sets a tone of fevered horror: You don't know quite what's going on, but it smacks of both youth and violence and humans in a state of siege. The tunnel seems not a place to hide but a symbol of a society's downward spiral.

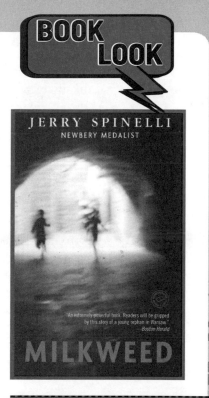

CHARACTERISTICS	OUR RATING
Appeal	★★★
Opportunities to Develop Empathy	★★★
Representation	★★★
Accessibility to Readers	★★

How to handle ambiguity at the start of a text: *Wait a minute! I am a bit confused. Let me figure out what I do know and what questions I have. Who is this narrator, and where is he or she?*

Memory

I am running.

That's the first thing I remember. Running. I carry something, my arm curled around it, hugging it to my chest. Bread, of course. Someone is chasing me. "Stop! Thief!" I run. People. Shoulders. Shoes. "Stop! Thief!"

Sometimes it is a dream. Sometimes it is a memory in the middle of the day as I stir iced tea or wait for soup to heat. I never see who is chasing and calling me. I never stop long enough to eat the bread. When I awaken from dream or memory, my legs are tingling.

Graphic Novels

Texts written in graphic novel format are flying from bookshelves and into the hands of readers, and not just so-called reluctant readers. Although graphic novels are sometimes typecast as "easy read" comics, research shows that comprehending a graphic novel requires utilizing multiple constructs of the brain in order to synthesize the images together with the text in a meaningful way. Readers who may be daunted by reading an entire chapter book engage in comprehending narrative via the sophisticated sequential art.

Beginning in Grade 5, the Common Core State Standards list graphic novels as a requirement, which is a testament to their rigor and inference load. They are considered long-form narratives, and are now divided into several types. For example, *manga*, the Japanese word for *comic* in the United States, refers to the style. Manga graphic novels are read from top to bottom and right to left. The *superhero* story is another category of graphic novel where both epic and episodic stories are told. *Personal narratives*, often in the now popular perzines, are written about the author's personal opinions and experiences. We've found our students enjoy knowing these various types, and that this genre expertise boosts their reading confidence and helps them go into a reading experience anticipating a predictable structure. We love graphic novels because they are engaging and often fun to read.

Here are some general tips to consider when adding a graphic novel to your teaching text set and adding a shelf to your classroom library:

- Read on a tablet when possible as the interactivity of the digital platform is highly motivating.

- Attune to characters by studying their facial expressions, their internal and external dialogue, and their actions and reactions.

- Consider the illustrator's decisions about meaning based on the tone of colors in the background and foreground of scenes, the size and scale of images, the layout of each scene, and the size and style of font.

Teaching Text: *El Deafo* by Cece Bell

This is one of our choices because . . . Cece is a unique, lovable character who teaches us the importance of family and friends while figuring out how to handle her inner struggle with being different. At age 4, Cece was hospitalized with meningitis. As a result, she lost most of her hearing. She attended a special school where students were like her in terms of their hearing loss, and where they learned to read lips and grapple with sign language while wearing a new hearing device. Later in the story, Cece and her family move to a different neighborhood where making friends and coexisting in a hearing world provide challenges that reveal Cece's true character. Cece's inner monologues about being a superhero are inspiring, and remind us that we all have superpowers that help us overcome our differences (pinky swear bonds with friends help, too!). The cover design is appealingly simple. It draws us in with an almost preschool picture book appeal, but on closer examination, we notice the device strapped to the skyward body, and with that, we understand this is a story where the happy ending will be hard-won.

CHARACTERISTICS	OUR RATING
Appeal	★ ★ ★
Opportunities to Develop Empathy	★ ★ ★
Representation	★ ★ ★
Accessibility to Readers	★ ★ ★

(Continued)

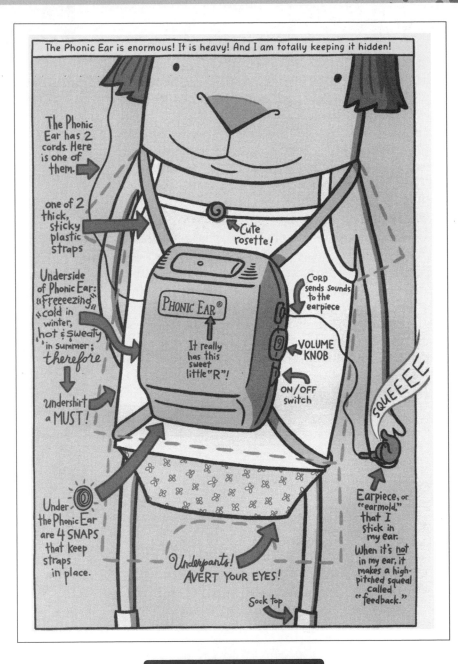

Thinking about character relationships: *Martha and Cece have the superpower of friendship!*

BOOK LOOK

Teaching Text: *Roller Girl*
by Victoria Jamieson

This is one of our choices because ... we're always game for learning about new adventures, particularly adventures involving sports, and we especially like stories with strong female characters. In *Roller Girl*, we've got it all! We meet Astrid who in many ways represents an average, typical kid living with her mom who spends a lot of time with her best friend. On the other hand, Astrid represents what we admire in characters—she is strong mentally and physically, and knows it, but has to learn she's emotionally rock solid, too, when faced with making some tough decisions about her fading friendship. The cover image will appeal to all readers, and its bright colors and comic book vibe reassure reluctant readers that the story line is accessible. Readers will discover all the significance in the details of Jamieson's deliberate choices in the cover design, including Astrid's hair color and her socks, as we journey alongside Astrid in not only a physical transformation but also an internal one, too.

CHARACTERISTICS	OUR RATING
Appeal	★★★
Opportunities to Develop Empathy	★★★
Representation	★★★
Accessibility to Readers	★★★

Thinking about the illustrator's decisions: *Wow! Look at this page spread. We see an entire scene of the park, and these three images below are interesting. The choice to create a red background reveals Astrid's frustration! We can imagine the tension without a lot of words!*

WAYS TO ENGAGE STUDENTS IN FICTION READ ALOUDS

ASK STUDENTS TO THINK ABOUT THE CHARACTERS AND THEMES THEY WILL LEARN ABOUT IN THE TEXT.

Before beginning a new fiction read aloud text, we tend to ask students to preview it by looking at the cover, title, back cover blurb, and a few pages. Then we give them the opportunity to discuss their predictions about what they will learn about. We do this instead of telling them exactly who the characters are or what the lessons will be. This way, students are empowered to make their own decisions and plans for reading as a way to engage their interest right away. As we begin reading, they are more eager to see if their predictions were accurate. We might ask,

- What do you think this story is *really* about?
- What lessons do you think the characters will learn?
- What lessons will *we* learn from the characters?
- Why do you think the author titled the story _____?

STOP PERIODICALLY TO SHARE THINKING.

We often put sticky notes on the parts of a read aloud text that we think will create a lot of deep thinking. These notes are reminders to stop and either share our own thinking or ask students what they are thinking. We might ask,

- What are you thinking now?
- What is the author really saying here?
- Why do you think the author included that?

KEEP IT COLLABORATIVE.

Ask students to help you understand the text. Enlist their questions, ideas, and theories as part of the class working together to learn from the text. Remember not to make it sound like a quiz or a game of "guess the right answer" (more on this in Chapter 4).

ASK STUDENTS THEIR OPINIONS ABOUT WHAT TO READ ALOUD.

As you read aloud and afterward, ask students to discuss or write and share their opinions about the text. You can use our rating system or create your own with the class. Let the students know that you value their opinions and will try to use as many of their recommendations as possible.

For example, the class might have a rating system that is tracked on a chart, such as

- We loved it. You must read us more books just like this!
- We liked it. We would be open to reading more books like this.
- It was OK. Some parts did not hold my attention or were too confusing.
- Don't read that again. It was so confusing and boring, and we just did not get it.

SHOW THE PICTURES.

Even if your students are older and "mature," make sure you show them how you read and study the images and not just the words. Give students time to ooh and aah over them. If some pictures are really detailed, project them on the board so everyone can read them closely.

Videos and viewing guide may also be accessed at
http://resources.corwin.com/GoldbergHouser-Fiction

**Setting Up a Classroom Library:
The Goal**

Video 2.1

**Book Selection:
The Goal**

Video 2.2

Previewing Books

Video 2.3

Student Book Talks

Video 2.4

Decisions About Reading Notebooks

3

"WE UNDERSTAND LANGUAGE BY SIMULATING IN OUR MINDS WHAT IT WOULD BE LIKE TO EXPERIENCE THE THINGS THAT THE LANGUAGE DESCRIBES."

(Benjamin K. Bergen)

Laura sat down next to a table of students and observed them for a moment. They were in the midst of independent reading and forming ideas about the characters in their novels. One student, Danny, stopped briefly to add a few more ideas about the book's main character in an entry he created in his reading notebook. After about thirty seconds of writing, he got right back into his book and began reading. A minute later, another reader, his partner Julia, stopped and added a few examples of what the character said and did to her notebook entry. She also returned to her reading quickly and kept going. What was happening in Laura's classroom was not magic, but it might look like that to others. The class spent the first month of school studying why and how readers use writing as an important tool in their reading and thinking process.

After about thirty minutes of independent reading, students met with their reading partners to discuss their thinking about the characters in their books. The first thing students did was take out their reading notebook entries and their books. The students in the class valued their reading notebooks and chose to write in them on their own for specific reasons. They were aware of the many ways their writing could help them remember what they were thinking and explain it to others. As Julia began to explain her thinking to her partner, she glanced at her notes and then began talking.

In this chapter, we look closely at how we can use writing to help make the thinking involved in interpreting fiction more accessible to students and how it can become an important window for teachers to decide what to teach next. We have seen the ways writing can become a tool for understanding fiction, yet many students don't choose to write or only do so in school when it is required. Most classrooms do not yet look like Laura's, but hers did not always look like this either, and in this chapter, we will explain the key lessons that helped create this "magic" that you can use tomorrow.

When working in classrooms, we see such variety in the types of writing that students create and huge differences in terms of what this writing offers students in their reading process. These differences create limitations in the types of information teachers gain about their students. So our hope is to offer what does work and what does help students use writing to deepen their thinking. The key is authenticity and choice, and in this chapter, we show you how to set this up.

This chapter can help you decide what to teach tomorrow if

- Students do not write about their reading
- You are unsure how to get reading notebooks started
- Students do the minimum required and see writing as a chore

In this chapter, you will learn

- How to help students see the value in writing about fiction
- Lessons for introducing student-directed reading notebook entries
- Key lessons to teach students to collect, develop, and revisit their thinking
- Common approaches to writing about reading and their limitations
- Ways to use student notebook entries to decide what to teach next

- Writing about reading has become stale and robotic in your classroom
- You are unsure how reading notebooks can help students interpret fiction

We begin this chapter by showing you how to teach writing about reading in genuine ways that connect to your students, offering you a window into students' thinking about fiction so you can decide what to teach next. The majority of the chapter will then take you into classrooms and students' writing so you can learn the lessons that have the biggest impact on students' thinking about fiction. You will leave this chapter knowing where to put your attention and the practices you might want to reconsider because they don't necessarily offer you or your students ways to develop more thoughtful reading practices.

Why We Really Use Writing as a Tool for Understanding

When researching writing as an access point for understanding, I decided to study my own practices. Over the course of a weekend, I tracked the reasons and ways I genuinely used writing as a tool to help me. As a researcher and teacher, I predicted that most of my writing would be in response to ideas and articles I was reading, and while this was part of my weekend, I also found many other organic ways I wrote. On the next page is a list of what I found.

I did not set aside special time to write over the weekend, but when I looked at how I spent my time, there were several moments and contexts where writing helped me. Some of the writing was about *remembering* such as grocery and shopping lists. Some of the writing was about *organizing* my thinking such as the comparison chart and running workout summary. Some of the writing was about *sharing* with others such as my emails. Some of the writing was about *recording my thinking* for reflection such as my outline and margin notes. I asked

OVER THE WEEKEND, I WROTE

- Emails to friends about upcoming plans
- Emails to colleagues about our shared projects
- Tweets to teachers, authors, and others I follow on Twitter in response to their posts
- A grocery list
- A holiday shopping list
- Margin notes in a book I was reading
- A summary of my weekly running workouts and what my goals were for next week
- Plans for my demonstration lessons coming up
- A comparison chart about what I noticed was similar between dystopian literature and apocalyptic literature for my book club sessions with eighth graders next week
- An outline of what I thought I would speak about at an upcoming parent workshop
- Answers to questions that were sent to me about word study
- Notes from our veterinarian about one cat's health issues
- Meal ideas for a holiday party

several groups of teachers to replicate this task—to track and record how they were using writing authentically in their lives. When we shared the lists, most of us were surprised at how often we used writing as a tool. After looking across dozens of teachers' lists, we consolidated our reasons why we write authentically into a few categories. We noticed that none of us wrote because we were told we had to or because we were "accountable." Instead, we wrote because it served a real and important purpose in our lives. "Writing is often our representation of the world made visible, embodying both process and product" (Emig, 1977, p. 122).

REASONS WHY WE USE WRITING AS A TOOL

- To remember
- To record our thinking
- To share with others
- To organize our thinking
- To discover our thinking

After examining the ways we use writing in our everyday lives, we wanted to understand the reasons why we write about fiction reading. In one memorable professional study group activity, we asked participating teachers to list the real reasons why they write about the fiction reading in their lives. We used a T-chart to guide the discussion. The left side read, "Types of Fiction I Read," and the right side read, "Why I Choose to Write About This Reading." Below is a sample chart that shows the types of responses we collected and how the teachers used their writing as an access point for understanding.

TYPES OF FICTION I READ	WHY I CHOOSE TO WRITE ABOUT THIS READING
Picture books	To jot down my thinking to share with students in a read aloud
Young adult novels	
	To keep track of my ideas about the character
Mysteries	
	To flag parts where the author's style and craft struck me
Realistic fiction	
Fantasy	To track clues, predict, and react
Historical fiction	To collect ideas and lessons being learned
Comics and graphic novels	To list questions to discuss and ideas to share with others
Book club books	

After we made this chart of reasons why we write about fiction, we discussed what was common among most of us. One teacher had an aha moment when she commented, "Ha! No one wrote down that we write because we were given questions to answer or because we are going to be tested on it." Everyone laughed and nodded.

Our goal is for students not just to write in school when being told to do so, but to choose to write as an access point to understanding when they see a real need for it. These reflective exercises helped us better understand writing as a tool for understanding, and we wanted to help our students develop these tools too.

Your Turn

Track your "writing as a tool" moments for a full day or weekend and reflect on what you notice. Share these findings with your colleagues. Explain to your students the genuine reasons why you choose writing as a meaning-making tool. Invite them to share their own noticings.

Current Reality: Why Students Write About Reading in School

In order to better understand students' perspectives about why they write about their reading, we were part of a group of teachers who decided to interview students. We are sharing this with you because we found a common pattern that can help you get to know your students' perspectives and, if needed, shift them. We took one period and went to every fourth-grade student in a class and asked them two questions:

1. Why did you write about your reading today?

2. Who is the audience for this writing?

After listening to every student, we tallied up the findings. Students explained the reasons why they wrote about their reading. Most common was the response "To show the teacher I did my work," a few students shrugged and explained they did not know why they were writing about their reading, and one student explained she wrote about her reading to remember things that she felt were important. Wary of not overgeneralizing the findings from one classroom, we asked the same two questions in dozens of other classrooms—students from a variety of grade levels and from different parts of the country. The chart on the next page shows the most common responses students gave for why they write about their reading in school.

When asked about the audience for their writing about reading, most students shrugged and said they did not know, a few students said "the teacher," two students said "my reading partner," and one student responded in a way that sounded like a question by tentatively saying, "I am?" Without a real purpose or audience, students often admit they get through writing with the minimal amount of work and effort because it is a chore and obstacle, not a tool to help them access meaning.

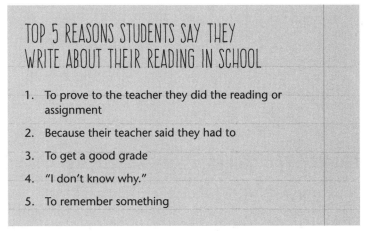

TOP 5 REASONS STUDENTS SAY THEY WRITE ABOUT THEIR READING IN SCHOOL

1. To prove to the teacher they did the reading or assignment
2. Because their teacher said they had to
3. To get a good grade
4. "I don't know why."
5. To remember something

These findings were not surprising to any of the teachers with whom we worked. Many students view writing about reading as purposeless busywork. Rather than groan, complain, or blame students for their views, we rolled up our sleeves and spent time rethinking our practices. We can all reflect by discussing

- *What are we communicating to students about writing about reading?*
- *What are we modeling for students?*
- *How are our practices and moves creating these students' perspectives?*
- *What else could we try?*

Your Turn

Interview your students to find out why they write about their reading. Use our two questions or create your own.

1. Why did you write about your reading today?
2. Who is the audience for this writing?

Once you find out their perspectives, design your lessons based on what you might want to help them shift. Students' perspectives are an important piece of deciding what to teach next.

© Daryl Getman, DAG Photography

Ask yourself: Why do your students write? Is it for you or for them? It's got to be the latter, or else we risk disengaged students missing opportunities to explore their own identity through their writing about reading.

Lessons That Wake Up Writing About Reading

History and literacy teacher Baynard Woods (2009) explains the power that students experience when they begin to view writing as not just a school task but a life-changing tool: "When students recognize the thinking inherent in writing, they start to recognize their own thinking and then the thinking that invests the world around them with meaning. When they recognize that the human world is made of thought, they realize that the world can be changed" (p. 19). Students' sense of agency can be developed when they realize the connections between thinking, writing, and changing their worlds.

In the following lessons, we help students understand the many genuine reasons why readers use writing as a tool for understanding fiction texts. If your students do not use writing authentically right now, these lessons offer you a starting point. What follows are five key lesson ideas. You can use one of these lessons, a few, or all five based on the students in your classroom. For the purposes of this book, we numbered them in this order, but you really could start with whichever one you think would best engage your students. All five address the same goal of helping students understand the genuine reasons why readers write about their thinking. While it makes sense to teach these lessons at the start of the school year, it is never too late to reboot your students' understanding of using writing as a tool.

LESSON 1
Starting With Why
MODEL WHY PEOPLE WRITE ABOUT READING

In this lesson, the goal is for students to get a glimpse into our reading lives as teachers and for them to understand that writing about reading is not a "school task" but a real reading tool. Try to be as real with your students as possible and show your process.

thin slice

Decide to Teach This Tomorrow if Your Students

- Do not write when they read
- Do not understand why they write about their reading
- View their audience for writing as the teacher
- Seem to think writing is a chore to get through when reading

What You Need:

- Several of your favorite fiction texts (for examples of our favorites, refer to Chapter 2 and Appendix B)

Tell Why: Explain to students that you read a variety of fiction texts and often write about them for various purposes. Tell the students you want to take a few minutes to show them what you have been reading and how writing has helped you.

Show How: Bring in a handful of fiction texts you are reading and show students why you are reading them and why you are choosing to write about them. If you have margin notes, stickies, or notebook entries, you can show them too. Aim for a blend of jots that express emotional responses and responses that help you work through confusion, and flag what you think may come up again. Keep tying your examples back to the *why*.

A Few Tips:

- If you do not really write much about your reading, dig deeper. Consider "out of the box" ways you do this like we explained in the intro to this chapter. What about grocery and to-do lists?

- Take a few of your favorite fiction books and try writing down your thinking about them if you have not done this before. Remember there is no wrong way to record your thinking. It can be as simple as "Wow! Great metaphor" or as complex as likening a character and theme to something in your life.

What are we after, ultimately? To instill in our readers a sense that reading and writing isn't school work but life work.

LESSON 2
You Got This!

AFFIRM WHAT STUDENTS ALREADY DO

In this lesson, your goal is to engage students in learning more about how they already use writing as an important tool for learning, especially in ways they might not have connected to reading fiction.

Decide to Teach This Tomorrow if Your Students

- Do not understand why they write about their reading
- View their audience for writing as the teacher
- Seem to think writing is a chore to get through when reading

What You Need:

- Chart paper and markers
- A fiction read aloud book
- Short video clips

Explore Why:

- Write the inquiry question on chart paper: *How does writing help us think?*
- Take a few days to watch a video, read aloud a fiction book, tell stories, and participate in any other fiction experiences.
- Offer students a few minutes throughout the day to reflect and write a response to the inquiry question after each experience.
- Conduct a class discussion about what the students found by going back to their reflections after each experience.

A Few Tips:

- This lesson can be extended for a few days and done for homework as well.
- If you teach in departments, you can ask your colleagues to help out by doing the same lesson in social studies or science so students understand this is not just an English class practice. Fiction does not just happen in English class. Consider science fiction and historical fiction.

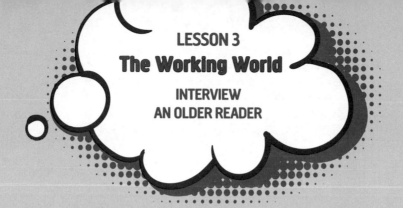

LESSON 3
The Working World
INTERVIEW AN OLDER READER

If you choose to teach this lesson, your goal is for students to see how adults they look up to use writing as a tool. In addition to adults, you can involve older students in middle or high school. You will want students to walk away understanding just how important writing is in the reading and learning process for people at different ages and in varying professions.

Decide to Teach This Tomorrow if Your Students

- Do not understand why they write about their reading
- Seem to think writing is a chore to get through when reading

What You Need:

- Chart paper
- People to interview
- Webcam technology if doing the interview via the web

Tell Why: Explain to students that older students and adults use writing for authentic purposes too, and this is not just a "school skill." Discuss how lawyers' reasons and doctors' reasons would be different, and so would moms' reasons and college students' reasons for why they write about what they are thinking as they read.

Discuss Why:

- Invite older students or adults from the community to be interviewed about why and how they write about their reading. Remember this can even be done via web conference or email if a live visit is not possible.
- Generate a list of questions with the students about how this person reads fiction and writes about it.

(Continued)

- Prep the people being interviewed so they know the questions you will be asking them ahead of time and let them know that you want students to really see the value of writing about reading.
- Let students see the variety of people who write as a way to learn by doing this a few times if possible. (Variation: Have a few people in during one period and run it like a panel discussion.)

A Few Tips:

- Try to find a few people whom you know the students respect and look up to.
- Be creative about whom you invite. For example, a soccer coach might not seem like an obvious choice, but he has to read and write notes and ideas too.
- Remember the power of positive role models. Even inviting a few older students sends the message that this is important and powerful.

LESSON 4
Chart It!

CREATE AN ANCHOR CHART OF REAL REASONS FOR WRITING

This lesson is aimed at helping consolidate and document what students have learned so far about why and how people write about their reading. This chart will anchor the lessons that come up later in this chapter and in the year. Take time to create it with the class and enlist the students' thinking and ideas.

Decide to Teach This Tomorrow if Your Students

- Are ready to share their new understandings about why people write about their reading
- Need a visual reminder and support to refer to
- Are ready to share their thinking about their own writing about reading with their classmates

thin slice

What You Need:

- Several of your favorite fiction texts (for examples of our favorites, refer to Chapter 2 and Appendix B)

Tell Why: Remind students of all you discussed in Lessons 1, 2, and 3 about why we write about reading in our lives. Refer back to the charts or books you used in those previous lessons as a concrete reminder for students.

Create an Anchor Chart:

- Create a class anchor chart that lists the reasons you discovered for why people authentically write about their thinking and fiction reading.
- Refer to this chart every time you model writing about reading for the next few weeks. Begin every lesson where you model writing about reading by explaining the reason why you are doing this and point out that reason on the chart.

(Continued)

A Few Tips:

- Anchor charts work well when used a lot. If we create them once and rarely look back at them, they become wallpaper. Keep the chart visible and point to it often. Students will begin to use it if they see you using it too.

- Also know when to take a chart down. After about six weeks or when students no longer need it because it is a part of what they now know how to do, you can take a photo of the chart as a reminder and then take it off the wall. Some teachers create a document with all the charts and share it with students so they can always refer back to them digitally.

- Remember to ask yourself if you know why students should write about their reading each time you ask them to do it. If you don't have a genuine reason, consider not asking them to do it. If we contradict what we say about authenticity, students will still view writing about reading as a chore to get through.

LESSON 5
Rising Tide

CREATE AN INSPIRATION WALL TO UPLIFT ALL STUDENTS

This is really the kick start to a classroom structure that you can keep up all year long. Much like the adage "a rising tide lifts all boats," displaying students' writing about reading gives all students the opportunity to learn from—and aspire to—the ways of thinking of peers. You can change the work displayed across the year as your students develop and grow.

Decide to Teach This Tomorrow if Your Students

- Are writing about their reading and are ready to learn from one another
- Benefit from examples and visuals
- Are working on building a community of fiction readers who help one another

thin slice

What You Need:

- Bulletin board and staples
- Copies of students' reading notebook entries
- Colored paper or big sticky notes and markers

Tell Why: Explain that you see amazing examples of students beginning to use writing as a tool for understanding their fiction books. Make this a point of celebration.

Show How:

- Use large paper to create headings on the bulletin board that correspond to the genuine reasons why readers write about their fiction texts. For example, there could be a section that says, "I write to record big moments," and another that says, "I write to keep track of the characters."
- Choose some student examples that match the reader's purpose to hang up under each category.

(Continued)

This is a sample of one classroom's inspiration wall with student examples of notebook entries (from Aimee Carroll's seventh-grade classroom in Paramus, New Jersey). Students use this wall to get ideas for their own notebook entry choices.

- For each student example, take a few minutes to examine and admire it with your class. Ask the students what they notice about it and label the moves the writer made with large sticky notes. There are many examples throughout this book of how we label student work with callouts that you can use to guide what you might write.

A Few Tips:

- Throughout the year, try to post examples from all the students. In this way, each student's writing is a possible mentor text to others.
- If you don't have the wall space, this could be a digital wall or presentation that students can access as an inspiration tool.
- We suggest you do not grade or write on these entries as then the focus becomes the grade and not the process the reader took to develop his thinking.

CLIPBOARD NOTES: READING NOTEBOOK ENTRIES

After teaching these lessons on why we authentically write about our fiction reading, you might use an observation tool like this to collect information about your students. These clipboard notes can help guide those "what next" questions.

NAME AND DATE	OBSERVATIONS
	☐ Writes to remember
	☐ Writes to record thinking
	☐ Shares writing and thinking with others
	☐ Organizes thinking
	☐ Uses writing to discover thinking
	☐ Other
Notes:	

Once you observe the kinds of writing about reading students are or are not doing, you can focus your lessons on what seems most underutilized. This can be taught in whole class lessons if most students need more practice, in small groups if it is just a few, or one-on-one in a conference.

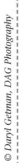

When students choose how to use their reading notebook as a tool, they experience the process of thinking through their reading, which often leads to engaged and empowered readers.

Students Create Self-Directed Reading Notebook Entries

Many teachers we support have decided to introduce and model the use of reading notebooks with their students. **What we mean by a reading notebook is a place to collect, develop, and revisit ideas about a text.** Students choose genuine and purposeful ways to record their thinking as needed, not because the teacher assigned them to write. In classrooms where reading notebooks are used, students make the choices about what, how, and when to record their thinking. The notebooks are filled with a variety of entries where the reader himself is the audience, not just the teacher. "Students must feel free to own their own thinking and aspirations . . . otherwise they will simply do what is asked and nothing more" (Swinehart, 2009, p. 33). Of course, the teacher models how she uses her reading notebook and then allows students to make their own choices of what and how to write in them. Let's clarify what an entry is, and in the next section, we will explain how to teach students to develop thinking with their notebook entries.

The word *entry* means the act of entering or the right of entering, gaining admission, or access. We choose to use the word *entry* because we see this type of writing as an entering—entering into the world of the book's deeper meanings, entering into our thoughts, and entering into an experience with intention. For example, think about the way yoga studios set up intentional ways of entering the space. First, the yoga students take off their shoes and place them outside of the studio doors. Then the yoga students enter the room and find a location that feels right for them that day, and they place their mats down on the spot. Next, the yoga students decide what props and supports they will likely need that day and gather blocks, blankets, and belts and place them next to their mats. Finally, they sit quietly and consider how they want their practice to go, checking in with themselves and how they are feeling. These practices become intentional rituals that help the yogis prepare and get ready to begin. This is just like how we envision the use of a reading notebook practice. While someone can practice yoga without the mat, it serves as a reminder and container for going deeply into meditative movement. While someone can think deeply without a notebook, it serves as a reminder and container for going deeply into generating and developing ideas. The props and tools of yoga are like the language prompts and organizers chosen in the reading notebook.

Readers choose how to collect their thinking, develop it further, and then revisit it as needed. When students are reading books that take several days to read such as longer picture books, early chapter books, or longer works of literature, the writing they do in the notebook helps them remember what they were thinking and then go back to those thoughts and continue where they left off. In this way, the reading notebook is also like a more sophisticated bookmark. Bookmarks are used to save our places and remind us where we left off in the book. Notebook entries can help us save our *thinking* in those places and remind us where our *thinking* left off in the book. Notebook entries that are developed over time across an entire book can help readers identify patterns in their thinking, critique their own thinking, and synthesize ideas across time and sometimes across texts. Linda Reif (2007) explains why she encourages her students to use notebooks: "For me, it's having a place where students can gather their ideas so they don't lose their thinking. . . . It's a place to look back at what they were thinking about themselves, their reading, and their world that might merit further development" (p. 195).

In *Visible Learning for Literacy* (2016), Fisher, Frey, and Hattie explain that the writing practices we teach in reading notebooks are highly effective at improving learning. For example, when students create their own concept maps and use a variety of ways to summarize in writing, more visible learning is likely to happen. They claim that "writing should be a means to uncover one's own thinking in the process" (p. 125). But writing about reading is much more effective when students create their own thinking maps as a tool for understanding rather than filling out worksheets or creating an entry without purpose. Purposeless writing does not help with learning.

Types of Entries That Grow Out of a Thriving Reading Culture

TYPE OF ENTRY	EXAMPLE
Writes to remember	characters ParVana Nooria Ali -girl 6th grade -Not allowed high school -2 years old -not in school -likes to be left alone -misses mother -helps father walk -acts like a typical teen -wants to go to school -very close to mom -wishes life was normal -has a lot of responsibility -stuck in the middle/trying to help Mother and with the delema of her stolen/help Parvana recover father The reader created a character chart to remember details about each character and to ensure she did not confuse who was who.

TYPE OF ENTRY	EXAMPLE
Writes to record thinking	 Images source: Basketball hoop; boy: clipart.com; shoe, giraffe, flooring, crumpled paper, paperclip: Pixabay This is a digital notebook entry where the reader compares two characters' similarities and differences.
Shares writing and thinking with others	 The reader made a list of possible topics to talk about with her book club. These topics are ideas she generated from previous entries.

(Continued)

TYPE OF ENTRY	EXAMPLE
Organizes thinking	The reader created a visual representation of the setting of the book and included details from the text and also her thinking about the setting. Rather than simply use words, she also used pictures to organize the parts of the setting.
Uses writing to discover thinking	The Taliban had really harsh rules One of these harsh rules is that girls had to wear chadors, which are cloths that cover most of your face and body. Also women had to wear a burqua, which covers all of your face and body with a screen for her to look out of. Women had to wear these outside. They could not be outside without a man. Another really harsh rule that the Taliban had was that nobody was allowed to work or school. They thought that they would get too much information. It makes me think that the Taliban wanted to be in absolute control of Afghanistan, and they didn't want anybody to figure out ways to defeat them. Maybe it was like the Holocaust The reader started with an idea and wrote it at the top of the page. Then she wrote about the idea to discover new ideas that stem from the first one.

Your Turn

Begin your own reading notebook practice. During read alouds, begin to model how you

- Set up your entry

- Decide what to write down

- Keep going back to your notebook to look at your thinking on the page

- Use the notebook entry to have a discussion

Then invite your students to do the same. Students can bring their reading notebooks to the class read aloud area and begin their own entries that they can use for partner, group, or whole class conversations. The following chart can help you get started.

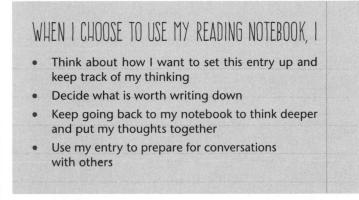

WHEN I CHOOSE TO USE MY READING NOTEBOOK, I

- Think about how I want to set this entry up and keep track of my thinking

- Decide what is worth writing down

- Keep going back to my notebook to think deeper and put my thoughts together

- Use my entry to prepare for conversations with others

How to Collect Thinking in Notebook Entries

"Writing lets us think of things we don't know we knew until we began writing. Writing is one way of representing and communicating our thinking to others, using our experiences, our knowledge, our opinions, and our feelings to inform and negotiate our understandings and misunderstandings of ourselves and the world in which we live" (Reif, 2007, p. 191). If we want to encourage students to use their reading notebook entries to collect the kind of thinking Reif describes, we likely need to model for them first what we mean and how they can get started. Over the next few pages, we highlight some key lessons and teaching ideas for helping students understand how to make choices about using their reading notebooks. Our intentional teaching helps students become intentional readers.

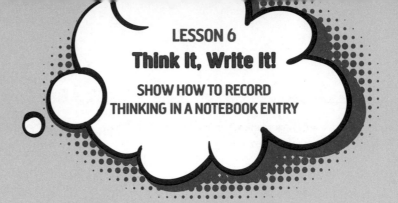

LESSON 6
Think It, Write It!
SHOW HOW TO RECORD THINKING IN A NOTEBOOK ENTRY

In this lesson, we show students the process of stopping, thinking, and creating a fiction reading notebook entry. This is a foundational lesson for students who are just learning the power of using writing as a tool for understanding their fiction texts.

thin slice

Decide to Teach This Tomorrow if Your Students

- Are not sure how to begin a reading notebook entry
- Are not writing in their reading notebooks at all
- Need help connecting their thinking process to their writing of entries

What You Need:

- Your own reading notebook or chart paper for modeling
- A familiar read aloud fiction text (such as *Extra Yarn* by Mac Barnett, 2012)
- Students' reading notebooks or whiteboards

Tell Why: Remind students why we write down our thinking. Refer back to the anchor chart of reasons (created in Lesson 4).

Show How:

- Reread a part of the text.
- Stop and think aloud about why you have a hunch this is something you want to recall and revisit.
- Then record your thinking in an entry. Narrate your process as you show it.
- Tell students we write when we have an idea we want to remember, share, or revisit later.

Practice How:

- Read another section and guide students to stop, think, and write down their ideas.
- Invite students to share the ways they wrote their thinking down and how it helped them.
- Emphasize there is no one right way to make an entry. As long as it helps them develop their thinking and understanding, it works.

A Few Tips:

- If students are brand new to writing about their thinking, they might need charts and examples hanging up of your notebook entries to refer back to.
- Remember we are assigning these entries to students not as tasks to complete for us, but rather as tools they can use to hold on to their thinking. Watch for language that conveys assignments.
- If students are experienced with reading notebooks, end by asking them how else they tend to record their thinking.

LESSON 7
Swap Meet
STUDENTS SHARE NOTEBOOK ENTRIES

The following lesson helps students understand how they can use their notebook as a powerful tool in more deeply understanding characters and themes when reading fiction.

Decide to Teach This Tomorrow if Your Students

- Do not understand what we mean by writing as a tool
- Write about reading but not in ways that help them understand their fiction texts better (They simply write something quickly at the end of the period and never look at it again.)

What You Need:

- Chart paper and markers
- Students' reading notebooks
- Some of your reading notebook entries

Discuss and Develop:

- Ask students to write down a list of the ways they could use their notebooks when thinking about characters and themes in fiction.
- Conduct a class or small group discussion to share what students wrote down.
- Ask students to jot down any new ideas they heard after the conversation.

The following is an example of a class's list of ways the reading notebook entries can help them understand characters and themes more deeply.

How Reading Notebooks Can Help Us Understand Fiction
– characters & themes

- get to know characters really well
- uncover patterns
- make ideas bigger and deeper
- change our "minds" – revise ideas
- find lessons to use in my life
- prepare to talk and share ideas

A Few Tips:

- If you worry that your students will not know what to say, you can show them your notebook examples and then ask them what they notice.
- This lesson is not about character and theme analysis, but more about how a reading notebook entry can help your students *think* about those two elements.

LESSON 8
I Got This!

DEVELOP GOALS
AND INTENTIONS

In addition to showing examples and modeling how to collect thinking in notebook entries, it is helpful to ask students to set their own goals for how to use their notebooks. Setting their own goals allows students to take more ownership of the reading notebook entries. Even if students struggle trying to answer the questions in the following lesson, it is helpful to go through this process as they will not learn without practice.

Decide to Teach This Tomorrow if Your Students

- Still view reading notebook entries as a task for you, the teacher
- Are working at a variety of levels and experiences and you want to offer more personalization
- Need to develop more ownership of their reading notebook entries

What You Need:

- Reflection questions for students
- Students' reading notebooks
- Your reading notebook
- Any notes you take during reading conferences with students

Tell Why:

- Explain how it is important to take time often to reflect on how a tool is being used and to set goals for how we can use it even better. You might even make a connection to another out-of-school tool you use like a dishwasher or running shoes. Tell students that our reading notebooks are tools and we can reflect on how we are using them and what is working and not working so well so we can set personalized goals for next steps.

Show How:

- Take out your reading notebook and display a list of reflection questions. Some examples follow, but feel free to create your own that match your students.
  - *What are some of your strengths as a reader of fiction?*
  - *How can your reading partner help you?*
  - *What are some goals you have for yourself when reading fiction?*
- Remember to *show how* you generate your answers to these reflective questions by explaining and modeling in front of students.

Practice How:

- Give students time to answer each reflective question in their reading notebooks.
- As students are writing, walk around and meet with them in conferences. If you currently take notes when you confer, you can refer back to them to help students remember what you have been working on together.

Below is one student's reading notebook entry with reflection and goals. She was able to do this because her teacher modeled the process of reflecting and setting goals.

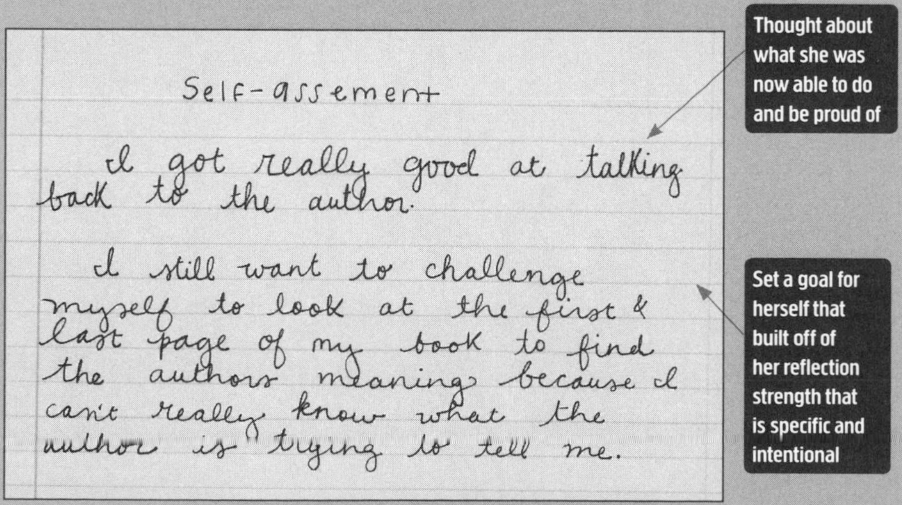

Self-assement

I got really good at talking back to the author.

> Thought about what she was now able to do and be proud of

I still want to challenge myself to look at the first & last page of my book to find the authors meaning because I can't really know what the author is trying to tell me.

> Set a goal for herself that built off of her reflection strength that is specific and intentional

A Few Tips:

- If your students are not yet collecting entries, save this lesson until they have several collected to reflect upon.

- For more information on helping students take charge and set their own goals, you can read *Mindsets and Moves: Strategies That Help Readers Take Charge* by Gravity Goldberg (2016).

- Taking conference notes can help you keep track of what you already taught each student, and these can be referenced as students set goals. If conferring is new to you, consider reading *Conferring With Readers: Supporting Each Student's Growth and Independence* by Gravity Goldberg and Jennifer Serravallo (2007).

Once students really understand authentic reasons to write about reading fiction and how they might record their thinking, it does not guarantee that all students will use writing as a powerful tool. The following lessons are designed for common challenges that we see in classrooms and are meant to help students refine their entries and make the most of them.

LESSON 9
Make It Mine

TEACH STUDENTS HOW TO AVOID COPYING FROM THE BOOK

Once students are in a routine of thinking about their goals and intentions and then choosing how they will collect that thinking, you might want to teach them the difference between copying and thinking on the page. When we paraphrase rather than copy, we are doing the vital mind work that leads to comprehension and a transfer of learning. One way to do this is to look at an entry and ask, "Is this from the text, from my head, or from both?"

Decide to Teach This Tomorrow if Your Students

- Copy information from the book
- Don't understand the difference between details in the text and thinking about them
- Have trouble making inferences

What You Need:

- A familiar read aloud fiction book
- Chart paper and markers

Tell Why: Explain that copying details directly from the book has limited value because it takes a lot of time and we could simply just reread the page or part if we need to know verbatim what it said. Remind your students that notebook entries are more useful when we record and develop our thinking about the details of the text.

Show How:

- Use a familiar read aloud fiction book that both you and your students know well. This means you don't need to read the whole book and can simply begin by rereading a small part.
- Create a T-chart in front of your students and write, "Details From the Text" on one side and "My Thinking" on the other side.

(Continued)

- Show students how you stop as you read and at first are quite literal. Jot down exact details from the book almost verbatim.
- Then show students how you think about the literal details and add your own thinking.
- Compare the "Details From the Text" column to the "My Thinking" column.
- When students understand the difference, remind them they can create their own ways of combining details from the book and thinking together into an entry and that the T-chart is just one way.

The example below is one we used to model this for students.

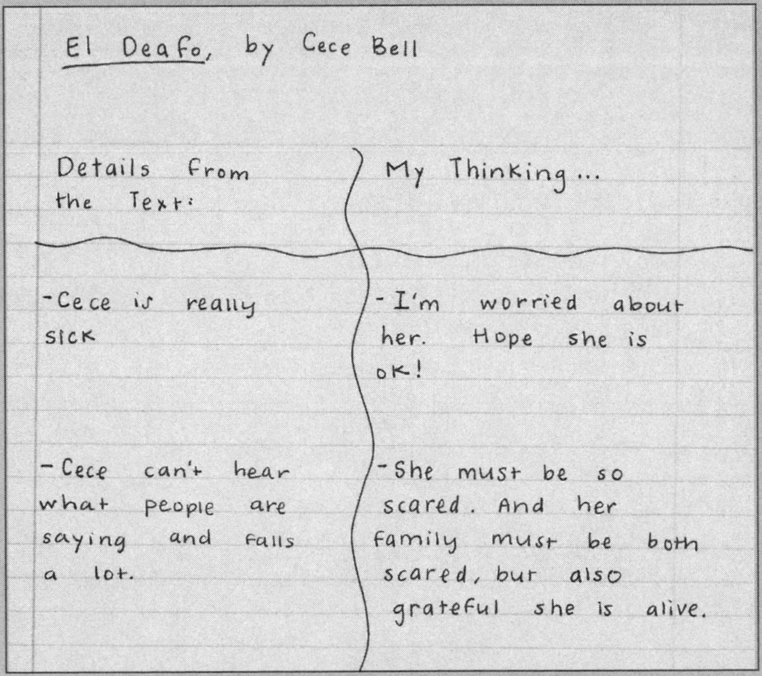

El Deafo, by Cece Bell

Details From the Text:	My Thinking...
-Cece is really sick	- I'm worried about her. Hope she is ok!
- Cece can't hear what people are saying and falls a lot.	-She must be so scared. And her family must be both scared, but also grateful she is alive.

A Few Tips:

- Inevitably, some students begin to create entries in their notebooks where they copy details from their fiction books rather than collect their own thinking about the information. We suggest you let this happen at first so you don't end up dampening students' willingness to try out notebook entries.
- Letting students be literal and copy a bit from the text at first allows them to clearly see how copying and thinking are different.
- Remember these are first-attempt approximations and will get better with more modeling and practice over time.

LESSON 10
Shake It Up!
TEACH STUDENTS HOW TO TAKE CREATIVE RISKS IN NOTE TAKING

Once students have been shown different ways they can choose to collect their thinking, it is easy for them to go on autopilot and simply do whatever you modeled from the class chart. If students seem to be mindlessly choosing a way to collect thinking from your modeling, then you can teach students they can create their own ways to make notebook entries.

Decide to Teach This Tomorrow if Your Students

- Always write in the same ways over and over again
- Seem stuck in a rut with how they record their thinking
- Write in ways that box their thinking in and narrow it rather than expand it
- Underutilize their graphics and image-based thinking

thin slice

What You Need:

- Creative examples of notebook entries
- A chart of possible ways to create entries

Tell Why: Tell students how thinking can get stuck in a rut in the same ways our notebook entries can be stuck. Explain how we can and often should be creatively thinking about how to show our ideas in concrete ways on the page. Hold up colored markers, highlighter pens, and other tools to signal that notebook entries aren't just black and white words! Also acknowledge that these techniques for collecting and organizing thinking can feel new and strange if we are not used to doing this, and that is OK.

Show Examples:

- Display a few creative examples from other students and allow students time to try to figure out what each student was creating. They might even ask the student who created the entry questions about how she came up with the idea.

(Continued)

- Give students permission to make their own creative entries. We like to use the phrase "What if . . ." and then try something out to see how it works.

- Create a class chart that lists some possible ways fiction readers might make reading notebook entries so students can refer back to it and even add to it over time.

A Few Tips:

- If your students are not yet being creative with their entries, then use the ones shown in this book, create your own, or collaborate with colleagues to see if they have examples.

- If your students are used to being given explicit directions for exactly what to do, they might need permission to be creative. It might be enough to just let them loose.

- One group of middle school teachers in New Jersey took photos of creative entries tied to clear thinking and purposes and made extensive slide shows. This served as a motivating incentive, and students wanted their work to be chosen. These teachers continue to show these examples to students years later.

One student example appears below. This student chose to create a card for each character in his novel. He turned the cards into a flipbook so he could easily flip through them and remind himself who the character was with important information. He chose this on his own as a tool to keep track of characters.

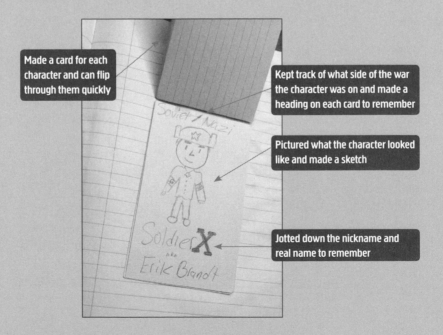

Made a card for each character and can flip through them quickly

Kept track of what side of the war the character was on and made a heading on each card to remember

Pictured what the character looked like and made a sketch

Jotted down the nickname and real name to remember

Let's look at another example. This student wanted to show the relationship between the two characters she was thinking about. She used a combination of images, words, and both her native language and English to create this entry.

Drew a heart with a broken line down it to symbolize the characters' relationship at this point in the text

Wrote down her thinking in her native language

Chose key quotes to show their relationship

Below is a chart that the teacher, Pam, created with her class after studying what other readers in the class were beginning to try out in their notebooks.

Different Types of Reading Notebook Entries

1. Green-Blue-Reds
2. Expanded Post-It (10 different kinds!)
3. T-chart: Character Feeling ... Evidence
4. T-chart: Character Trait ... Evidence
5. Close Reading... First Impressions
   Vocab/words
   Patterns
   Now I think...
6. Character Feeling Timeline
7. Thoughts → What From the Book Maker Me Think This
8. "What my character is doing → How I feel about that" chart
9. Character "web"
10. Letter to character

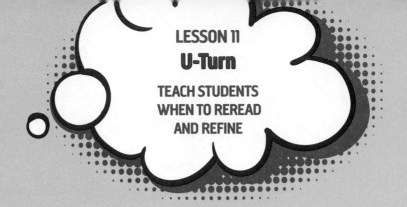

LESSON 11
U-Turn

TEACH STUDENTS WHEN TO REREAD AND REFINE

Once students know how to collect thinking in their notebook entries, you will likely want to show them how to develop their thinking even further. It can be easy for the entries to become something that students get through fast—like a product to complete—rather than a tool to develop and refine ideas. A few key lessons can help students break the focus on completion and remember to revisit their thinking once it is collected.

thin slice

Decide to Teach This Tomorrow if Your Students

- Rarely revisit and reread entries
- Skim the surface and could go deeper with their entries

What You Need:

- Your reading notebook
- Sticky notes
- A book you wrote about to refer back to

Explain When: Explain how you take a few minutes to reread what you collected in your notebook entries at specific times. You can display a list of when you might choose to do this rereading of an entry.

REREAD AND RETHINK ABOUT ENTRIES WHEN YOU

- Finish reading a chapter of the text
- Finish reading the whole text
- Come across a new event that supports your thinking or that challenges your thinking
- Are about to discuss your thinking with a partner or book club
- Have not stopped to think about the characters or themes for a while

---

Show Examples:

- Take out one of your more quickly created reading notebook entries and show students how you reread it. When you reread your entry, you can ask, "What am I thinking about all of this now?"
- Show students how you put a sticky note on top of the original entry or simply add to the entry you first created.

This is a chart that Pam used with her students to show them how and why we revise our thinking in an entry.

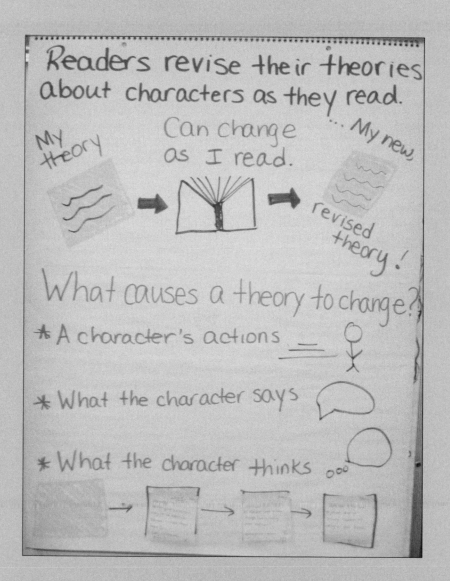

A Few Tips:

- Try giving students a few minutes toward the middle and end of reading time to reread and rethink on the page. You can build in time explicitly for this purpose until it becomes more natural for students and you can stop telling them when to do it.
- Find student examples of rereading and rethinking and show them off to students.
- Remember to highlight the importance of thinking and not just writing more for the sake of it.

Let's look at an example from a student who went back and added more to one of his entries about a character's motivation. As he read further in his book, he came up with a revised idea. This rereading and rethinking allowed the student to come up with ideas he did not originally have when he began reading the novel.

Acknowledges he had a different thought at first	At first I thought the guy was doing graffiti on purpose. Now I think he did it for a reason so he could make his family happy.
Uses the thinking language of "Now I think ..." to show a change	
Adds why his thinking changed	*because he was doing it in a black suit in a black night. ☺ because his family enjoyed it.

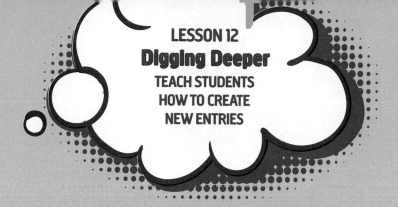

LESSON 12
Digging Deeper
TEACH STUDENTS
HOW TO CREATE
NEW ENTRIES

Once students have created a few entries with a common focus, it is helpful to show them how to consolidate their thinking and to create a new entry that highlights the biggest ideas from across several entries or texts.

Decide to Teach This Tomorrow if Your Students

- Don't see how the parts of their text go together
- Don't connect entries and thinking
- View each entry as its own separate thinking rather than part of the whole of the text

What You Need:

- Your reading notebook
- Sticky notes
- A book you wrote about to refer back to

Tell Why: Tell students how each entry with the same focus or from the same text can go together in some way. Rather than view each entry as standing alone, they can look across entries to see bigger ideas, themes, and commonalities.

Show How:

- Model how you read through a few entries with the same focus from your reading notebook.
- Show your thinking about the patterns and bigger ideas you are seeing across each entry. These could be common themes, ideas, or questions that came up across pages.
- Create a new entry that shows the common ideas in one place. This could be a new list, chart, or visual.

(Continued)

Let's look at one student's new entry she created after reading through a few entries from two different novels. She wanted to look closer at the expressions the characters faced. She read her past entries from both books and used a combination of visuals and words to show her newer and more developed thinking.

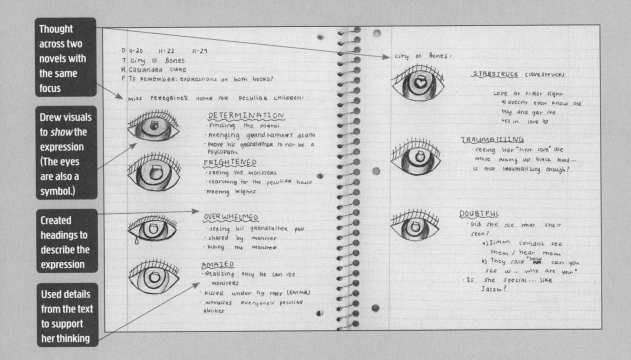

Thought across two novels with the same focus

Drew visuals to *show* the expression (The eyes are also a symbol.)

Created headings to describe the expression

Used details from the text to support her thinking

A Few Tips:

While conferring with students and looking at their notebook entries, you might ask the following questions. You can use these questions to guide your note taking and decide what to revisit and teach again.

- Why did the reader write this entry?
- How is this entry helping the reader understand this fiction text?
- What are the reader's intentions, and how are they being met?
- How is the student making decisions about the type of entry he is making?
- Is the student revisiting entries and going deeper with his thinking?
- Often students need to see another model or have a shared practice with another class read aloud text.

What's Next?

So far in this chapter, we have discussed why authenticity is important, the role of the reading notebook, and several key lessons for teaching students to use their writing to collect, develop, and revisit thinking. In the next section, we take a brief interlude to examine some common writing-about-reading practices and how they might actually be limiting our students and our decision-making processes. Now that we know what is possible to decide to teach, it is helpful to reflect on how we currently teach students to write about their reading. This can help us identify shifts we might make in our practices. The next section starts with a reflective questionnaire you can take to decide how to use the next section, where we discuss the common limiting practices and why they might not be serving us or our students.

© Daryl Getman, DAG Photography

Reading notebook entries helps students not only develop their thinking, but *trust* their thinking, which serves them well as they read new books and study characters.

SELF-REFLECTION QUESTIONNAIRE
READING NOTEBOOKS

Check all that apply. Celebrate what is checked off and use what is not checked off to set goals for your students.

When I listen to and observe my students, I notice they

- ☐ Have a clear intention for why they write about their reading
- ☐ Vary the ways they write to match their intentions
- ☐ Use the entries to more deeply understand their texts
- ☐ Revisit their entries to add to and refine their thinking
- ☐ Use their entries to begin conversations with others
- ☐ Collect information and thinking in the entries
- ☐ Value and are proud of their entries
- ☐ View their writing as a valuable part of the reading process

The area of my students' reading notebook entries I am most proud of is . . .

If I could change one thing about my students' reading notebook entries, it would be . . .

One goal I have for my students' reading notebook entries is . . .

What We Might Let Go of When Asking Students to Write About Reading

As we wrote this book, one of the current best sellers was *The Life-Changing Magic of Tidying Up: The Japanese Art of Decluttering and Organizing* by Marie Kondo (2014). All of our friends were reading it, and one of the big takeaways everyone mentions is how they must not take their time and go little by little as they declutter their homes. Instead, they must decide to go all in and get rid of the things they own that no longer bring them joy. It is in this fast and complete fashion that the decluttering happens and the joy can come forth. We see a lot of connection to making changes in our classrooms. If a practice is not bringing you or your students joy, then maybe it is time to swiftly remove it, declutter your teaching, and make room for joyful reading. In this chapter so far, we have examined several key lessons about how to set up reading notebooks with students so they are self-directed, motivated, and able to think deeply. Let's turn now and look at a few common practices in schools that may be cluttering up our time and getting in the way of this deep and joyful reading. Like Marie Kondo, we suggest you take an honest look and then "tidy up" the ways you ask students to write about their reading.

Worksheets, Reading Guides, and Comprehension Questions

One of the most widely used practices we see in classrooms is giving students questions to answer about what they read. These questions are typically in the form of worksheets, reading guides, or quizzes, and most are called comprehension questions. Some are part of a basal series, some are teacher created, and some are part of test preparation materials. While we understand this is a common practice, we see many limitations for both teachers and students when the majority of students' reading is followed by answering someone else's questions.

The following example is a worksheet that students filled out in response to the short story "The Fight" by Adam Bagdasarian (see *First French Kiss*, 2003). The story is about a teenage boy who challenges another boy to a fight and then reveals how much he regrets the decision. Much of the story centers on his tension between not showing his weakness to his classmates and realizing how poorly he has treated them because he was a "popular" kid. Most of the story builds around this tension until the final fight scenes where the narrator is beaten up and has a self-realization that he deserved to be "de-crowned" as the king of the school because of the way he abused his social power. Shannon filled out the questions as she read, and her work is shown on the next page. We used arrows to point out what we noticed in her answers.

These are accurate and literal facts from the book.

She identified one detail from the text accurately, then made a very general statement. She is missing other key details revealed by the narrator's internal thinking.

This is not totally accurate. There was lots of discussion about whether there should be rules or not, and they did go back and forth about whether kicking and scratching should be allowed.

This shows a misunderstanding of the motivation for the fight. Yes, they did elbow each other in basketball, but the narrator was talking about how he could beat Mike up after school and was bragging about his ability, and this got back to Mike who took the challenge. Reputations and pride really caused the fight.

This is accurate and directly from the text.

While this is true, the reader is missing the other fight going on in the story—the internal fight between right and wrong and pride and common sense for the narrator.

Again, she is missing the other meaning of the fight and how it was a fight between his pride and his own survival. He would rather be beaten up than show weakness.

The Fight
By Adam Bagdasarian

1. What game was the narrator playing in gym class?

   Basketball

2. Which friend did the narrator walk home from school with?

   Kevin

3. Why don't most of the kids at school think the narrator will win the fight?

   Because the narrator ~~wasn't~~ was 3 inches shorter than Mike. ~~and~~ Also, Mike was better at other stuff.

4. What are the rules of the fight?

   There were no rules to the fight.

5. What is the main conflict in the story?

   Two boys got into a fight because one of them elbowed the other witch made them fight.

6. Who wins the fight?

   Mike won the fight.

7. Why did the author title the story The Fight?

   Because two kids got into a fight.

8. Is this a good title for the story? Tell why or why not?

   Yes it is a good title for the story because two kids got into a fight.

If we look at Shannon's answers to the questions, we do gain some information about her understanding of the story. The following lists what we and her teacher were able to learn about Shannon as a reader when we studied her answers together.

- Able to answer some literal recall questions and get them correct (1, 2, 6)

- Identifies who wins the fight (6)

- Seems to be missing the tension going on around why he really does not want to fight but does anyway (3, 5, 7, 8)

- Missed some of the explanation around the rules of the fight (4)

After we looked at this list, we asked, "So what does this show us about what to teach Shannon next? Why did she miss some things, and how can we help her?" The room was silent as we really had no idea. We knew there were some big gaps in her understanding from looking at these answers, but we were not sure where they came from.

The Limitations. When we are given a set of questions to answer, what we pay attention to is already chosen for us. Our main goal in reading then becomes to find the correct answers. Frey and Fisher (2013) explain, "If students are asked only recall and recitation questions, they learn to read for that type of information" (p. 60). This is so limiting, because in reality engaged readers have many questions running through their minds as they read, and these self-created questions help them better understand the text than any given to them by others. It's no surprise, then, that in surveys of student readers they often say that the questions given to them by others never match the real questions they have as they read.

When we look at answers to reading questions, we can guess what went right or wrong and why, but we really don't have a clue about what and how the reader was thinking as he read. For example, perhaps Shannon did not think about the character's motivation or the many layers of the fight. Or perhaps Shannon struggled to understand the meaning of some of the words. Maybe Shannon had little background knowledge on the topic, or maybe she knew a lot about fights and trying to be "top dog." These questions did not let us know any of this. By only looking at her answers, we really don't know why and how Shannon went about reading this text. This means as teachers we may end up making our best guess about what Shannon needs to learn next and getting it wrong. We might end up using trial and error and wasting lots of time teaching strategies she does not need.

The following chart shows the possible limitations in the decision-making process when using worksheets and comprehension questions created by someone who is not the reader herself.

POSSIBLE LIMITATIONS OF BASING DECISIONS ON WORKSHEETS AND COMPREHENSION QUESTIONS	
For Readers	• Narrows the focus for what is worth paying attention to • Creates a "hunting for answers" experience without really reading • Takes away some of the joy of reading • Can interfere with students' understanding of information • Presents reading as a task to prove to the teacher students can answer questions correctly • Takes away from actual time spent reading • Provides little room for reflection or personalization of the reading process
For Teachers	• Unclear why a reader got a question right or wrong • Unclear what strategy to teach next • Could lead students to think that reading is about skimming the surface and not understanding • Could waste a lot of time trying to guess what to teach next • Could be turning students off to reading • Leaves little room for reflection on which parts of one's teaching are effective and which are not

Your Turn

Ask your students to list the questions they have as they read a short story, then compare them to the questions you were planning on assigning. Then consider asking students to focus more on their own questions as they continue reading. Watch what happens to students' engagement and their ability to understand the text.

Self-questioning (as opposed to teacher questions) has a huge impact on student learning with an effect size of 0.64 (Fisher, Frey, & Hattie, 2016).

Teacher-Assigned Written Responses

Many of the schools we support have moved away from giving students worksheets and questions, and instead assign students to write responses to their own reading. These written responses are usually selected from a menu of options. In our early careers, we gave students bookmarks that listed options for what and how they could respond, and then we collected and graded the responses weekly. Some of these options included writing a summary, writing a review, making a map, and choosing a key fact to describe in their own words. Students in many classrooms are given similar lists of options and then expected to create a written response daily at home or at school. The following written response was created by a reader who also read "The Fight." This student, Amanda, chose to write a summary of the story. Her response and our noticings follow.

The Fight

Summary

She wrote a topic sentence about what the story was mainly about, but missed the other layer about the internal struggle with pride.

This is a story about a boy who fights another kid at school. The characters are Mike, Kevin, Linda, and the narrator. The setting is at school and outside of school. The problem is that the two boys fight each-other. The solution is that Mike wins the fight. I recommend this story to boys who like fighting stories.

She wrote a topic sentence about what the story was mainly about, but missed the other layer about the internal struggle with pride.

She identified the characters and setting, but with no elaboration about which characters are more important than others and the roles they play, and no mention of how the setting impacts other elements of the story.

This is missing the real problem and solution because it focuses solely on the external events and misses what the characters are really feeling and motivated by.

She considers whom to recommend this book to but sees this only as a story about fighting and misses the internal struggle to fit in, save face, and maintain a reputation. It is also unclear if the reader enjoyed the story herself.

If we look at Amanda's written response, we do gain some information about her understanding of the story. The following lists what we were able to learn about Amanda as a reader when we studied her response together with our teacher group:

- Able to identify the characters by name

- Unsure if she knows who is who and what each character's role was

- Able to name the setting for most of the story

- Unsure if she sees any connections between the characters and the setting

- Seemed to recognize the external conflict between the characters (the fight) but not the internal conflict about what was motivating the fight and what was going on for the main character

- Misunderstood the problem and solution

- Only views the story from a plot layer—thinking it is just about the fight—and misses the tension between appearing tough and being tough and between the popular boy and trying to keep his power and status with his peers

After we made this list, one teacher commented, "Well, we really only get such a small glimpse into what Amanda understood because we just are getting to see her paragraph summary." End products in the form of written responses give us very little to go on when deciding what to teach tomorrow.

The Limitations. These types of written responses feel like a fill-in-the-blank activity. What we mean by *fill-in-the-blank activity* is that the student writes, "This is a story about . . . The characters are . . . The problem is . . ." and then all but one sentence in the paragraph are literal details she took from the text. The problem with formulas for reading is that they oversimplify what reading really is and send the message that if you can fill in the blank, you fully understood.

Years ago, we sat in the audience at Teachers College to hear one of the master reading teachers, Ellin Keene, speak. She stood in front of hundreds of teachers and explained that she wished she had never written about connections in her book *Mosaic of Thought* (Keene & Zimmerman, 2007). There was a collective gasp in the room as everyone was shocked. In almost every classroom across the country, teachers had been telling students to make self-to-text and text-to-text connections. When the murmurs of the teachers finally died down, Ellin went on to explain how she saw so many students mimicking the language of connections and using the terminology, but what they were actually saying, writing, and doing with connections was not helping them better understand their books. I am sure we have all heard a student (or a hundred) explain, "I have a self-to-text connection! I have a cat!" And then there is the uncomfortable pause because the pet cat was not relevant or important in the book at all. We might have to fight the urge to say, "So what?" What Ellin was pointing out was that filling in the connection blank with a detail from the text is not the process of making meaning. Many of the written responses we see are versions of this. This is true not just for connections but for many of the written response menu options. Most of what Amanda wrote was filling in the "I learned" blank and then writing down the parts she recalled.

Another of the main limitations for teachers when we try to use teacher-assigned responses to assess and understand students as readers is that we gain such limited information when students *write to fit a formula*. Amanda's teacher commented, "This could be anyone's summary. Nothing about it seems to be unique to Amanda. Anyone in my class could have written this." Another limitation of teaching students written responses in this way is that all students' work starts to look the same and we don't get glimpses into how readers think and develop ideas differently across time. In this book, we show you several examples of how students' thinking developed over time using student-directed reading notebook entries.

The following chart shows the possible limitations in the decision-making process when using written responses chosen from a menu of options.

	POSSIBLE LIMITATIONS OF BASING DECISIONS ON ASSIGNED WRITTEN JOURNAL RESPONSES
For Readers	• Narrows the focus for what is worth paying attention to • Creates a formula for reading and writing about it • Takes away some of the joy of reading • Can mask whether students are understanding the text • Presents reading as a task to prove to the teacher students can write a good response • Takes away from actual time spent reading • Leaves little room for reflection or personalization of the reading process
For Teachers	• Doesn't clarify what strategy to teach next • Might end up teaching formulas instead of reading strategies • Might end up asking students to simply fill in the blank without impacting meaning making • Could waste a lot of time trying to guess what to teach next • Could be turning students off to reading • Leaves little room for reflection on which parts of one's teaching are effective and which are not

Your Turn

Read through some recent student responses you assigned and ask yourself three questions:

1. How did this help the reader more deeply make meaning and understand the text?
2. What am I learning about the way this reader thinks about fiction text?
3. Can I see the individual differences in student thinking from these written assignments?

If you are not getting the type of information that would help you make an intentional decision, and if students do not clearly benefit from their notebook writing, consider shifting this practice to include more genuine student entries. Remember you can declutter your reading time so more joy and deeper thinking happen by letting go of some of these common practices.

It can be tricky to see the differences between assigned written responses and reading notebook entries because sometimes they both happen in a physical notebook. In *Writing About Reading* by Janet Angelillo (2003), the difference between a reading journal and a reading notebook is clarified: "A reading journal serves the purpose of proving to the teacher that the student has read the book by requiring students to write summaries or retellings after most or every reading session. . . . The journal exists to prove the act of reading to the teacher. However, the reading notebook differs in that it is for the reader's benefit, not for the teacher" (p. 47). Let's compare how these two types of writing are actually very different in the following chart.

ASSIGNED WRITTEN JOURNAL RESPONSES	READING NOTEBOOK ENTRIES
Audience is the teacher	Audience is the reader and maybe the reader's partner or book club members
Purpose is to prove a student read and understood the book	Purpose is to record thinking and then develop it even further—to create meaning from the text
Written at the end of the reading session or book	Written as the reader is reading whenever an idea is worth writing down
A product created at the end	A part of the reading process done throughout the reading time
Often ignored after created	Often used for conversations with partners or book clubs, for revisiting ideas over time, and for self-reflection
What the Teacher Learns: If a student read the book If the student can follow directions and create the product If a student had some understanding at the end	**What the Teacher Learns:** How a student organizes thinking Types of thinking a student chooses to focus on The reader's process of thinking and forming ideas How thinking changes over time Aspects of narrative structure the student seems to understand or needs more support with Aspects of craft the student seems attuned to or seems to be missing

When students self-direct what, why, and how, they will create entries in their reading notebooks in which they are more motivated to think deeply than when we assign the task. By taking the time to teach students what a reading notebook is and the authentic ways we use the entries, we are beginning to invite students into the real ways readers use writing as a tool for thinking. In this chapter, we looked at several key lessons and examples of notebook entries you can teach your students. While it does take time and modeling, the benefits for students are totally worth it. The following chart shows some of the benefits for both readers and teachers when using student-directed reading notebook entries.

	BENEFITS OF MAKING DECISIONS BASED ON STUDENT-DIRECTED READING NOTEBOOK ENTRIES
For Readers	• Allows students to choose how they want to track and organize their thinking • Allows students to pursue their own ideas and questions as they read • Invites more ownership of the process • Allows students to transfer experiences and ways of using writing as an access point • Can improve comprehension • Reveals the real reasons why students are writing • Allows for less time spent writing during reading class
For Teachers	• Provides a glimpse into how readers think as they read • Gives opportunities for thin-slicing student thinking • Shows the reading process closer to how it unfolds and not just as a product at the end • Allows teachers to more clearly figure out where confusions came up or where thinking was generated in the text • Allows teachers to see the unique ways a reader is making meaning • Involves less to read but more information gained • Leads to knowledge of what to teach next

READING NOTEBOOKS: AN ACTION PLAN

As you get started teaching students how to use writing as a tool in the reading process, consider the current reality in your classroom. Think about whether a reboot of the initial lessons on authenticity and writing about reading is needed or if your students just need some further modeling of how to use reading notebooks for deeper understanding. Use the information you gather from these conferences to decide what to teach next.

GETTING STARTED WITH WRITING ABOUT FICTION READING

- ☐ Find out the reasons why your students currently write about reading (see page 60).

- ☐ Introduce genuine writing-about-reading lessons to students (see page 64).

- ☐ Explain to and show students what reading notebook entries are and why we create them (see page 64).

- ☐ Show students different ways to record their thinking in notebook entries (see page 80).

- ☐ Reflect with students and help them set personalized goals and intentions (see page 84).

- ☐ Inspire creative notebook entries by showing examples (see page 89).

- ☐ Take the **Self-Reflection Questionnaire** on page 98 and decide on some goals.

- ☐ Consider the practices you might want to let go of (see page 99).

Videos and viewing guide may also be accessed at
http://resources.corwin.com/GoldbergHouser-Fiction

 The Power of Using a Reading Notebook: The Goal

Video 3.1

 The Power of Using a Reading Notebook: Small Group Discussion

Video 3.2

 The Power of Using a Reading Notebook: Deciding What to Teach Next

Video 3.3

 Conferring About Reading Notebook Entries

Video 3.4

 Conferring About Reading Notebook Entries: Deciding What to Teach Next

Video 3.5

 A Reading Notebook Conference: The Lesson

Video 3.6

 Reflecting on a Reading Notebook Conference: Deciding What to Teach Next

Video 3.7

Decisions About Discussion

4

"WHEN WE READ TOGETHER, WE CONNECT.
TOGETHER, WE SEE THE WORLD. TOGETHER,
WE SEE ONE ANOTHER."

(Kate DiCamillo)

It was my very first day of teaching students in my own classroom. I survived a few months of substitute teaching during the previous school year. I attended a few professional development conferences over the summer and read a few books that stressed the importance of building community and reading aloud. As a result, that was the first item on the list of lesson plans for my very first day. I gathered the students in a meeting area and selected a book I hoped they would enjoy. Halfway through the read, Bakari raised his hand and interrupted what I thought at the time was a fairly successful read aloud: "Excuse me, but this is the time you are supposed to let us say something about the book." I placed the book on my lap and looked around the room only to see eager faces and bright-eyed smiles. "Ummm, OK" was all I could muster. But before I knew what had happened, as if on cue, each student turned and faced a peer nearby and began talking. I don't recall what they were talking about. But I do recall how impressed I was then, and I'm impressed to this day. They naturally took turns, talked about their own ideas, invited one another to share their thinking, asked for clarification, summarized, and pushed one another to see new ideas. It was incredible. Looking back at that moment now, I realize how fortunate I was to step into a school where conversations were at the heart of teaching and learning in each and every classroom. At this particular school, students are raised in a curriculum where conversation is an integral part of everyday life—in the hallways, at recess, and during physical education. I'd even go so far as to say, by the time students entered my classroom, conversations had shaped their identities.

When conversations are at the center of strategic curriculum design rather than an afterthought, students are empowered, gain autonomy, become critical decision makers, gain constant opportunities to practice self-regulation techniques, and experience a variety of social and emotional scenarios. This chapter will serve as a guide in your decision-making process for enhancing the classroom conversations already established for starting conversations in your classroom. Our focus will be on the ways in which conversation deepens students' understanding of fiction, and also serves as an assessment tool for you.

INTENTIONAL MOMENT

Think about the role of conversations in various aspects of your life. For example, think about moments of sheer excitement when you share news through a conversation, times when you need a sounding board, or times when you seek advice. Conversations play an important role in our everyday lives, and the purpose of our conversations is to serve as a well-rounded balance of our identity. Imagine creating time and teaching for a variety of conversations in our classrooms for the students we teach.

In this chapter, you will learn

- The benefits of classroom conversations as access points to understanding fiction texts
- How conversations serve as a tool for students and teachers
- Key lessons for teaching authentic conversations
- Common teaching approaches to classroom conversations and their limitations

In this chapter, we will look closely at how conversations serve as access points into deeply understanding fiction texts by helping readers clarify and extend their thinking. We'll do this by studying several transcripts of classroom conversations between students. We'll read these transcripts closely with an admiring lens, asking, "What are these students already doing well?" Following each transcript, we'll turn the strengths we noticed students using into lessons that we can teach other students who have not yet learned these skills. Finally, we'll reflect on common ineffective practices and the payoffs when you let them go. You'll leave this chapter with the building blocks for teaching students to have conversations, become contributing members of their community, and recognize the power in their voices. Once your students are engaged in *meaningful* conversations, you will have a whole lot more information to use when answering the "What next?" question.

The Benefits: Finding What's True for Us in Texts and Life

Conversations serve as access points for making meaning not only in the texts we read, but also in our everyday lives. They are an important part of the learning process, and when conversations happen, they become an important tool that yields information about the thinking process of readers, which contributes to our decisions about what to teach next.

Benefits for Readers. Conversations give readers a chance to process their experience in reading with others. As readers of fiction texts, we meet characters who may confirm or challenge our current belief systems. Conversations between readers serve as a platform to debate issues within a text brought on by characters' decisions, authors' decisions, and even our own decisions in our reactions as readers. Conversations also serve as a guide for readers who, through fiction, experience traveling to places and meeting people different from those in their own neighborhoods. Reading fiction opens the door to possibilities; having the opportunity to participate in conversations with other readers gives students the knowledge that too often has been limited because someone thought they couldn't access the text because they didn't have the background knowledge. When students discuss their reading with each other, they are forced to articulate their understanding of the text, and they also gain access to their conversational partners' understanding of the text, thus both deepening and expanding their comprehension. Therefore, giving our students time to read and talk about their reading provides opportunities for them to gain knowledge through experiences from the texts they read.

Benefits for Teachers. Let's face it—the teaching of reading and thinking about reading is challenging for many reasons, one of them being that when the act of reading happens, it's invisible. When you are teaching something invisible, how do you know where to start, let alone where to go next? Having conversations and writing in notebooks (discussed in the previous chapter) are two ways to help make thinking about reading visible (audible). When we listen to conversations, we listen in a way that treats them as reflections of the thinking readers practice while they read. We listen for evidence of comprehension in students'

BENEFITS OF CLASSROOM CONVERSATIONS FOR STUDENTS	BENEFITS OF CLASSROOM CONVERSATIONS FOR TEACHERS
★ Conversation provides opportunities for students to be social and forge relationships with peers.	★ Conversations make learning visible/audible.
★ Reading and discussing texts with others often increases engagement.	★ Conversations provide a platform for students to self-regulate and rehearse everyday life skills needed to engage with others in the community.
★ Reading and discussing texts with others exposes students to ways of thinking and feeling through text that may become part of their own repertoire.	★ Conversations provide an opportunity for immediate feedback.
★ Conversations provide a platform for articulating one's own experience and learning from others about their experiences.	★ Listening to conversations helps us decide what to teach next.
★ Conversations provide an opportunity to apply problem-solving skills and self-regulation techniques with peers.	★ Listening to conversations helps us know what types of thinking students are doing.
★ Conversations provide an opportunity for immediate feedback from others.	★ Listening to students helps us identify students' possible confusions or misconceptions.
★ Authentic conversations offer an opportunity to feel known and valued.	★ Creating space for conversations honors students' identity.

conversations. For example, when a reader describes a scene to her partner by saying, "I was really picturing Rob and Sistine when they were sitting on the bus, and I imagine it was weird and awkward," we have a hunch this reader is envisioning the text. Our next step might be to analyze the quality of the skill level and then decide whether or not to teach the same skill or a different skill based on a quick slice of the conversation. This is an example of conversations as a helpful tool for our decisions about what to teach next.

Regardless of where you are in your own journey of implementing classroom conversations, we hope you use this chapter to reflect on how you can gain new insight on how to use them in your decision-making process. Set aside time to listen to student conversations. Release yourself from the pressure of having to teach in this initial listening phase. Create a note-taking system where you can capture the observations you make and perhaps transcribe parts or entire conversations. Return to these notes and look for patterns or connections to specific skill sets.

The chart below shows what you might listen for and hear when students are having conversations. The left-hand column has questions that will guide your listening. In the center column are examples of what students might say as they reveal their thinking. In the right-hand column, we listed the terminology used by reading teachers to describe this thinking. The precise terms we listed are not sacrosanct, and you may have other terms to guide your note taking. Regardless of how you organize your clipboard notes, your aim is to *use what students are already doing* to decide what to teach next. So you are always building from the known to the new, building from strengths.

QUESTIONS WE MIGHT ASK READERS ABOUT THEIR THINKING	WHAT YOU MIGHT HEAR STUDENTS SAYING	AN EXAMPLE OF THIS READING STRENGTH
What are you doing as a reader when you read scenes and can see a movie in your mind?	★ *I'm picturing . . .* ★ *I hear . . .* ★ *I see . . .*	☐ Envisioning
Can you reread a part of this text where you had a strong reaction and walk through the steps of your thinking? What was the first thing you did? Then what did you do?	★ *No way!* ★ *I can't believe . . .* ★ *I can't imagine why . . .* ★ *Why would the character . . . ?*	☐ Critique
Describe some of the thinking you have about this character. What in the text is making you think that?	★ *I think this character is . . .* ★ *A pattern I'm noticing is . . . and that makes me think . . .* ★ *I'm not sure . . . but maybe . . .*	☐ Theories about characters

Teach Students to Have Meaningful Conversations

If classroom conversations are new for your students, or students need a few reminders, you might start by exploring conversational *behaviors* (making eye contact, taking turns, inviting others to join the conversation, etc.). Set up an inquiry by asking students to listen to and observe conversations all day long. Invite them to watch friends in conversations at recess or lunch, or listen to conversations at home with family members. Take photos of students demonstrating these behaviors and make a chart. The following ideas can guide your teaching decisions:

- Ask students to observe people having conversations and notice what they say and how they speak to one another. Create a chart with the results of this inquiry.

- Rehearse conversational behaviors with nonacademic topics that are highly engaging and offer opportunities for all students to participate (social events, current events, etc.).

- Introduce improv games as a way to create community guidelines that set up the foundation for risk-taking and sharing new ideas. For more practical ideas about classroom improv, check out *The Second City Guide to Improv in the Classroom* by Katherine McKnight and Mary Scruggs (2008) and web resources such as www.secondcity.com/network/10 -reasons-teachers-use-improv-classroom/.

- Engage in shared experiences around community events, such as taking an opportunity after lunch or recess to discuss an event.

- Give time to students to practice storytelling. Our friend, performer, and storyteller Antonio Sacre reminds us that the practice of stringing together events that change a character is one way of telling a story, and many pieces of fiction follow this same pattern. Therefore, by storytelling, our students are rehearsing for understanding their fiction reading.

- Vary the types of formats students use to engage in conversations between whole class, small groups, and partnerships.

Making Decisions Based on Student Conversations

In this section, we use student conversation transcripts to set up the key lessons that begin on page 123. In essence, this is the same process you will use to decide what to teach next: You notice what was successful in the conversation,

When students choose their own books based on their affinities and their ability to read accurately, fluently, and with high levels of understanding, they are setting themselves up for reading experiences that lead to genuine conversations.

and by naming the characteristics that were most productive, you are building on strengths and discovering what to teach to other students. Essentially, by thin-slicing conversations, we are able to make decisions about what to teach next, allowing the students' conversations to show us the next day's teaching and answer, "What do I teach tomorrow?"

We are about to enter a classroom where genuine conversations happen around thinking about books. In this classroom, the students use reading notebooks to record their thinking, and they have ownership of what, how, and why they write about their reading as well as what, how, and why they talk about their reading. During independent reading time, we observe and overhear the following as we listen to a partnership conversation.

Students are seated in various places around the room. Some are at tables, some are on the floor, and others are sitting on benches of various heights. The teacher is sitting next to a student while the student reads aloud from his text. After a few short minutes of conversation, the teacher leaves the student, moves to the center of the room, and raises her hand. This quiet motion signals to the readers that their attention is needed. We listen, and we hear:

"Readers, we have a few minutes left. If you think a conversation will help you today, take a moment to prepare for that conversation and then move into your partnership spaces." The room remains silent as students prepare. Some are flipping through pages of their books, others are writing in notebooks, and others are placing sticky notes within their text. They begin to shift from independent reading spaces to new spaces throughout the classroom next to students who are holding the same text or a text in the same series. We sit next to a partnership holding *The Tequila Worm* by Viola Canales (2005). The book is opened to the chapter titled "Taco Head." The students start a discussion, and the transcript follows.

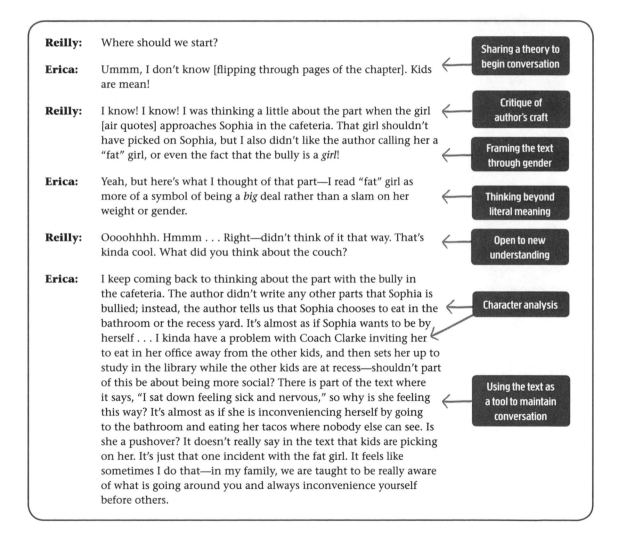

Reilly: Where should we start?

Erica: Ummm, I don't know [flipping through pages of the chapter]. Kids are mean!

Sharing a theory to begin conversation

Reilly: I know! I know! I was thinking a little about the part when the girl [air quotes] approaches Sophia in the cafeteria. That girl shouldn't have picked on Sophia, but I also didn't like the author calling her a "fat" girl, or even the fact that the bully is a *girl*!

Critique of author's craft

Framing the text through gender

Erica: Yeah, but here's what I thought of that part—I read "fat" girl as more of a symbol of being a *big* deal rather than a slam on her weight or gender.

Thinking beyond literal meaning

Reilly: Oooohhhh. Hmmm . . . Right—didn't think of it that way. That's kinda cool. What did you think about the couch?

Open to new understanding

Erica: I keep coming back to thinking about the part with the bully in the cafeteria. The author didn't write any other parts that Sophia is bullied; instead, the author tells us that Sophia chooses to eat in the bathroom or the recess yard. It's almost as if Sophia wants to be by herself . . . I kinda have a problem with Coach Clarke inviting her to eat in her office away from the other kids, and then sets her up to study in the library while the other kids are at recess—shouldn't part of this be about being more social? There is part of the text where it says, "I sat down feeling sick and nervous," so why is she feeling this way? It's almost as if she is inconveniencing herself by going to the bathroom and eating her tacos where nobody else can see. Is she a pushover? It doesn't really say in the text that kids are picking on her. It's just that one incident with the fat girl. It feels like sometimes I do that—in my family, we are taught to be really aware of what is going around you and always inconvenience yourself before others.

Character analysis

Using the text as a tool to maintain conversation

Erica:	So, back to the book, I was thinking that being different is hard. But what does it mean to be different? Where do we get the idea that being different is bad? Is it bad?	**Approximating theme**
Reilly:	Yeah, I'm not Mexican American reading this, so I don't know what it's like to be different as a Mexican American—but I have a lot of difference too. I wonder if different is different in different places? [The girls laugh.] If the setting of this school in this book was in Los Angeles, Sophia probably wouldn't feel different for being Mexican American. She may feel different for other reasons, but there are many students who are Mexican American in classrooms all over Los Angeles.	**Growing thinking through interpretation of possible ideas** **Frames: Setting, culture**
Erica:	[Nodding] Uh-huh, yep. So, what are we really trying to say? We are running out of time!	
Reilly:	I think we're really trying to say something about difference. I want to go back and think more about why we think difference is a bad thing. Or maybe, when do we think it's good, and when do we think it's bad? Like, I like that I'm a girl who plays on sports teams with mostly boys—that makes me different, but I like that because I'm just as good as most of them!	**Moving closer to themes (less cliché)**
Erica:	So, are we agreeing we want to think more about this difference thing?	
Reilly:	Yeah, I think so.	
Erica:	OK, so let's agree to read the next chapter, and we can talk more about it tomorrow.	**Student-generated reading plans**
Reilly:	Yeah, I want to come back to this chapter. We didn't get to talk about Sophia's parents—like, did you notice the author didn't include any details about Sophia telling her parents? Only Coach Clarke—and I want to talk more about this Coach Clarke thing, and how Coach sets up Sophia to think about revenge. So weird!	**Questioning the characters, the author**
Erica:	OK, yep!	

Learning From Reilly and Erica

Let's thin-slice the discussion between Reilly and Erica.

Reilly and Erica know how to

- Engage and navigate talk in authentic ways
- Actively listen
- Analyze text in diverse ways
- Use partnership discussions as part of their reading plan

When we look back to this classroom scenario, we find that listening to student discussions is just one way of making the invisible act of reading visible. For example, when Reilly and Erica speak about the author's decisions in creating the character of Coach Clarke, we have the opportunity to bridge reading and writing. It's likely these students are working on narrative writing and, therefore, making decisions firsthand as writers. In this partnership, Erica and Reilly are bringing their writing experience into their reading, which enables them to think critically in texts—in this case, about the author's decisions and the impact on the reader.

Effective Fiction Conversation Characteristics

CONVERSATION CHARACTERISTICS	DESCRIPTION	WHAT STUDENTS MIGHT SAY
Negotiate the Conversation	Students actively participate in conversations by • Showing up with ideas to discuss • Listening openly and building and challenging ideas • Self-regulating • Taking turns, making eye contact, leaning in, etc.	• *What do you mean?* • *So what you are saying is . . . ?* • *Another example is . . .* • *I don't know what that word means.* • *What are you really saying?* • *Can we go back to the part about . . .* • *This reminds me of . . .*
Negotiate Their Thinking and the Text	Students develop thinking in conversations by • Referring back to the text • Sharing their theories • Building an idea together • Considering the decisions of the author	• Character: *A theory I have about this character is . . .* • Character: *When I think about the relationship between these characters, it makes me wonder . . .* • Theme: *This is really about the big idea . . .* • Theme: *In the text, the characters are learning . . . so that makes me think in our everyday lives we should be thinking about . . .*
Negotiate a Reading Plan	Students reflect on thinking and make plans for future reading by • Sharing their process • Talking about their intentions • Showing challenging parts and what they did to try to get through them • Asking for help • Planning together for future reading and conversations	• *Let's reread . . . because we need to think about . . .* • *When I got to this challenging part, I . . .* • *Can you help me with . . . ?* • *Tomorrow when I read, I am going to . . .* • *I think I need to focus more on . . .*

Moves for Analyzing Text in Diverse Ways

Here, we want to focus on one area of the chart on the previous page because it's the heart of the fiction reading process, and most of the decisions you make about what readers need will arise from here. Fiction writers are often likened to tapestry makers who deliberately use threads of character's details, setting, themes, and other strands to create a story world that a reader has to envision. And to extend this analogy, there are many hundreds of threads and patterns each of us teachers could try to teach our students in reading fiction! But for the sake of framing this book, or framing this tapestry of the landscape of fiction, we find it useful to mine students' understanding of characters and themes along three planes: understanding text, understanding people, and understanding self. This frame can then be used to listen to student conversations, make decisions about what to teach next, and reflect on the rest of the chapters in this book.

When readers think about characters, they pay attention to what the character needs and what the character wants. To do so, readers live in the character's world in a copacetic, but high-alert, state. They

- Pay attention to both the internal and external roadblocks characters face

- Study patterns in the characters' responses to the world around them

- Think about patterns in the characters' physical surroundings and situations

- Linger in the complexity and uncertainty of not knowing how the conflicts will unfold

- Journey alongside the characters as they grow and change as a result of each particular element of the plot created intentionally by the author

- Synthesize all they read, intuitively knowing that they need to understand the characters' journey as well as why the author might think it matters to them and to others

- Interpret ideas and themes as they study what a character says, thinks, and does along with what a character does not say—and notice patterns in when things are said and when they are left unsaid

- Look for symbolism in the setting, objects, and patterns

When readers think through texts in these ways, the result is often that their conversations mirror their thinking. Therefore, by leaning in and listening, we're able to hear patterns in readers' thinking, name them, and use them to answer the "what to teach next" question.

In the chart that follows, we give a quick preview of the kinds of language students might use when they think deeply about fiction. Notice the focus on understanding characters (more in Chapter 5) and interpreting themes (more in Chapter 6). By focusing on these, many other literary elements naturally get attended to as well. You'll notice we present three categories of understanding—text, people, and self—as all three are major benefits of reading fiction. We use Kate DiCamillo's (2005) *The Tiger Rising* to illustrate, because it's such a rich, accessible, and elegant book in terms of characters and themes.

	UNDERSTANDING CHARACTERS		INTERPRETING THEMES	
	WHAT HAPPENED IN THE TEXT	WHAT STUDENTS MIGHT SAY	WHAT HAPPENED IN THE TEXT	WHAT STUDENTS MIGHT SAY
Understand text	Rob's mother has died, and he suppresses his feelings because his father wants him to move on.	*"In Chapter 1, Rob keeps using the word not—not thinking about anything—so I think he isn't over his mom's death or something."*	Suitcase Contrast of darkness and light is used by DiCamillo to allude to emotions of the characters. The caged tiger is a symbol of emotions that have been avoided.	*"When he says the suitcase is bursting, I realize the suitcase is a metaphor for all the sadness he's locked inside."* *"Throughout the book, both light and dark get mentioned a lot. I wonder if this is connected to how Rob feels."* *"Both Rob and Sistine are avoiding dealing with major life changes. Rob won't let himself grieve his mom's death, and Sistine needs to deal with the reality of her parents' separation. It's like they both have caged-up emotions."*

(Continued)

(Continued)

	UNDERSTANDING CHARACTERS		INTERPRETING THEMES	
	WHAT HAPPENED IN THE TEXT	WHAT STUDENTS MIGHT SAY	WHAT HAPPENED IN THE TEXT	WHAT STUDENTS MIGHT SAY
Understand people	The hotel maid, Willie May, tells Rob his rash is a result of his sadness.	*"I can tell she's had a hard life and seen a lot. She's got wisdom. There is a checkout person at the grocery store in town who talks to my mom like that. I bet she hasn't gone to college, but she's wise just like Willie May."*	Rob's father reads the note from the principal at school about Rob's rash and then cooks him a macaroni-and-cheese dinner on the hot plate and gives all of the food to Rob.	*"I think Rob's father isn't a bad guy—it's just maybe he thinks he's supposed to be strong for his son, and he doesn't realize Rob would heal faster if he didn't completely stop talking about the mom."*
Understand self	DiCamillo developed young characters who face common obstacles and react in common ways.	*"I didn't cry at my grandma's funeral, but last summer I did when my mom gave me her old wristwatch."*	Sistine and Rob are walking through the woods in search of the tiger. Sistine asks Rob several times about his mother; Rob shrugs it off until Sistine leaves. Rob runs to catch up with Sistine and tells her his mother has died.	*"I think Rob realizes that he doesn't want to lose Sistine's friendship even though it's hard to talk about his mom. There are lots of times I avoid conversations, but then when I finally do talk about it, I end up feeling better. It's almost like a relief to find someone you can share hard things with."*

Lessons for Talking About Fiction

What follows are key lessons inspired by Reilly and Erica that you can decide to teach if you have students who are either just beginning or returning to conversations and need support with utilizing them as a more effective tool.

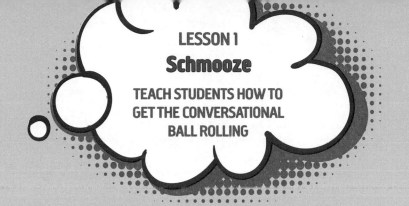

LESSON 1
Schmooze
TEACH STUDENTS HOW TO GET THE CONVERSATIONAL BALL ROLLING

This lesson is designed to teach the basics of getting conversations started. Students know how to talk to one another, and they also know how to talk about their books. In fact, there is a really good chance they know how to recall and repeat out loud literal aspects of the texts they listen to or read. Therefore, this isn't a lesson on "how to talk" to your reading partner, or (only) repeat what is in the text; instead, it teaches students how readers navigate or plot the course of their conversations about *thinking* about reading in a way that benefits understanding of texts, one another, and ourselves.

Decide to Teach This Tomorrow if Your Students

- Are new to conversations about their own thinking about reading
- Need support in understanding the purpose of conversations about reading
- Are ready for a reminder of a few tips about the basics of conversations

thin slice

What You Need:

- A topic to talk about—something from the local headline news, for example, or a shared experience of the class community (a field trip, a nail-biting foursquare game at recess, etc.). The important consideration is that the topic is something the entire class participated in so that every student has equal access to the topic and the conversation about the topic.

Tell Why: Describe the importance of conversations for knowing one another in our everyday lives and make the link to knowing one another as readers, knowing texts we read, and knowing ourselves through conversations. Explain to students the expectation of participating in daily conversations. List the various structures conversations will take: whole class, small groups, partnerships, and individual with you, the teacher.

(Continued)

Explore How:

- Gather: Ask students to move to a central meeting space away from the possible distractions at their desks. In another effort to limit distractions, have them leave all notebooks, books, pens, and papers at their desks. They should sit next to a partner in the meeting area.

- Start: You might begin by saying, "I was surprised to read in the newspaper this morning that . . . What are your thoughts about . . . ? Talk with your partner."

- Listen: As students talk with their partners, your job is to observe and collect information about them. Consider giving yourself a few lenses to research:

> ○ *Behaviors.* How are the partners talking? Are they taking turns? Are they making eye contact? Are they showing they're listening?
>
> ○ *Content.* What are they talking about? Is it related to the topic? Are they able to return to the topic when they stray? Are they able to give examples that support their opinions about the topic?
>
> ○ *Conversations.* How are they able to negotiate the conversation? Are they able to initiate and get started? Are they inviting others into the conversation? Are they clarifying and checking for understanding?

- Support: Encourage students when you observe them utilizing strategies in their conversations. You might give them an encouraging gesture such as a thumbs-up and a smile, or name what you noticed in a way that allows them to replicate it in the future.

Name How:

- Ask students to gather back as a whole group. Spend the remaining two to three minutes naming observations that seemed to really help conversations. When students hear what they were doing well, you have an opportunity to infuse your classroom with optimism and create a strong foundation for next step teaching.

- Create a chart that evolves across the year. Add to the chart every time you teach a new aspect of conversations. See the sample that follows.

CONVERSATIONS LOOK LIKE

* Using your body to show you are listening
    * Leaning in
    * Making eye contact
    * Smiling :)
    * Facing one another

* Taking turns
* Inviting all members to participate and contribute to the thinking of the group
* Pointing to the text and reading notebook entries as examples

CONVERSATIONS SOUND LIKE

* Clarifying
    * *I wasn't sure what the author was trying to say here . . .*
    * *What do you mean when you say . . . ?*
    * *Are you saying . . . ?*

* Starting
    * *Who has an idea to start?*
    * *Where do we begin?*
    * *Let's all turn to page . . .*

* Turning
    * *Can we move on?*
    * *How does that connect with what we are saying about . . . ?*
    * *We need to get back to the idea of . . .*

* Ending
    * *OK, it's time to wrap up . . .*
    * *What do we want to do next?*
    * *We did a great job today of . . .*
    * *Let's try . . .*

A Few Tips:

* Our friend and storyteller Antonio Sacre reminds us how important storytelling is to building stronger brains: "Storytelling makes pictures in your head, and these pictures solidify and codify memory and experience in an unforgettable way. When these strong memories or pictures or stories connect in any way to a piece of fiction we read, both are enhanced." This lesson prepares students for conversations using a storytelling platform. Let's consider when we can carve out a few minutes each day for students to share a few moments with one another by telling stories and practice using conversational behaviors.

* While listening to students talking to one another, take a few photographs of expected outcomes (students showing they are listening by leaning in, making eye contact, smiling, etc.). Add these photos to the chart you create to support conversations.

Many students benefit from both visual and written cues on classroom charts.

- Create a special space in your classroom dedicated to supporting classroom conversations. This might be a different-colored bulletin board or a centrally located, easily accessible chart that students can visit as often as they need to support their conversations.
- Design a quick "on the go" system to note observations. Focus your observations by creating lenses through which to observe your students. See the sample option below.

STUDENT NAMES	BEHAVIORS: WHAT DO PEOPLE *LOOK* LIKE IN CONVERSATIONS?	TALK: WHAT DO PEOPLE *SOUND* LIKE IN CONVERSATIONS?	CONTENT: WHAT DO PEOPLE TALK *ABOUT* IN CONVERSATIONS?

Talk Show Tricks

TEACH STUDENTS HOW TO CREATE PLANS WITH PARTNERS

This lesson is designed to be taught after the initial stage of getting conversations started. Our goal is to *shape* conversations by teaching students effective time management skills. We are not suggesting that students move methodically through conversations; however, to start, it's often helpful to explicitly guide students through a variety of activities before they begin to utilize them independently.

Decide to Teach This Tomorrow if Your Students

- Have a routine for starting conversations and need support maintaining focus
- Need support in building stamina in conversations
- Need support in engaging with one another in conversations
- Are reading for a few time management tips
- Are having conversations and need support in making them productive

thin
slice

What You Need:

- Chart paper
- A student or colleague to model being your reading partner
- Students gathered in the meeting area next to a partner

Tell Why: Explain to students the importance of managing time effectively in order to be productive in reading and in conversations about our reading. Tell students they will have a chance to collaborate in their partnerships to create an agenda for their time together. Afterward, they will test out that agenda and then determine if it needs revising before their next meeting.

(Continued)

Show How:

- Model starting a conversation with your partner (either a student or a colleague) with the goal of collaborating to stay organized, focused, and productive.

- Create a chart to organize reflections. See the sample below. Think aloud as you reflect about the process with your partner. The chart below shows three categories to discuss and reflect upon.

LOVE IT!	NOT SO GREAT . . .	IDEAS TO TRY INSTEAD
★ Reading parts of the text to our partners that we want to talk about	★ Running out of things to talk about and then ending up not talking or talking about recess	☐ Looking for confusing parts of the text and asking a question that could help clarify them

- Explain to students that agendas are a way of making a plan and keeping organized. Based on the reflections, model creating a *Partnership Agenda*. See the example that follows.

Partnership Agenda

3 minutes ☐ Dramatic reading of favorite scenes

☐ Ask clarifying questions

☐ Share theories and themes

1-2 minutes ☐ Make a reading plan

Practice How:

- Give students a few minutes to reflect on their conversations with the same three-column chart you just created in your model.
- Students use the reflection in order to create a Partnership Agenda about what they want to try next.

A Tip:

- Co-author a chart with students to support their reflections and problem solving. See the sample below.

PRODUCTIVE PARTNERSHIP CONVERSATIONS

IF WE WANT	WE CAN TRY
★ Ways to start	★ Rereading a scene and asking our partners to react or even act it out
	★ Reading aloud part of a notebook entry and asking for feedback or thoughts
	★ Asking a question
★ To understand our books	★ Giving a quick summary
	★ Asking clarifying questions
	★ Rereading a part of the text together
★ Everyone to participate	★ Inviting others to add to a specific idea or question
	★ Asking readers to share part of their notebook entries
	★ Having a *conversation* by writing in our notebooks followed by a discussion
★ To find themes	★ Asking our partner questions:
	○ What lessons does this part teach us?
	○ How do you think the author feels about . . . ?
	★ Sharing reading notebook entries
	★ Comparing the current book to previously read books

CLIPBOARD NOTES: STUDENT CONVERSATIONS

The following tool can be used when observing students as part of your conversation clipboard notes. You might look for conversational behaviors, tools, or thinking when making your observations.

NAME AND DATE	OBSERVATIONS
	Conversational Behaviors ☐ Initiates ☐ Listens ☐ Takes turns ☐ Clarifies ☐ Summarizes
	Conversational Tools ☐ Uses notebook entries ☐ References the text ☐ Uses classroom charts
	Conversations and Thinking ☐ Supports thinking ☐ Challenges thinking ☐ Inspires a plan ☐ Encourages rereading
	Other Notes:

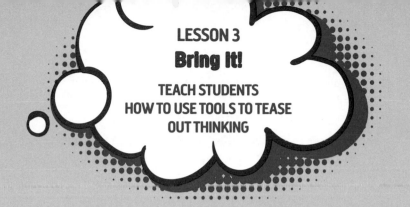

LESSON 3
Bring It!

TEACH STUDENTS
HOW TO USE TOOLS TO TEASE
OUT THINKING

Bring all of it! Bring materials and tools to each conversation you have about your reading, and most importantly, bring your thinking! Materials serve not only to support our thinking while we read but also to support the conversations we have about our reading. In this lesson, we'll model for students how to effectively use tools such as text excerpts, reading notebooks, sticky notes, or any other tools readers create to add to the productivity of conversations and ultimately help build understanding of fiction books.

Decide to Teach This Tomorrow if Your Students

- Run out of things to talk about
- Need support with keeping conversations focused
- View tools such as notebooks and sticky notes as school tasks rather than real reading tools

thin slice

What You Need:

- Your reading notebook
- A familiar read aloud with a few sticky notes prepared ahead of time, such as *Rules* by Cynthia Lord (2006) (for more book options, see Chapter 2)

Tell Why: Explain to students the natural ebb and flow of conversations. In some of our conversations, we will run out of time because we have so much to talk about. Other times, it will feel like we have too much time. Describe to students the goal of striking a balance in our conversations as a tool to support our thinking.

Show How: Model for students a two-minute scenario of preparing for partnership conversations.

- Think aloud as you scan the previously created chart, Partnership Agenda (created in Lesson 2), and remind yourself of your plans as a reading partnership.

(Continued)

Preparing for Conversations

☐ identify part of the text you'd like to discuss

OR

☐ create a notebook entry to use in conversations

OR

☐ jot a question or reaction

OR

☐ share your opinion and back it up.

- Model rereading a short excerpt from a read aloud book. Pause and think aloud about the ideas you have about your reading. For example, you might ask questions about the characters or describe images you envision.

- Demonstrate either marking the page with a sticky note or jotting the page number in your reading notebook.

- Draft a notebook entry or think aloud about the process of what you would write (if you don't want to take the time to write the whole entry in front of students).

- Show students how to use the materials you just prepped in a conversation by inviting a student or colleague to act as your reading partner.

- Name the steps you modeled when preparing for the conversation and create a chart for future reference. See the following sample.

A Few Tips:

- Instead of having students move to independent reading after this lesson, let students prepare and meet in partnerships so they can apply the learning immediately.

- For younger or less experienced students, divide this lesson into a few parts and teach it across a few days.

- Create a bulletin board in your classroom to display examples of student-generated tools and how they support thinking and understanding of texts. As a way to organize the bulletin board, try creating a chart similar to the one below.

READING TOOL I CREATED	HOW IT HELPS ME IN MY READING

Mia and Angie—Next we'll study a conversation between reading partners Mia and Angie. Get your clipboard notes ready. We'll listen and name what they are doing well. Let's take note of what they already know about initiating and maintaining a conversation. Let's also note what they are talking about and how they are talking about it. From our analysis of these notes, we'll think about students in our class who are similar to Mia and Angie and are ready to learn these same transferable strategies. We'll also think about how we might scaffold these lessons for students who are developing in their conversational collaboration with their peers.

Mia:	I'm thinking about something different in my book.	Student initiation of conversation
Angie:	What?	
Mia:	I'm thinking about the frames we have been trying in read aloud. So I'm trying out reading some of this by framing gender [holds up her copy of *The Tiger Rising*]. So, in this book, Sistine fights a lot in school. That's not what most girls do. Most girls probably, like, talk to their friends and just do girly stuff. That's what most books are usually about—boys fighting and things like that. So I think that this book really does bring, kinda like, equal rights. This book doesn't just show us about Sistine. Sistine does a lot of things that I don't think boys would even do. So I like the book!	Transfer of class strategies to independent understanding Frame: Gender (see Chapter 6)
Angie:	In my book, the girls act like normal girls—well, not Agatha. Agatha— I feel like she wants to get into fights like Sistine. Sophie wants to hang out with girls, and Agatha should do what boys do. She seems like the type of person to me, like Sistine, who would get into fights a lot.	
Teacher:	Say more about what you mean when you talk about things that girls or boys do.	Character analysis (see Chapter 5)
Mia:	Well, if you relate it to life, like today, if I go to soccer and I'm the only girl on the team, sometimes the coach will tell the boys, "Even the girl can do it," and I don't get that! It's just saying, "She can do it, so that means you can do it," but really not. I can do different things that maybe boys can't do. It doesn't just have to be in soccer.	
Angie:	I agree with you. Sometimes, like, ummm.... if a girl is trying to do something she likes to do, then a boy says, "No, you can't do this because you are a girl!" just because of being a girl! I think that's not fair. Just because they are different genders doesn't mean they can't do the same thing.	Grappling with gender roles both in text and in life
Teacher:	Hmm. Where do these ideas that people have come from?	

thin slice

Learning From Mia and Angie

When we thin-slice their conversation, we see evidence of several independent routines around the management and social behaviors of co-authoring thinking and understanding through conversations. These students can

- Initiate conversations on their own without a prompt or worksheet from the teacher
- Listen to one another and build ideas from each other's thoughts
- Ask one another questions to clarify or brainstorm theories and ideas
- Stay focused on a topic
- Share their current thinking about the books they are reading
- Connect ideas from the book to their everyday lives
- Consider objectives and decisions authors make in their writing

We also observe Mia and Angie approximating higher-level thinking around the characters and themes. They are approximating

- Ideas about characters
- Messages and themes around gender roles
- The historical impact on gender representation in fiction stories
- Cross-text thinking with each of their independent books and secular media

When we study what they are discussing and how, we're able to generate a list of strategies for the readers in our class who are similar to Mia and Angie, as well as for those students who are on their way. The following lessons are inspired by our observations of Mia and Angie.

LESSON 4
Extreme Sport
DARING TO TALK ABOUT EDGY IDEAS

This lesson is designed to support students to think about complex ideas in their reading and discuss them in their conversations. Before this lesson is taught, it's important to ensure there has been enough teaching and collaboration around building a community that honors intellectual risk-taking. Then, teach students a variety of ways to grapple with ideas. This lesson provides concrete scaffolds of questions that can later be removed, or added to and revised. The goal is to encourage asking powerful questions that can lead to powerful thinking.

Decide to Teach This Tomorrow if Your Students

- Need support thinking beyond literal and cliché ideas
- Talk about the same things most days and need support with diversifying their conversations
- Are playing it safe in their conversations instead of using them as a place to explore new ideas and thinking
- Are afraid of having the "wrong" answer or not getting it right
- Have a strong sense of trust in one another and are willing to take intellectual risks

What You Need:

- A chart with questions written ahead of time (see an example on the next page)
- A familiar read aloud text—for example, *The Tiger Rising* by Kate DiCamillo (2005) (see Chapter 2 for more book ideas)
- A provocative or edgy scene that will push the boundaries of your classroom status quo conversations

Tell Why: Explain to students that conversations are opportunities to grapple with ideas that are new or challenge our current set of beliefs and thinking.

(Continued)

Show How: Display questions like those shown here. Make clear that these questions are ones we can ask ourselves or one another in our conversations.

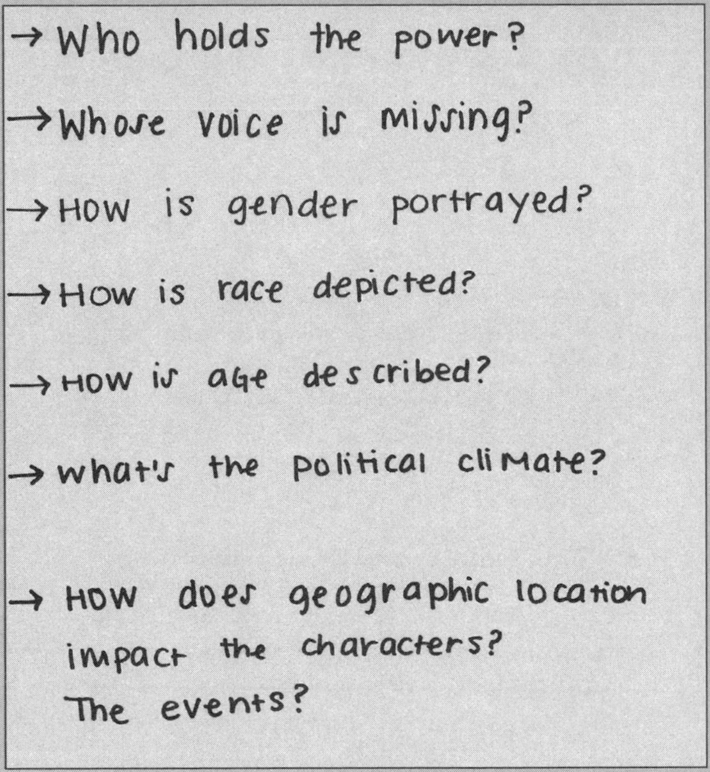

→ Who holds the power?

→ Whose voice is missing?

→ How is gender portrayed?

→ How is race depicted?

→ How is age described?

→ What's the political climate?

→ How does geographic location
   impact the characters?
   The events?

- Show students the chart of questions that help us be a bit edgier in our thinking and conversations.
- Choose a question from the chart and be sure to think aloud about how you made that choice and why you think it will help your conversation.

Practice How:

- Plan for two to three minutes of time for students and their partners to practice trying out their thinking using different questions from the chart. Students can discuss the class read aloud with these questions in mind.
- Let students know they can use these same questions when they discuss any fiction text—read aloud books or their independent reading books.

A Few Tips:

- When you confer with students, it can help to model the "messiness" of thinking. You can use these same sentence starters later to coach students. For example:

PUSHING THE LIMITS OF MY THINKING

★ Normally I would think about . . . but I'm trying to understand . . .

★ On the other hand . . .

★ I understand . . . but let's think about another perspective . . .

★ Conversely . . .

★ Maybe it could be . . .

★ Maybe . . .

★ What about . . . ?

- Modify this lesson by writing questions on 3 × 5 cards or sentence strips and place them in an envelope. Distribute the envelope to each partnership or club. Students can take turns pulling a question from the envelope, placing it in the center of the group, and then starting a conversation.

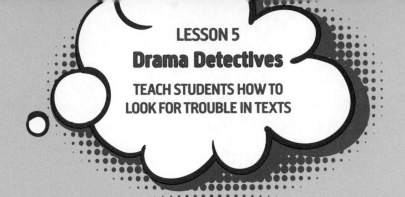

"In literature, only trouble is interesting. It takes literature to turn the great themes of life into story," said scholar Janet Burroway. And by extension, then, the drama of fiction lends itself to juicy discussion. This lesson reminds students to seek out the drama! In paying attention to these moments, they often pick up on the themes the author is toying with (see more in Chapters 5 and 6 for lessons about understanding characters and interpreting themes). Processing the twists and turns of the plot through conversation gives insight to multiple perspectives and helps readers develop great empathy for characters.

thin slice

Decide to Teach This Tomorrow if Your Students

- Are studying single dimensions of characters rather than multiple
- Need support engaging in conversations
- Think conversations are boring and tedious

What You Need:

- A familiar read aloud text that has a dramatic scene or two. We suggest using "The Fight" from Adam Bagdasarian's (2003) *First French Kiss and Other Traumas* or *Days With Frog and Toad* by Arnold Lobel (1979).
- Chart paper
- Students sitting in a gathering area in partnerships
- A colleague or student to model a partnership conversation with you

Tell Why: Ask students to (mentally or in their reading notebooks) list their top three favorite stories and reflect on why they like them. Remind students that we are often drawn to stories because of the drama! Explain that this lesson is designed to help them think through elements of the drama (plot) in their conversations as a way to deepen their understanding.

Show How:

- On a piece of chart paper, sketch an example of a plot with the characters facing roadblocks with every attempt to get what they want, which ultimately causes tension and drama.

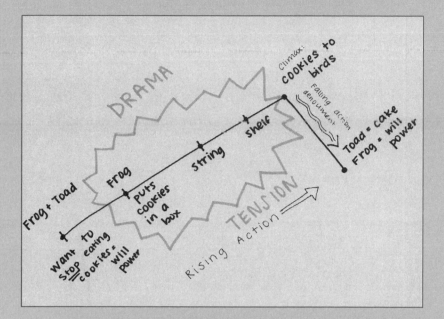

- Write the following questions on chart paper:

> Let's study the *drama*!
> - Who are the characters, and what do they want?
> - What are the roadblocks that prevent them from getting what they want?
> - In their attempts to get what they want, what do they learn? What do we learn?

- Think aloud as you model answering the questions with your partner using the characters from a familiar class read aloud.

Practice How:

- Give students two or three minutes to practice this same thinking in the familiar read aloud text by jotting down a few ideas in their reading notebooks.
- Give students a few minutes to share their thinking with their partner. Lean in and listen to students' conversations. Many students benefit from support in how to start a discussion from a question rather than moving robotically through the list of questions.

A Few Tips:

- Teach this lesson first, during a read aloud rather than an isolated lesson. Make sure you plan where you will stop and what you will say. Plan for places for students to rehearse for the conversation during the read aloud with their partners.

- Use the following chart to help you notice what students are doing and what you might teach them next in a partner conference.

IF STUDENTS ARE	SUPPORT THEM BY
• Jumping from one talking point to the next • Not giving examples for their thinking	★ Saying, "Can you tell me more about the part about . . . ?"
• In a one-sided conversation with one student doing all the talking	★ Asking the silent partner, "What do you think about what your partner is saying about . . . ?"
• Stuck in a retell and need help getting to the plot	★ Asking, "Where did this story start to turn?" ★ Prompting, "Let's find the place in the text where events started to change, turn, or twist . . ."
• Not making eye contact	★ Asking, "How can we show one another we are listening?"
• Discussing turning points and twists	★ Asking, "So what is that *really* about?" ★ Asking, "Could there be a bigger idea there?"
• Discussing themes	★ Asking, "What did you notice about the author's choices?" ★ Asking, "Why would the author include that scene?"

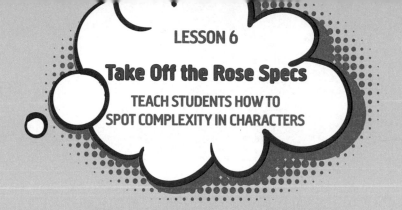

LESSON 6

Take Off the Rose Specs

TEACH STUDENTS HOW TO SPOT COMPLEXITY IN CHARACTERS

What are your favorite fiction books? Why? We're often drawn to the people in stories. It's important to understand characters. This lesson is designed to encourage readers to see multiple perspectives of a character through debate. If we examine characters from one point of view, we're limiting our chance to explore the dynamics of characters and their relationships.

Decide to Teach This Tomorrow if Your Students

- Have a limited view of the character(s)
- Need support in providing evidence for their opinions
- Are going to write an opinion or argument piece of writing this year

thin slice

What You Need:

- A familiar read aloud text, such as *Houndsley and Catina* by James Howe (2006)
- Chart paper
- Your reading notebook
- A colleague or student to demonstrate a partnership debate
- Students sitting in a gathering area in partnerships

Tell Why: Remind students how important it is to get to know characters just like we get to know people—by studying all aspects of what they look like in mood and dress, what they say, and how they act over time. Tell them that this lesson is a chance to see multiple aspects of characters through *debate*.

Show How:

- Draw a box in the middle of the chart paper. Write the name of a character in the middle of it. Write opposing opinions on either side of the box. See the sample on the next page.

(Continued)

- Choose one side to support. Think aloud as you prepare your notebook to support that side.
- Ask for a student to serve as your partner who has the opposite opinion he wants to support. Model a quick two- or three-minute debate with this student acting as your debate partner.
- Swap sides. Prepare an argument for the other point of view.
- Again, model a quick two- to three-minute debate, this time supporting the opposite side.
- Remind students the importance of thinking about both sides. Arguing for one side and then the other is an exercise to help us see multiple perspectives.

A Few Tips:

- If students are not familiar with debate, invite members of the debate team to join the class during this lesson or an interview.
- Watch a short video clip of a student-to-student debate as a strong model.
- Teach students a few introductory steps to debate protocol. For example, state your claim or opinion and support it with evidence. Prepare for the counter-argument. Think about a logical and compelling progression to organize your debate.
- Instead of debating a character or event from a text, first try the protocols of debate with a short video clip, a headline from the local newspaper, or a piece of art or music.

What's Next?

Let's take a moment to check in. In this chapter, we've discussed the benefits of classroom conversations, how conversations serve as a tool for both students and teachers, and several key lessons for teaching genuine conversations. In the next section, we'll take a look at common classroom practices and consider how they might not be as helpful as we'd like in our decision-making process. Take a moment to check in by having a conversation with a colleague on your thoughts so far, jotting an entry in your reading notebook, or using the following questionnaire to reflect.

© Daryl Getman, DAG Photography

When students choose the parts they want to discuss and are free to explore their own ideas and questions, they are more engaged, they build better understanding of the text, and we teachers have a front-row seat to their thinking.

SELF-REFLECTION QUESTIONNAIRE
STUDENT CONVERSATIONS

Check all that apply. Celebrate what is checked off and use what is not checked off to set goals for your students.

When I listen to and observe my students, I notice

- ☐ Students are mostly on task
- ☐ Conversations help the students understand their reading and thinking more deeply
- ☐ Students actively participate and show up prepared for the conversations
- ☐ Students independently solve problems
- ☐ Students help one another
- ☐ Students build off each other's ideas
- ☐ Students sustain attention and stamina
- ☐ Students leave the conversation with more ideas and new insights

The area I am most proud of in my students' conversations is . . .

If I could change one thing about my students' conversations, it would be . . .

One goal I have for my students' conversations is . . .

What We Might Let Go of When Asking Students to Talk About Their Reading

Teacher-Led Question-and-Answer Talk

In much the same way that writing about reading is often done through a predetermined worksheet, novel guide, or quiz, discussion structures often undermine readers' thinking and comprehension by being, well, too tightly wound! As well intentioned as they may be, the net effect is that they keep the teacher on a pedestal of knowing all the "correct" insights about a text. Let's step into a classroom and look at a transcript of students answering the teacher's questions after a read aloud. Make note of what seems different than the authentic conversation transcripts we just read and why.

Learning From William

In this fourth-grade classroom, the teacher has allocated fifteen to twenty minutes of the daily schedule to gather students together for an interactive read aloud. An interactive read aloud occurs when a teacher models her thinking in a class text and prompts students to share their thinking. One goal the teacher has in mind is to build in time for students to process their thinking through planned interactions in the text. This teacher has indicated the times she wants to stop and ask questions by placing sticky notes throughout the text as reminders. When we enter the classroom, the teacher has the students gathered. She is the only one with a copy of the text, *One Green Apple* by Eve Bunting (2006). The students are sitting next to their partners. The teacher finishes reading a page, places the book on her lap, and looks to the students to begin asking questions. A transcript of the talk follows.

Let's take a look at what happens when discussions are teacher led in a question-and-answer structure. When we study with teachers about this topic, we are often told that students can't sustain a conversation, stay on topic, or listen to one another. We caution thinking of it in this way, but rather push you to think about what students can do. They can talk. Really talk. Walk through the cafeteria or the yard at any given time, and you'll hear it. So, then, perhaps we want to think about *how* we set students up to talk about books and their thinking. There are so many things to think about, and therefore talk about, in books. Just like writing about reading, when students answer someone else's question, it feels forced and compliant rather than natural and exploratory. In essence, we're robbing students of the opportunity to think through the text.

Teacher:	Anna and Farah are on the class trip at the apple orchard. Farah is feeling different. She describes part of that feeling is because her clothing feels different. She describes her dupatta. Who can tell us what a dupatta is? (She waits for someone to raise their hand. She calls on a student).
Jerome:	It's a cloth you wear on your head.
Teacher:	OK, and who can tell us why this makes Farah feel different? (Nobody raises their hands.) William, what do you think?
William:	Uh, I guess because nobody else is wearing one.
Teacher:	OK, good. Anyone else? (No one raises her hand). Let's read on. (The teacher picks up the book and continues to read a few more pages until the next sticky note).
Teacher:	The author writes, *"laughs sound the same at home...it is the words that are strange. But soon I will know their words. I will blend with the others the way my apple blended with the cider."* What does the author mean by blend with the others the way my apple blended? (The teacher waits for students to raise their hands. It's quiet and she begins to call on students).

Side annotations:

- Teacher asks a right/wrong question.
- Student answers with a simple sentence and no explanation or sharing of ideas.
- Teacher asks a question that asks students to prove her idea about the character.
- Student gets called on and makes a best guess. There is no explanation or discussion of his idea.
- Teacher chooses a quote she thinks is important and asks students to consider word choice.

In the transcript above, the teacher meant well by sharing her thinking, but she also inadvertently narrowed the students' thinking and talking. When we share our thinking, there is a chance students will become complacent and simply move through the motions and in the end experience a false impression of real reading—that reading means coming to someone else's ideas and answering someone else's questions. Teacher-driven discussions often feel more like evaluations and "guess what's on my mind" teaching. Sometimes teachers ask questions where they are looking for one answer related to the book, rather than setting up a bigger question that guides discussion like the first question in the above transcript. When this happens, we come back to one of our basic beliefs: We teach students; we don't teach books.

When we take time to read aloud to students and have conversations, we can begin with a few questions that stir "big idea" thinking, rather than asking literal questions about the book. Questions that stir big idea thinking are often transferable from text to text. In this way, we are teaching students to think deeply rather than quizzing them on the book. Students can take the same question from a read aloud experience and try it in their independent reading book of choice. These big idea questions become the type of questions students begin to ask themselves when they read on their own.

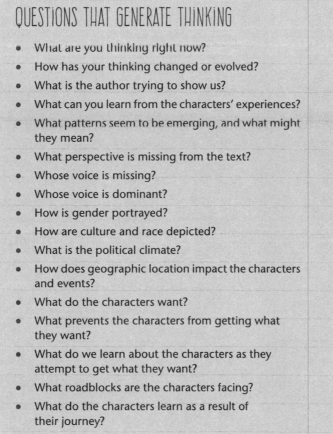

QUESTIONS THAT GENERATE THINKING

- What are you thinking right now?
- How has your thinking changed or evolved?
- What is the author trying to show us?
- What can you learn from the characters' experiences?
- What patterns seem to be emerging, and what might they mean?
- What perspective is missing from the text?
- Whose voice is missing?
- Whose voice is dominant?
- How is gender portrayed?
- How are culture and race depicted?
- What is the political climate?
- How does geographic location impact the characters and events?
- What do the characters want?
- What prevents the characters from getting what they want?
- What do we learn about the characters as they attempt to get what they want?
- What roadblocks are the characters facing?
- What do the characters learn as a result of their journey?
- What do we learn from the characters' journey?

When teachers drive the talking, it decreases the opportunity for the conversation to be a genuine access point in the process of making meaning of a text. Why? In essence, because students subvert their own creative and critical thinking to be compliant and impress the teacher, even in the most egalitarian classrooms. What's more, when teachers overfacilitate, it can skew their perception of students' understanding. In other words, a teacher creates a question from the text and asks the student, the student answers, and the teacher moves on, thinking the student understands the text, when in fact, this may not be and often is not the case. We find that when students answer someone else's questions, it's often an indication of recall or strong memory, and not necessarily true comprehension or understanding of the text. Teachers may also be more apt to assume the entire group is on board with the answer, causing a more generalized false assessment.

By contrast, when we shift away from questions about books and move toward questions about thinking, we are able to assess with greater accuracy. And best of all, we have much more time back in our lives. Creating questions for each text we read aloud is time consuming! You'll find that as you read this book, you'll feel better equipped to create a few big idea questions that generate thinking and can be transferred from text to text. With all that extra free time on your hands, you can get back to your personal reading life. When we ask the same big idea questions over and over, we have one less decision to make too.

	POSSIBLE LIMITATIONS OF TEACHER-LED QUESTION-AND-ANSWER TALK
Readers	• Begin to view reading as an act of compliance • Become disengaged from deeper thinking • Demonstrate a lack of ownership in the reading process • Have an inaccurate image of authentic reading • Only hear one idea or perspective and miss other interpretations
Teachers	• Inaccurate assessment of student comprehension • Time consuming • Temporary (teaching of books) • Creates dependence on the teacher • Prohibits the teacher from seeing the types of thinking students initiate on their own

AUTHENTIC FICTION DISCUSSIONS: AN ACTION PLAN

In this chapter, we explored the benefits of classroom conversations, how they can serve as a tool for both students and teachers, and key lessons to teach authentic conversations, and we reflected on a few classroom practices we might choose to let go of. When readers are well versed in the routines of having student-led conversations, the patterns of their conversations become patterns in their thinking. When we listen to these conversations, they become an important element in our decisions about what to teach next. We hope that conversations are planned as a key element of strategic curriculum design rather than an afterthought. The following list summarizes some of this chapter's big ideas that can help you take action in your classroom.

GETTING STARTED WITH DISCUSSIONS ABOUT FICTION READING

- [ ] Find out reasons why students are in conversations throughout the day by surveying or interviewing them.

- [ ] Investigate characteristics of quality conversations (page 119).

- [ ] Video or fishbowl students having conversations. Create a chart of the qualities.

- [ ] Listen to student conversations and transcribe a few. Study these transcripts with your colleagues and name what the students are doing well. These can be turned into lessons.

- [ ] Teach students strategies for keeping their conversations on task (page 131).

- [ ] Teach students how to use conversations as a tool to help them understand the interactions of characters they are reading about in their fiction texts and big ideas and themes.

- [ ] Dedicate five minutes a day for classroom conversations.

- [ ] Use the **Self-Reflection Questionnaire** on page 144 to decide on some goals.

Videos and viewing guide may also be accessed at
http://resources.corwin.com/GoldbergHouser-Fiction

 Supporting Student Conversations During a Read Aloud: The Goal

Video 4.1

 Supporting Student Conversations During a Read Aloud: The Lesson

Video 4.2

 Supporting Student Conversations During a Read Aloud: Deciding What to Teach Next

Video 4.3

Decisions About Understanding Characters

"PLOT IS NO MORE THAN FOOTPRINTS LEFT IN THE SNOW
AFTER YOUR CHARACTERS HAVE RUN BY ON THEIR WAY
TO INCREDIBLE DESTINATIONS."

(Ray Bradbury)

What does it mean to study characters? We begin this chapter by assuring you that we are going to help you get away from what can feel like an endless map of possible teaching paths. We will focus on a few key ways to study characters that have a lasting effect on readers' thinking and understanding.

Our motto is that to understand the characters is to understand the theme. To understand characters, readers need to not only be able to describe what they look like, how old they are, where they live, and so on, but also be willing to take a deeper, closer look at who they are. When we guide students to study character, it's not enough to meet the characters and ride along with the plot like a boat bobs up and down with the waves. Instead, we read with questions continually dancing in our heads: *What motivates these characters? What are their relationships like? How do they respond to struggle? Why do they always seem to react that way? What is going to help them get what they need? What am I seeing about their life that they don't yet see?*

Let's begin by clarifying one of the pitfalls that readers often end up in when trying to determine characters. More often than not, readers put a label on a character such as *brave* (Harry Potter) or *sassy* (Junie B. Jones). When we oversimplify characters with a single word or label, we are not fully studying who they really are. And we unwittingly may send our students the message that it's OK to reduce or label people in our lives with a single word. As teachers, we have to guard against the tendency for us or our students to typecast classmates as the smart one, the cute one, the sporty one, and so on. Think about this in your own life—even seemingly positive descriptors like *sweet* or *brave* can chafe or seem to box us in, right? So, as you read this chapter on character and try some lessons, we encourage you to consciously choose to teach students what it means to study something or someone.

The word *study* comes from the Latin word *studium* and means "to be busy with, devote oneself to, concentrate on." When we teach students to study characters, we are asking them to devote their attention and concentration to the characters and all their nuances. An early definition from the 1300s defines *study* as "reading a book or writing intently and meditatively" (Harper, 2016). To read intently and meditatively might mean feeling the heartbreak of Auggie from *Wonder* (Palacio, 2012) when he is teased or cheering for Jonas when he escapes his community in *The Giver* (Lowry, 1993). But studying characters meditatively also means to contemplate and consider them from multiple perspectives and to acknowledge we will never really know them any more than we will really know another person. We will know only what the author reveals to us. This makes the study so powerful, as each reader might pay attention and consider different ideas about characters and in turn take away different lessons from reading about their experiences.

In this chapter, we show examples of students' thinking that range from single-word labels about a character to complex theories and ideas the reader developed over time. We will show you how to introduce the complexity and humanity of characters to your students so they can study them deeply. One of the best things about reading fiction in general and studying characters in particular is that it raises our students' awareness that we are each complex, ever changing, and memorable in our flaws. We will also show you how to look at students' reading notebook entries and conversations and decide what to teach next.

Why Understanding Characters Is So Important

By studying characters, we begin to better understand people in our lives. The same questions we ask about characters can be asked about ourselves, our friends, and our families. *Why did they do that? What do they really mean? What is really going on?* A recent study found that people who regularly read fiction developed more empathy and understanding for others (Kidd & Costano, 2013). In a time when researchers like Sherry Turkle are writing about the ways children today are less empathetic than previous generations, we can use fictional characters to help teach this essential human skill. I still recall the first time I read *Bridge to Terabithia* (Paterson, 1977) as a child and crying so hard my mom came running into the room to check on me. Through books, I experienced losses as well as triumphs. It is essential all students get to do the same.

Joseph Campbell, mythologist, scholar, and professor, spent his career showing the benefits of studying stories. One of his major contributions was to show how every culture has its own version of the hero's journey. Each version includes different characters, settings, and obstacles, but they also all have the same qualities and lessons within them. When we teach students to study the character's journey in their books, they are learning the timeless lessons of an entire planet of people. By looking closely at characters, we can look at ourselves: "Our life evokes our character. You find out more about yourself as you go on. That's why it's good to be able to put yourself in situations" (Campbell & Moyers, 1988, p. 159). When we look at characters' situations, we can begin to examine our own.

Of course, there are also very practical and school-based reasons to focus on studying characters. For one, every state's standards include a focus on characters such as being able to describe and compare them. It is also not uncommon for standardized tests to ask questions like "Why did the character do . . . ?" or "What do you think the character learned from . . . ?" There are both school- and life-based reasons to teach students to study characters.

What Other Reading Skills Fit With Understanding Characters?

Shonda Rhimes, screenwriter, producer, and director of popular television shows like *Grey's Anatomy*, explains that she does not know a character she is creating until she looks at how he handles conflict (quoted in *Rising Strong* by Brené Brown, 2015). When we study characters, we are also studying plot—the conflicts, rising and falling action, and resolution—all through the lens of the characters. But when we ask students to identify each of these plot elements, they often forget they are all created by and driven by the characters. We can simplify our teaching by focusing first on characters, and the other elements will follow.

Some of these other skills that come along with studying characters include using figurative language to make inferences and predicting what the character will do next based on previous events and the conflicts of the story. We make sure to model how to use strategies to figure out the unfamiliar vocabulary such as using the clues in the sentences and reading for figurative and connotative language rather than simply doing a literal read. These skills are not the goals for students but are essential parts of the process of helping us study characters. Rather than teach these skills in isolation, we model them *as needed* when we show students how we think about and study characters. Think of characters as our anchor in a sea of story elements.

In Chapter 5, we introduce daily practices and key lessons that you can begin with today. See the following list for of what we describe in detail in the following sections.

In this chapter, you will learn

In Chapter 5, we examine how a reader can study characters first in one fiction text and later across more than one text.

- We will step into classrooms to learn how we introduce character studies to students. You will find anchor charts and lesson descriptions.
- You will learn the three most common types of thinking students tend to do when studying characters and what they look like in writing and conversations.
- We offer a thin-slicing "cheat sheet" to help you look quickly at student notebook entries and conversations and identify the types of thinking they are doing.
- We show examples of the most common notebook entries students make when studying characters. These can be shown to your students as inspiring examples.
- We simplify the number of choices we make as teachers and show you the three main choices we have when deciding what to teach next.
- We leave you with a clear action plan for getting started in your own classroom.

thin slice

Lessons on Understanding Characters

If your students are new to understanding what it means to really study characters by thinking deeply, having conversations, and creating reading notebook entries to document and develop their ideas, then you might want to begin with the following three introductory lessons. These lessons can be taught at the beginning of the year or when you are ready to teach students what it means to study characters and form opinions about them. These are foundational lessons for students who only look at the plot or who focus on literal elements of the characters such as their names, ages, and physical descriptions. You can teach all three or choose the ones that match your students.

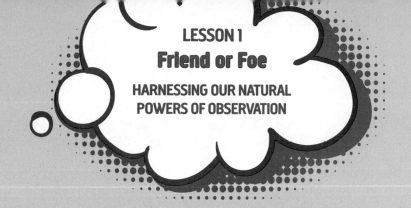

LESSON 1
Friend or Foe
HARNESSING OUR NATURAL POWERS OF OBSERVATION

In this lesson, you can show students that they already know how to study characters, because they have been doing so since the day they were born. We are hardwired to sense friend or foe in order to survive, and then sharpen this capacity to form opinions as we build relationships, live in communities, read, and watch movies. This lesson will become one you refer back to again and again. It can hook students into the study of characters.

Decide to Teach This Tomorrow if Your Students

- Focus solely on plot and what is going to happen next
- Have trouble coming up with their own thinking and ideas about characters
- Stick so close to the literal elements of characters that they are unsure how to form opinions about them
- Are new to talking and writing about their thinking about characters

thin slice

What You Need:

- A short video clip of a popular book turned film (choose one that is appropriate for your students; in the following example, we used *The Hunger Games* [Collins, 2008] because the students were older)
- Several sheets of large paper or chart paper
- Markers and sticky notes

Tell Why: Explain to students that they already know how to form opinions about people in their lives and characters in movies and that they are now learning how to do this with characters in books as well. Let them know there is no such thing as a wrong opinion as long as it is based on what happens in the text. Tell students that when we form opinions, share them, and then revisit them with other readers, we learn so much about people in general. You might

(Continued)

show a chart that lists some of the benefits of studying characters such as the one that follows.

WHEN WE STUDY CHARACTERS, WE CAN LEARN TO

- Form opinions about specific characters and people in general
- Track characters' behaviors so we can learn how people's choices impact their lives
- Interpret characters' feelings and also the feelings of people in our lives
- Understand how characters' relationships impact their lives

Explore How:

- Show a short video clip of the scene from the movie. Tell the students to focus on what they think of the main character in this clip.
  - *For example, show a two-minute clip from* The Hunger Games *when the main character, Katniss, volunteers as tribute to save her sister.*
- After showing the video clip, divide the class into groups of four students and place a large piece of blank paper in between them. Students each move to a corner of the page where they will write down their opinion about the main character (for example, Katniss). Make sure to explain that this is a "silent conversation" and they will have time to talk later.
  - After about twenty seconds, prompt them, "Now list the parts of the video clip that impacted your opinion. What did Katniss do or say to give you this idea? Jot your thinking under your opinion." Give the students a minute to write.
  - Tell students to rotate the group's paper and read and respond in writing to what the first person wrote. If they agree, have them tell why. If they disagree, have them tell why. Give them about one minute to write a response. (You can connect this activity to commenting on a blog post as it uses the same skill set.)
  - Keep rotating every minute until all students are back to where they began. The final minute is time for the student who originally wrote the opinion to have the last word and respond to all the comments in that corner so far.

- After the "silent conversation" about the character, give the groups about ten minutes to look at each corner and discuss as a group what their opinions were.

Below is an example of one group's silent conversation page.

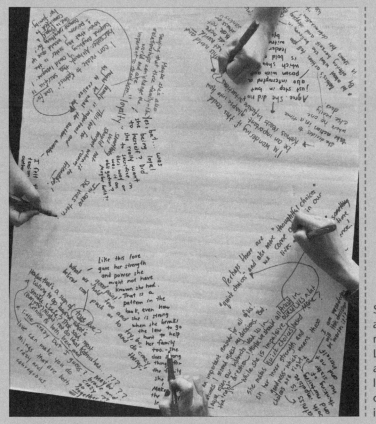

Students read one another's responses and respond back in writing. Like a live blog, this activity helps students learn to build on or challenge one another's ideas about characters.

- After the group conversations, come back together as a whole class and create a class chart of opinions about the character. You can make this chart collaboratively by asking the members of each group to decide on one of the opinions from their paper that had the most evidence from the movie clip. They can write that opinion on a sticky note and share it with the class. The rest of the class can decide if there is sufficient evidence from the video to hang it on the chart.

Below is an example of a chart created about Katniss from *The Hunger Games*. Notice that, collectively, the opinions bust the notion that anyone can be defined by a single attribute.

OPINIONS ABOUT KATNISS

- overprotective
- impulsive
- brave

A Few Tips:

- The page of writing offers students talking points and helps them prepare for what opinions are worth their time to discuss and really think about. For example, if a group had a comment in a corner that read, "She is a good character," the students would likely not spend time discussing the idea because the comment was not compelling. Comments like "She is impulsive" or "She is overprotective" would give the groups lots to discuss and spark conversations that went into why and how and if they agreed or not. You can point this out to students.

- If you have younger students, they might need more time than one minute to record their ideas, but still keep it short so they focus on getting just the essential ideas down and they are excited to have a conversation off the corner of the page.

- When students use only a single word to show an opinion as these students did, we can teach them how to expand their thinking beyond a single-word label.

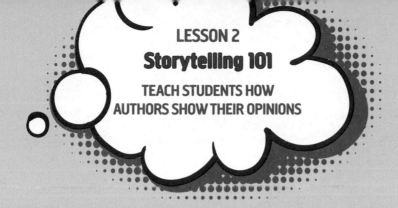

LESSON 2
Storytelling 101
TEACH STUDENTS HOW AUTHORS SHOW THEIR OPINIONS

In this lesson, students learn that the way a story is told shows us the author's opinions about a character and allows us as readers to form our own opinions. We can listen to or read a story in this new way.

Decide to Teach This Tomorrow if Your Students

- Focus solely on plot and what is going to happen next
- Have trouble coming up with their own thinking and ideas about characters
- Stick so close to the literal elements of characters that they are unsure how to form opinions about them
- Don't see the connections between the characters and plot

What You Need:

- A story you know well

Tell Why: Explain that our opinions of people and characters impact the ways we tell their stories. Authors have opinions about characters they create, and they don't always tell us exactly what these opinions are. We can think about the details the author shows us about what a character says and how a character speaks, or what a character does and thinks. We can listen to or read a story and form opinions about the characters.

Show How:

- Tell a story in two different ways to highlight how a character can be seen differently depending on the information we receive.
  - *For example, tell a story in which the main character steals food from a neighbor's garden and seems to be sneaky and deceitful. Then tell the same story, but this time explain that the character's family is struggling to get food and there are young children at home who need to be fed.*

(Continued)

- After each telling, pause and ask the students to record their thinking on a sticky note or notebook page and then to discuss it with a partner.
- Then discuss why the opinions may have been different in each telling.

Practice How:

- Students pair up and try out the same storytelling practice.
- First they tell the story showing one opinion about a character.
- Then they tell it a different way to show another opinion.
- Partners debrief on how the opinion changed the story.

A Few Tips:

- If students have trouble hearing the differences, change your voice and pause dramatically to show the differences. Make them obvious.
- If you have trouble coming up with a story, you can retell a true story from your life or borrow a story from a book you have read.
- Since this is just an introductory lesson, don't be too concerned if students have trouble articulating a specific opinion word and instead use words like *nice* or *mean*.

There are several ways to introduce the concept of character opinions to students of different ages and experiences. Since some students will already come to reading experiences with this focus and line of thinking developed, you can either choose to deepen this even further or introduce it to students who don't necessarily form opinions as they read. What follows are a few activities for introducing character opinions to students.

Sketching: Project an opinion about a character on the board and ask students to picture what this would look like and draw an example of someone (not with names) who illustrates this opinion. For example, project the opinion "competitive" on the board and give students a few minutes to picture, sketch, then discuss their examples. Someone might say, "The character has to win everything and even rushes to be the first person to line up in school." Ask students to add speech or thought bubbles to the sketch if you want to teach how what characters do, say, and think also gives us opinions about them.

Interviews: Students can work on their own or in pairs. Ask them to choose a person they have a positive opinion about in their school or local community. Perhaps model by choosing a colleague. Then list a few opinions you have about this person that you respect and admire. Perhaps you would write down "thoughtful and generous." Then ask students to interview one another about why they have that opinion about a person and give examples that show the opinion. Students might ask me why I think my colleague is generous, and I could tell the story of the time she stayed after school to help me plan a lesson or the time she shared her lunch with me because I forgot mine. After the interviews, have students discuss in groups what they learned from the interviews about opinions.

Self-Reflection: Once you have built a safe classroom space for students to honestly reflect and share, you can ask students to think about their opinions about themselves. They can make a T-chart and list opinions about themselves they carry and then examples of things they did, said, or thought that gave them these opinions. For example, a student might list "hardworking" on the left side of the chart and "I stay after baseball practice for extra work on hitting the ball even farther" as the example on the right side of the chart. As students make these charts, remind them that these are opinions and not fixed traits so they can and likely will change if the students want them to. Also, make sure students generate multiple opinions about themselves so they acknowledge all the many facets and qualities they possess.

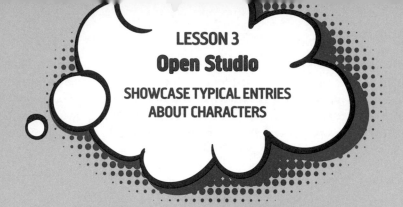

LESSON 3
Open Studio
SHOWCASE TYPICAL ENTRIES ABOUT CHARACTERS

These introductory lessons and activities are meant to immerse students in the thinking process of understanding what it means to study characters. Once students understand this concept, you can begin to show them how to create reading notebook entries to document and develop their thinking about the characters. One powerful way to teach this is to show students examples of the most common ways these notebook entries look while making sure to let them know they have choices. It can be hard to make a choice without examples of what those choices might be first. This is why we show some common examples as starting-off points.

thin slice

Decide to Teach This Tomorrow if Your Students

- Do not yet use their reading notebook entries to help them study characters
- Create entries in their notebooks that do not help them understand characters
- Do the same sorts of writing every day and need some help imagining other ways they could develop entries about characters

What You Need:

- Either student or teacher examples of common notebook entries (or create your own like the ones we have listed in this lesson)
- Chart paper and markers

Explain Why: Tell students that the way they set up their notebook entries can help them understand characters. Explain that they can absolutely create their own ways of recording this thinking, but if they want to see what other readers tend to do, you are going to show them some examples. These examples can inspire their own choices.

Show Examples:

- Project a few notebook types like the ones in the left column of the chart below. Use your own notebook or students' examples as models. (Based on the experience level of your students, you can show one at a time or several at a time in this lesson.)

- As you show each example, model for students how you look at the entry and name what you notice.

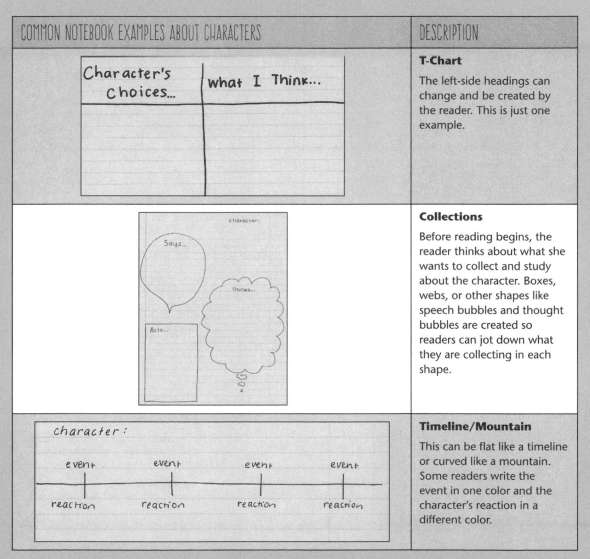

COMMON NOTEBOOK EXAMPLES ABOUT CHARACTERS	DESCRIPTION
Character's Choices... / What I Think...	**T-Chart** The left-side headings can change and be created by the reader. This is just one example.
character: / Says... / Thinks... / Acts...	**Collections** Before reading begins, the reader thinks about what she wants to collect and study about the character. Boxes, webs, or other shapes like speech bubbles and thought bubbles are created so readers can jot down what they are collecting in each shape.
character: / event, event, event, event / reaction, reaction, reaction, reaction	**Timeline/Mountain** This can be flat like a timeline or curved like a mountain. Some readers write the event in one color and the character's reaction in a different color.

(Continued)

Box and Bullets

Sometimes the idea box is clear up front, and other times the character details are bulleted first and after the reading the idea is written down. The bigger thinking can come at the end.

```
┌─────────────────────────────┐
│  Idea about character       │
└─────────────────────────────┘
   •  ⎫
   •  ⎬  support from
   •  ⎭  the text
   •
```

Columns

Readers can create columns to track thinking down and across. For example, it could be one column per character to compare them. Or it could be something to focus on with one character like motivation.

character A	character B	character C

Character:

Actions (what and how)	Motivations (why)

Conversation on the Page

Readers write in sentences and think of it like a conversation with themselves, their partners, or the author about their thinking. It is not formal and structured writing. The purpose is to develop deeper and more refined thinking.

Character: Peter

I am so upset for Peter!! His dad was such an unbelievable cold-hearted man! He didn't even care that Peter loved Pax and was attached to him. Peter must feel powerless because his dad made him give up his best friend. And he also lost his mom recently. He must be so full of sadness and anger. I wonder how he will be able to be happy again or how he will ever forgive his dad.

- Ask students to talk to a partner about what they notice. You can use what they say to create an anchor chart like what we have listed in the right-hand column above.

- End by asking students to choose one of these types to try out in their independent reading and explain to a partner why they made that choice. They can even set up the notebook entry right there before going back to their seats to begin reading and studying characters. Of course, do not limit students to only the choices you showed them.

A Few Tips:

- We find that the way the students choose to set up their notebooks has little to do with their types of thinking. Instead, how they use the entry and whether or not they go back to the entry over time and do further thinking has the largest impact on the type of thinking about character.

- When students choose their own type of entry, they have more ownership and freedom to think about a narrative in ways that work for them.

- We suggest you explicitly introduce each type of entry to your students and then begin to offer choice to students.

- We always allow students to create their own entries that go well beyond what we model. As long as the entry helps them study characters and think deeply, it does not matter which way they choose to write.

- As an extension, you can use another read aloud experience to create some class entries together using some of these types.

What to Look for When Students Study Characters

While there is not one way students' thinking always develops, we notice trends in the ways they study characters. Recall that studying characters is one focus and therefore one aspect to pay attention to when reading a fiction text, but certainly not the only one. Within this one focus, there are ways readers tend to think. When we know the patterns and tendencies, we can thin-slice student entries and conversations, making rapid and informed decisions about what to teach next. In our work with readers of different experiences and age groups, we have found three main types of thinking for how a reader studies characters. The following list includes the three types—Right-Now Thinking, Over-Time Thinking, and Refining Thinking.

When students choose how they study characters, they develop ownership and empathy.

thin slice

- **Right-Now Thinking:** Early on, a reader may think about a character in little parts without putting the pieces together. The thinking is based on one small detail or event.

- **Over-Time Thinking:** A reader may begin to put thinking together across the text. This may be multiple events, choices a character makes, or relationships the character is in across time. These readers see the whole of the text and not just the current event.

- **Refining Thinking:** Partway through or at the end of a text, readers may refine their thinking based on additional information about the character. They take new information they are learning and use it to revisit thoughts they had earlier in the text. They move back and forth between acquiring new information about a character and seeing how it fits with what they are learning and already know about this character. The reader may go deeper with an idea, revise an idea based on new information, or connect an idea to a larger claim about the character.

UNDERSTANDING CHARACTERS

The following chart is meant to be an assessment tool you can use when looking at your students' notebook entries and listening to their conversations. It is your thin-slicing "cheat sheet," so to speak. We suggest you carry a copy around on your clipboard as you confer with students and make teaching decisions.

UNDERSTANDING CHARACTERS IN FICTION TEXTS		
RIGHT-NOW THINKING	OVER-TIME THINKING	REFINING THINKING
What to look for: Thinking is based on one part of the text.	What to look for: Thinking happens in multiple places in the text. Ideas are based on connecting information from throughout the section or text.	What to look for: Changes in thinking are based on new scenes or events, or the thinking is made more specific from an earlier broad idea.
What a reader might say: *This character action means . . .* *I'm thinking . . . in this one part.* *I think this part shows the character is . . .*	What a reader might say: *Based on this scene and this event, I am thinking . . .* *When I look at this part and this part, I think . . .* *A pattern I am noticing is . . .* *Another example is . . .*	What a reader might say: *I used to think . . . but now I think . . .* *I no longer think this because . . .* *Based on more events, I now think . . .* *To be more specific, I now understand . . .*

In the following sections, we look at student work to practice thin-slicing using these three types of thinking with student notebook entries and conversations. While looking and listening, we will first identify what a student *is doing* before deciding what to teach next.

thin slice

Thin-Slicing Students' Thinking About Characters

Let's step into classrooms and look closely at a few students' reading notebook entries and conversations as a way to identify the three main types of thinking students tend to do when studying characters in fiction texts. In the following examples, you will see some ways that we can identify Right-Now, Over-Time, and Refining Thinking based on what students write and say.

Teacher Tip

As we look at reading notebook entries, let's notice how students decided to organize the entry. Showing students their peers' entries as examples can inspire their own thinking and entries. Simply by showing students there are multiple ways to record our thinking, students find the ways that work best for them.

Right-Now Thinking: Michelle's Thinking About the Characters in *Fourth Grade Fairy*

She pictures what the characters are doing in the scene. She makes quick sketches and adds in the dialogue.

She thinks about the characters' thoughts and feelings after she pictures them and jots that down.

Each of these rows is its own scene and thinking. They do not connect. There is one for each of the two characters.

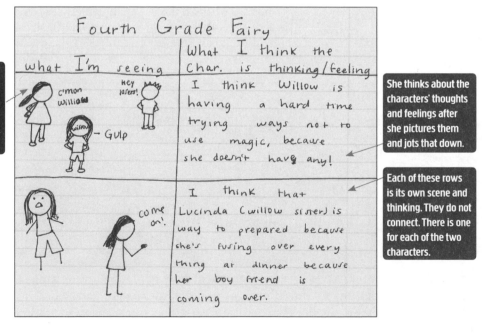

After looking at Michelle's reading notebook entry about the characters in *Fourth Grade Fairy* (Cook, 2011), we noticed the following.

- As she reads, she pictures the characters in the scene. She also thinks about what they would be saying to one another. This is shown in the left side of her chart in the sketch.

- She thinks about the character's feelings and thoughts. This is shown in the right side of the chart.

- She draws a line between scenes on her chart and does not connect the two ideas or parts in any way. Each part of her thinking on the chart stands alone right now.

After thin-slicing this entry, we found a pattern in the way Michelle was thinking. She pictured and thought about how the character was feeling in the right-now moment of the book without thinking about what came before it or what might come after it. She was doing a lot of Right-Now Thinking about each event, one at a time. When we notice students who mostly are doing Right-Now Thinking, we begin to model for them how to do some Over-Time Thinking. The following chart shows our moves for deciding what to teach next.

1. WE LOOK AND LISTEN TO STUDENTS.	2. WE NAME WHAT THEY ARE DOING.	3. WE IDENTIFY THE CURRENT TYPE OF THINKING.
What the Reader Said/Wrote	**What We Notice**	**Type of Thinking**
"I think Willow is having a hard time trying ways not to use magic, because she doesn't have any!"	She is thinking about the character's feelings in this one scene of the story.	Right-Now Thinking
"I think that Lucinda (Willow's sister) is way too prepared because she's fussing over everything at dinner because her boyfriend is coming over."	She is thinking about a different character in the book and what is motivating her behaviors.	Right-Now Thinking

Let's check out a different student's reading notebook entry to see what some Over-Time Thinking can look like.

Over-Time Thinking: Margaret's Thinking About a Character in *Divergent*

She pictures what the character looks like based on descriptions from more than one part of the text.

She forms the opinion that the character is relatable and mysterious.

She talks back to the text by having a different perspective about being different than the author describes.

This is how I think Tris would look because of the descriptions in the book. She was part of the abnegation faction so her face is very plain and simple. She has brown hair which is wavy. Her eyes are described as stunning and mesmerizing. she is confident a very indivi— dual so I did my best to portray that in my design. very she is but beautiful which is mysterious believe what I so relat— makes her able. I also believe that her being so different from everyone creates an aura which everyone is naturally attracted to. Being divergent is described as dangerous, but I think it would be fun to be different from the societal norms.

We also listened while Margaret had a conversation with her reading partner, Olivia, about this notebook entry. This is part of what we heard.

Margaret:	Have you read *Divergent* yet?
Olivia:	Yes. I read the first book twice and the others in the series once.
Margaret:	Well, I was picturing what Tris looks like and I drew it here [shows the entry and points to the picture].
Olivia:	I pictured her really pretty and tall too.
Margaret:	Really? But the author says she is in the Abnegation faction and they are really plain. Kind of like Amish people. I pictured her pretty but super plain. Like no makeup and no jewelry and her hair is natural and long.
Olivia:	I guess you are right. I was thinking more about how she looks later in the books. Because she changes and . . .
Margaret:	Stop! Don't tell me what happens. I am not done yet. [Olivia smiles and nods.] Veronica Roth says that Tris is Divergent later on in the book, and that did make me picture her differently. Like she was plain and also her eyes must look different and the way she moves might be different. Like I pictured her moving faster and more graceful than the others in her faction. I couldn't draw her moving in this entry, but it was like I saw her like a dancer and more playful than the others in her faction.

> They are summarizing what they pictured and comparing it.

> Margaret explains why she pictures the character this way. She is using her own background knowledge and details from the text.

> Margaret puts together what she read about the societal group the character is in, what the author describes, and what she was picturing when she put it together. Her description was based on several chapters of the book.

After looking at Margaret's reading notebook entry and listening to her conversation about the character in *Divergent* (Roth, 2011), we noticed the following.

- She pictures Tris, the character, based on details and descriptions from across the text. She puts the details together over time.

- She forms opinions about the character such as being mysterious, relatable, and different. She even describes her as having an aura that everyone is attracted to and being graceful.

- She is beginning to interpret the character's difference as positive rather than how the author has the society interpreting it, which is negative. She is "talking back" to the text.

thin
slice

1. WE LOOK AND LISTEN TO STUDENTS.	2. WE NAME WHAT THEY ARE DOING.	3. WE IDENTIFY THE CURRENT TYPE OF THINKING.
What the Reader Said/Wrote	**What We Notice**	**Type of Thinking**
"This is how I think Tris would look because of the descriptions in the book." (entry)	She is basing this on more than one part of the text.	Over-Time Thinking
"But the author says she is in the Abnegation faction and they are really plain. Kind of like Amish people. I pictured her pretty but super plain. Like no makeup and no jewelry and her hair is natural and long." (conversation)	She is backing up her thinking with details from more than one part of the text and from her own background knowledge.	Over-Time Thinking
"Veronica Roth says that Tris is Divergent later on in the book." (conversation)	She builds on her original idea by referring to information given later in the text. She is not basing her thinking on just one part.	Over-Time Thinking

Refining Thinking: Tom's Thinking About a Character in "The Fight"

Let's look at one more reader's thinking about characters and how he is refining his thinking.

> I'm thinking this character is a well respected, tough. I also think he's a tough guy and that he can take anyone. I also think he really isn't as tough as he thought.

> I now think the character isn't as tough as I thought he was in the beginning. I also think the character is not getting scared.

> I'm now thinking that the character is now doubting himself but still showing that he's better than everyone.

> We can learn that you shouldn't think so much of yourself and you shouldn't think that you're better than everyone else. We can also learn

1. He forms an idea about the character but then considers the difference between what the character shows others and what he thinks of himself.

2. The reader is beginning to question his own initial idea and is open to revising his thinking now that he is further into the story.

3. He now sees the internal struggle the character is facing. This is the main conflict of the story. His thinking is deeper over the course of the text.

4. The reader takes what happened at the end of the story to form a larger lesson he can learn from the character. This lesson stems from all the thinking he did across the story and his willingness to reread the thoughts he wrote down along the way.

After looking at Tom's reading notebook entry about the characters in "The Fight" (from Bagdasarian, 2003), we noticed the following.

- His thinking is changing and getting deeper even in the first few pages from being respected, to a "tough guy," to not as tough as he thinks.

- He is paying attention to what the character thinks of himself and what others think of him. He uses this to identify the central conflict of the story.

- He puts all his thinking together at the end and looks over his notes to form a larger idea and theme (more on theme in Chapter 6).

- All of this thinking was an accumulation across the text. He built on each idea from box to box of his entry.

thin slice

1. WE LOOK AND LISTEN TO STUDENTS.	2. WE NAME WHAT THEY ARE DOING.	3. WE IDENTIFY THE CURRENT TYPE OF THINKING.
What the Reader Said/Wrote	**What We Notice**	**Type of Thinking**
"I now think the character isn't as tough as I thought he was in the beginning. I also think the character is now getting scared." (2)	He questions his own initial idea and is open to changing his mind based on the new information he is getting.	Refining Thinking
"I'm now thinking that the character is now doubting himself but still showing that he's better than everyone." (3)	This idea is based on his thinking in Boxes 1 and 2 of his entry. It is evolving based on all he knows so far about the character and not just focused on the one scene he is reading now. His ideas are more nuanced and revised later in the story.	Refining Thinking

thin slice

CLIPBOARD NOTES: TYPES OF THINKING ABOUT UNDERSTANDING CHARACTERS

As you spend time looking at students' reading notebook entries and listening to their conversations, see if you can identify the type of thinking they are doing. You can use a chart like this one or create your own. Take a few days to sit with individual students to find out what type of thinking they are doing. Remember—it could be more than one type.

WHAT THE READER SAID/WROTE	WHAT I NOTICE	TYPE OF THINKING
Name: Date:		☐ Right-Now Thinking ☐ Over-Time Thinking ☐ Refining Thinking

Decide What to Teach Next

Let's step into a seventh-grade classroom, the same one that Tom is in. His class-mate, Tonya, also read the short story "The Fight" and thought about the characters. She set up her notebook entry with categories to help guide her thinking in the text. She wrote "character might be . . ." and then left a few lines blank to go back and list her thinking. She did the same thing with other categories such as "character feels . . ." and left space underneath to collect her thinking. Recall this is a short story about a high school boy who challenges another boy to a fight and then realizes he does not know how to fight or want to fight but does want to "save face" and not back down. Below is what we noticed when we looked at Tonya's reading notebook entry as she was creating it.

character might be... (1)
- concieted
- tough
- competitive
- wants to be a leader

> Tonya used "might be" to give herself permission to take a risk with her thinking because she was only at the start of the story. She listed her ideas about the type of character she thinks he is. This helps her better understand what is moving him.

characters feels (2)
- scared
- nervous
- not a person who doesn't want to fight anymore

> Now she is thinking about his internal feelings and recognizes that he is different from what he projects to others. Instead of being tough like she wrote at first, he is really feeling scared.

character thoughts (3)
- brave
- nervous but wants to fight
- still nervous but fearless

> She is grappling with her thoughts about this character and has some contradictory thinking because of the tension between how he presents himself to others and how he really feels.

what can we learn from the characters experience?

I learned that trying to be someone else can get you into trouble.

> She asks herself the main question (her purpose for reading) and then answers it based on all that she thought across the story. We can see her return to her purpose, and then she writes a lesson she learned and can share with her reading partner.

When Tonya met with her teacher in a reading conference, she had a conversation about her thinking. What follows is a portion of the conversation.

Tonya: So now that I am done with this story, I am so conflicted about the main character.

> Can separate her own thinking and feelings about the character from the character's feelings in the book

Teacher: What do you mean? How so?

Tonya: Well, at first I thought he was conceited and tough, but then I realized he was scared and nervous to fight, and then at the end when he was beaten up, I felt bad for him. Like I think it was so stupid for him to get in the fight at all, but also I did feel badly that he was now going to get made fun of and not be as "cool" as he was with his friends.

> Describes how her thinking about the character was revised and complicated as she read further into the story

Teacher: So you see that he created this problem for himself, but you also sympathized with him and this painful lesson he learned.

Tonya: Yeah. It almost seemed at times that he wanted to be taken down and not be the king of the school anymore. But I guess he did not know how to do it in a normal way, so instead he picked this fight.

Teacher: The author does not say he wanted to be taken down from being "king." What makes you think that?

> Interprets the character's motivation and then explains what parts of the story led her to the ideas

Tonya: Well, it just seemed like he was mocking himself and saying that Mike could have all the attention because he did not want it anymore.

By looking closely at what Tonya is writing and listening to what she says, we can get a glimpse into what she is thinking and the way she is approaching her character study. Before making any decisions about what to teach next, we first notice and name the type of thinking she tends to do. By looking closely at what the reader is already able to do, we have a springboard for where to lead her next.

thin slice Once we thin-slice readers' thinking and identify what they are already doing, we can begin the next phase of the decision-making process. We can decide what to teach next.

If a reader was not thinking over time, we could teach her to do this; or if a reader was not refining her thinking, we could choose that. These types of thinking guide the types of choices we might make. They narrow the choices down so we don't feel we need to teach everything or we have nothing to teach at all. As improvisers, we use these three types of thinking as "rules" or tenets to follow when thin-slicing and making in-the-moment decisions.

THREE TEACHING CHOICES WE CAN MAKE

1. Name and reinforce a type of thinking readers are already using.
2. Show readers a different type of thinking and model how to use it.
3. Coach readers to apply a currently used type of thinking in other sections or books.

What do we teach Tonya tomorrow?

In the first three columns of the following chart, we thin-slice Tonya's character study thinking. In the fourth column, we add our choice about what to teach next. We could teach this right now in the conference, or we could teach this to her tomorrow.

1. WE LOOK AND LISTEN TO STUDENTS.	2. WE NAME WHAT THEY ARE DOING.	3. WE IDENTIFY THE CURRENT TYPE OF THINKING.	4. WE DECIDE WHAT TO TEACH NEXT.
What the Reader Said/Wrote	**What We Notice**	**Type of Thinking**	**What to Teach Next**
"At first I thought he was conceited and tough, but then I realized he was scared and nervous to fight, and then at the end when he was beaten up, I felt bad for him." (conversation)	Tonya's thinking changes across the text as she learns more about the character. She realizes she was not wrong at the start and instead that as she reads more she will think more.	Refining Thinking	*Name and Reinforce This Type of Thinking:* Because this type of thinking was brand new for her, we decided not to teach Tonya anything new just yet and instead to explain what she did and how it helped her. We wanted her to understand what she was doing and how it helped her study characters.
"I learned that trying to be someone else can get you into trouble." (entry)	She formed this bigger idea based on all she learned from across the story and not just this one part.	Over-Time Thinking	

Choice 1: Name and Reinforce a Type of Thinking

Jacob is a fourth grader in a classroom where students are studying characters. He chooses books in a series where boys are the main characters and they tend to go on adventures. While Jacob has a reading partner, Matthew, the two are not reading the same book. The following notebook entry was created by Jacob while he was more than halfway through his book. He chose to write his thinking in sentences; notice it sounds like a conversation on the page, which is what we strive for. Let's take a look at the notebook entry.

> Andy is brave when he asked Terry "Why did you try to wash your underwear in the shark's tank?" and went to go get the underwear out of the shark's mouth. I would be to scared to go into the shark's tank, let alone go in its mouth!

He formed an opinion based on the current scene.

He includes a description of the scene that gave him the opinion.

He made a comparison to what he would do.

In this notebook entry, Jacob chose a character and formed an opinion (Andy is brave). This opinion seems to solely be based on this one scene where the character went into a shark tank to retrieve his underwear. He used a direct quote and a bit of summary to show where this opinion came from. At the end, he compared what he would do with the character choice and then formed an opinion about himself.

Jacob's teacher, Judy, sat next to him for a conference. The following transcript is an excerpt from their conversation.

After having a conference with Jacob, we identified a pattern in the ways he forms opinions about characters. As a reader, we noticed that he collected examples from the text to support his opinion, which was based on what the character did and chose in a particular scene. This pattern came up in his entry and his conversation with Judy. Let's use the four-step process to decide what to teach him next.

thin
slice

Judy: Jacob, you have a few entries in your notebook. What are you working on and thinking about?

Jacob: I'm forming opinions about Andy. I am now in Book 3 in my series!

> Chose an opinion to discuss

Judy: So what are you thinking?

[Jacob looked at his notebook entries and pointed to one in particular.]

Jacob: So right here, I was thinking about how brave Andy is.

> Formed an opinion

Judy: Why do you think that?

Jacob: Well [he giggles], Andy's underwear are in a shark tank, and he goes in to get them. He goes in while there are sharks there! That is so brave. There is no way I would do that with sharks there.

Judy: Wow! That *is* brave. I wouldn't go in with sharks either. So do you think he is brave in other parts too?

> Supports his opinion with an example and a comparison

Jacob: No. Not really.

1. WE LOOK AND LISTEN TO STUDENTS.	2. WE NAME WHAT THEY ARE DOING.	3. WE IDENTIFY THE CURRENT TYPE OF THINKING.	4. WE DECIDE WHAT TO TEACH NEXT.
What the Reader Said/Wrote	**What We Notice**	**Type of Thinking**	**What to Teach Next**
"Andy is brave when he asked Terry 'Why did you wash your underwear in the shark's tank?' and went to get the underwear out of the shark's mouth!"	Jacob forms an opinion about the character based on what is happening in this one scene.	Right-Now Thinking	*Name and Reinforce Current Type of Thinking:* Because this type of thinking was brand new for Jacob, we decided not to teach him a new type just yet. He was able to form an idea in one part of the text, and we would explain what he did and how it helped him understand the character, and encourage him to keep doing this same thinking in other parts of this book.
"I would be [too] scared to go into the shark's tank." (entry)	He compares himself to the character in this one part.	Right-Now Thinking	
"So right here, I was thinking about how brave Andy is." (conversation)	He points to the one part where he has this opinion about the character.	Right-Now Thinking	

Since Jacob had never done this type of thinking before and in the past only retold the literal information from his book, we decided not to teach him a new type of thinking just yet. Instead, we decided to reinforce this thinking by naming and describing what Jacob was doing and explaining why it was so helpful for him to continue to do this type of thinking. Sometimes, our teaching means not moving on to something brand new and instead sticking with something for a bit longer first. When students experience success, they develop more agency (Johnston, 2012), and it breeds the sort of internal motivation we hope all readers experience.

Choice 2: Show a Different Type of Thinking

Let's step into a third-grade classroom where we meet Tammy. Tammy's class has been studying characters in a variety of books that students self-selected with a few criteria in mind: They must be (a) books with characters, (b) books they can read with accuracy, fluency, and understanding, and (c) books they are interested in reading. This meant Tammy chose the book *Dork Diaries: Tales From a Not-So-Fabulous Life* by Rachel Renée Russell (2009), a popular book in this class. While this book might not be considered "high literature," it did meet the class criteria, and since Tammy chose this text, it had a greater chance of deeply engaging and interesting her. She decided on her purpose after seeing her teacher model her thinking and reviewing an anchor chart of possible purposes for studying characters. Tammy's purpose was to form opinions about the secondary character in her book, Mr. Snodgrass. Let's take a look at the notebook entry.

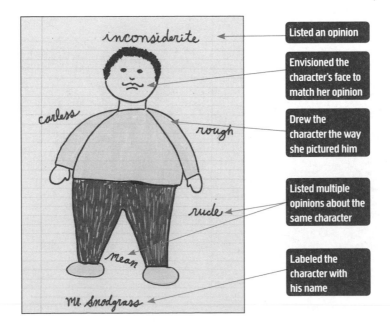

The following transcript was from a conversation between Tammy and her partner, Eliza.

Tammy: I think Mr. Snodgrass is really inconsiderate. What do you think? ← Listed an opinion

Eliza: Yeah, I guess so. He is also kinda mean.

Tammy: I agree and wrote down that he was mean too. ← Agreed on an opinion

Eliza: What else do you think?

Tammy: He is so rude, careless, and rough. ← Listed others' opinions

Eliza: What do you mean by rough?

Tammy: Like in this book he seems rough.

By applying the "types of thinking" framework—Right-Now, Over-Time, or Refining Thinking—to thin-slice Tammy's thinking, we can quickly figure out what she is already doing.

thin slice

1. WE LOOK AND LISTEN TO STUDENTS.	2. WE NAME WHAT THEY ARE DOING.	3. WE IDENTIFY THE CURRENT TYPE OF THINKING.	4. WE DECIDE WHAT TO TEACH NEXT.
What the Reader Said/Wrote	**What We Notice**	**Type of Thinking**	**What to Teach Next**
Listed opinions • Inconsiderate • Rude • Careless • Rough • Mean (entry) "Like in this book he seems rough." (conversation)	Tammy formed more than one opinion about the same character. Since her opinions are listed and not described and she is not referring to multiple parts of the text, it seems to be her current thinking right now. She lists "rough" in her entry and also when she speaks with her partner. She does not explain or elaborate in the entry or the conversation yet.	Right-Now Thinking Right-Now Thinking	*Show a New Type of Thinking:* Show Tammy how to do some Over-Time Thinking and revisit an idea across the book. Teach her how to form an idea, such as being inconsiderate, and then come back to that idea with examples from across the text and not just in one part. Possibly show her other ways to set up an entry that is not only a listing but builds off her lists to have a space for more elaboration such as a chart or bullets.

We decided to show Tammy how she could take an idea she had in one part of the book and keep thinking and writing about it across the text to do some Over-Time Thinking. She can form ideas right now and do some Right-Now Thinking, so we wanted to show her how to keep asking "Is he still inconsiderate?" across the text. Our goal in demonstrating this is twofold: First, we want to heighten a reader's awareness that when we read fiction, we are both reading for consistent patterns of behavior *and* continually looking for clues to a character change, a break in the pattern the author implants to develop the story of character growth. We can show her how to set up a notebook entry with more examples across the text or add to the entry she already has. We can explain that listing is one way to record ideas, and then we can go back to those ideas over and over again to see what we think about them later in the book. We are building off what she is already doing and extending it so that her thinking sustains her as she goes the distance of the entire novel.

Choice 3: Coach Readers to Apply a Currently Used Type of Thinking in Other Sections or Books

Krystina decided to think over time about the character's feelings in her book. She made this decision at the start of reading and used emojis and a plot line to track the character's feelings. By creating her entry in this way, she was setting herself up for Over-Time Thinking because she was able to focus on the feelings across the book. Let's look at her entry and thin-slice what type of character thinking she was doing and consider what we might teach her next.

At the end of the independent reading portion of the reading workshop period, Krystina shared her entry with the class and taught her classmates what she was doing and thinking. Here is part of what she said.

Krystina:	(Puts her entry under a document camera so it can be projected for the whole class to see as she explains her thinking process) "I set up my notebook entry with an emoji plot line by drawing the faces on the side. I drew them from bottom to top, and the bottom one is very upset, then sort of angry, then content, then happy, then exuberant. Then as I was reading, I would stop when something big happened and I wanted to think about the character's feelings. I thought about which emoji face it matched and drew a line there. I wrote what was happening to cause that feeling. I kept doing that throughout the book when big things happened. It was fun to see how the feelings changed and then to see when and why they changed in the book."
Classmate:	"Did anything surprise you as you looked back at this entry at the end?"
Krystina:	"Sort of. Well, I was surprised she went from super angry to exuberant. I think that was because of the conflict in the book and then it starting to be solved. But we have been learning about how characters are like real people and have all sorts of feelings and ups and downs like us, so that was not surprising to see."

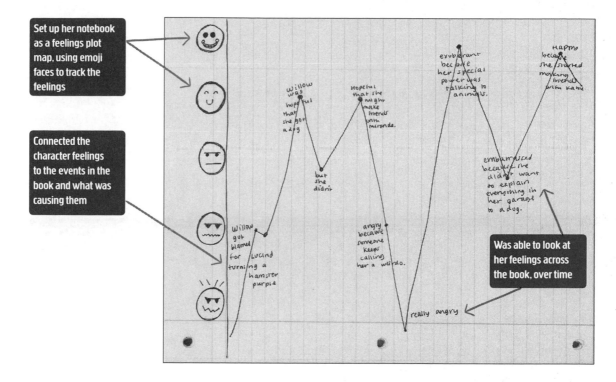

Set up her notebook as a feelings plot map, using emoji faces to track the feelings

Connected the character feelings to the events in the book and what was causing them

Was able to look at her feelings across the book, over time

Willow was hopeful that she got a dog

Hopeful that she might make friends with Miranda.

exuberant because her special power was talking to animals.

Happy because she started making friends with Katie.

but she didn't

embarrassed because she didn't want to explain everything in her garage to a dog.

Willow got blamed for Lucind turning a hamster purple

angry because someone keeps calling her a weirdo.

really angry

After looking at Krystina's entry and hearing her explain her process and thinking to her classmates, we were able to use our four-step process to thin-slice her thinking and decide what to teach next. Let's look at the chart on the next page see our process.

thin slice

Sometimes the students who are already doing so much deep thinking can be the most difficult for us to decide what to teach next. We decided to show Krystina how to use the same types of thinking in other books in this series and beyond. This thinking about how feelings go up and down across a text and are caused by events and conflicts is helpful to examine in any fiction book. We showed her how she could do similar types of thinking in the next book she was planning on reading. **Transfer is more likely to happen when we explain to students *what* they did, *why* it was helpful, and *when and how* they can do it again in other texts.**

Even though these examples of the choices we made were focused on individual students, many of the decisions we make about what to teach next are taught in whole group or small group lessons. Once we identify that most or several students are using the same types of thinking, we can consider if the whole class, a small group, or just one student needs this next step. This is another type of decision we can make. By taking the time to take clipboard notes, we can look at patterns in our classroom and decide which structure makes the most sense.

Teacher Tip

1. WE LOOK AND LISTEN TO STUDENTS.	2. WE NAME WHAT THEY ARE DOING.	3. WE IDENTIFY THE CURRENT TYPE OF THINKING.	4. WE DECIDE WHAT TO TEACH NEXT.
What the Reader Said/Wrote	**What We Notice**	**Type of Thinking**	**What to Teach Next**
Krystina set up the notebook to use emojis to track feelings across the book. (entry)	This shows Krystina already knows how to focus on one character area such as feelings across a text and not jump around or forget about her original thinking.	Over-Time Thinking	*Use the Same Type of Thinking in Other Texts:* Since Krystina is already doing so many things to study her character, show her how she can use the same moves and thinking in other fiction texts. This particular text is an easily read short chapter book that is part of a series. She can begin to look at other books in this series and beyond the series in the same way. This will help her learn to transfer her learning.
"I wrote what was happening to cause that feeling." (conversation)	She was connecting her feelings to the cause and thinking about what was motivating them. This was based on the current event and past events in the book.	Right-Now and Over-Time Thinking	
"I think that was because of the conflict in the book and then it starting to be solved." (conversation)	She connects the feelings and events to the conflict. This shows she is refining her thinking and going deeper by seeing how feelings are based on conflicts and struggles.	Refining Thinking	

Studying More Than One Character

Many readers focus solely on studying the main character of a book. While it is vital to focus on the main character, we gain even more insight when we look at the character's relationships and compare more than one character within a text or across texts. After all, the propellant of story is the tension between protagonist and antagonist, so it makes sense to have students become comfortable studying more than one character. In this section, we will explain two key lessons for teaching students to study more than one character and look at a few examples of how students study multiple characters. We apply the same decision-making process to their entries and conversations as when they study one character at a time.

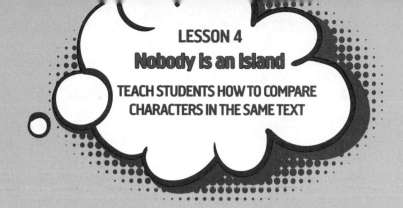

LESSON 4
Nobody Is an Island
TEACH STUDENTS HOW TO COMPARE CHARACTERS IN THE SAME TEXT

In this lesson, we show students how to study two or more characters from the same book and consider how they are similar to and different from one another. This includes how our thinking about the two characters is similar and different.

Decide to Teach This Tomorrow if Your Students

- Already know how to independently study characters in one book
- Are reading books with more than one important character
- Ignore secondary characters as they read and form ideas

What You Need:

- A familiar read aloud fiction book
- Your own reading notebook
- Chart paper and markers

Explain Why: Explain that when we focus on just one character in a book, we are missing some of the whole picture of the story. Now that your students know how to study one character, it is helpful to compare the main character to other characters in the text so they can see how each character has his own role and impact on the plot. You might also explain that it can be tricky to read a book with many characters, and it can be helpful to write about each of the important characters to keep them straight and not confuse who is who.

Show How:

- Refer back to a familiar read aloud book with memorable characters or back to a part of a read aloud you already did. This allows you to study the characters in front of students and model your thinking without having to spend time reading a brand-new text.

(Continued)

- Show students how you can use a T-chart or multicolumn chart to keep track of the characters within a book.
- Model how you look across each column to think about how they are similar and different. This can be done in a conversation and also in writing. You might use the following chart to help show the process of comparing characters and the different ways you might compare them.

WE CAN COMPARE CHARACTERS BY THINKING ABOUT

- The roles they play in the story
- What motivates them
- The choices they make
- How they respond to an event or conflict
- Our opinions about them
- The lessons they learn

Percy	Annabeth	Groves	Chiron	Rachel
·Son of the mayor god Poseidon ·Loves Annabeth and always protects her ·very gullible and always believes where they are told ·willing to do risky things to preserve the truth ·cares about his family and Olympus. ·Hates Kronos and wants to destroy him ·Best friends with Grover	·Daughter of Athena ·Fights with a knife Luke gave her when she was younger ·Is wise above her ages ·Ran away from home at a really young age ·a very independent individual with many worries and questions about her future. ·wants to be an architect when she grows up. ·very jealous of Rachel + Percy	·speaks for the trees ·Got the god Pan's powers when he died ·Is a sayrar ·very local and trustworthy ·Has a girlfriend named Jupiter ·"...Grover put his Reed to his lips and began to play the instrument	·camp director while Mr. D is gone ·He is a centaur so he is ½ man, ½ horse ·very stubborn when it comes to his father kronos ·Part of council of cloveneiders ·Is in technical terms the voice of the forest nyads	·mortal ·enjoys painting and being a part of society ·Hates her parents because they spoil her ·can see through the mist and see all the matters ·lives in NYC ·very expressive, happy and difficult to understanding at times ·Rebellious when she stole

Highlighted the main character

Created a column for each character

Listed character roles and behaviors

Pictured each character and drew what she saw based on the roles and behaviors

The chart on the previous page is from a student reading the book *The Last Olympian* (Riordan, 2009), which has several characters with unusual names. She made a five-column chart and listed the characters' roles and behaviors along with pictures of what they looked like.

A Few Tips:

- If you have younger or less experienced students, consider using a short story rather than a full-length book for this lesson.
- If students have trouble deciding which characters are important enough to compare, they can still add them all to their entries and then see which ones they have enough to write about. If they don't have much to say, that helps them decide who is important in the book.

Let's look at how another reader, Marcus, looked at two characters in the same novel called *Emil and Karl* by Yankev Glatshteyn (1940/2006), which is about two boys whose parents are taken away by Nazis during World War II. One of the boys is Jewish, and one is not. In Marcus's entry on the next page, we can thin-slice how he is thinking about both of these characters and notice his type of thinking.

Even though Marcus is studying more than one character, we can still follow the same process, naming what type of thinking he is doing and making a choice about what to teach him next. Notice we labeled the type of thinking in the callouts. Think about what you would choose to team him tomorrow. Would you reinforce what he is already doing, teach him a new way of thinking, or show him how to do this same thinking in a different text?

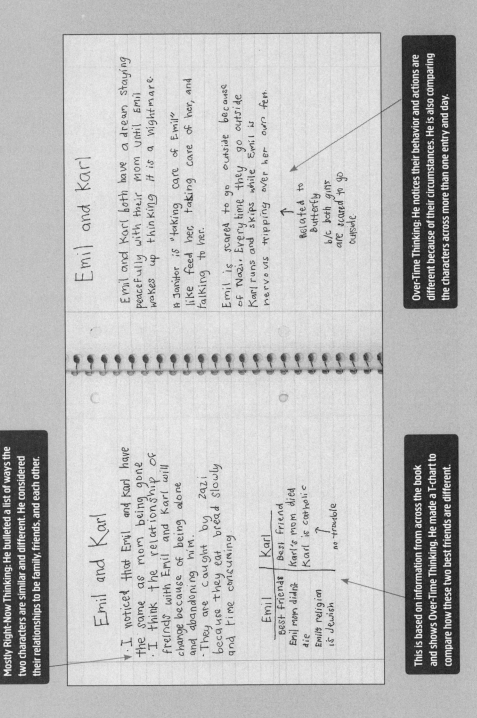

Mostly Right-Now Thinking: He bulleted a list of ways the two characters are similar and different. He considered their relationships to be family, friends, and each other.

Over-Time Thinking: He notices their behavior and actions are different because of their circumstances. He is also comparing the characters across more than one entry and day.

This is based on information from across the book and shows Over-Time Thinking. He made a T-chart to compare how these two best friends are different.

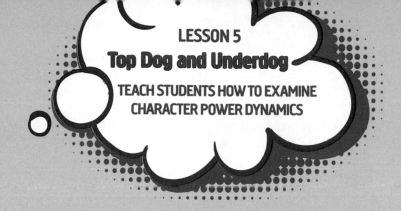

LESSON 5

Top Dog and Underdog

TEACH STUDENTS HOW TO EXAMINE
CHARACTER POWER DYNAMICS

In this lesson, we show students how important it is to examine how characters impact and influence one another. This means how they support or pressure one another, how they treat one another, and how they impact each other's choices.

Decide to Teach This Tomorrow if Your Students

- Already know how to independently study characters in one book
- Are reading books with more than one important character
- Ignore secondary characters as they read and form ideas
- Focus mostly on actions and not the motivation behind why characters make choices

thin slice

What You Need:

- A familiar read aloud fiction book
- Your own reading notebook
- Chart paper and markers

Explain Why: This lesson is important for students as readers and as people. If students begin to understand how characters impact and pressure one another, they can begin to see this playing out with their own relationships in their lives. Let students know that no person or character acts in isolation and that we are always impacted in some way by the people in our lives. When we consider this, we can better understand character motivation and why characters make the choices they do. We can also point out that characters tend to play particular roles, and figuring out their roles in the story helps us predict what they might do next.

Show How:

- Referring back to a familiar read aloud fiction text with at least two important characters, show students how you think about the way the characters impact one another.

(Continued)

- Create a notebook entry in front of students and possibly show them a few ways you write about how characters impact one another. Following are a few examples of notebook entries that show the impact characters have on one another. These were made in front of students, so the process of thinking about the impact was modeled and not just a product at the end.

Support and Pressure Flow Chart With Sketches

In this example, I modeled the process of making a column for each character that either supported or pressured the main character. In each column, I showed how I wrote the character's name, sketched him, used dialogue bubbles to show pressure or support, and then drew arrows to show the flow of how it impacted the main character. This is just one way readers could create an entry.

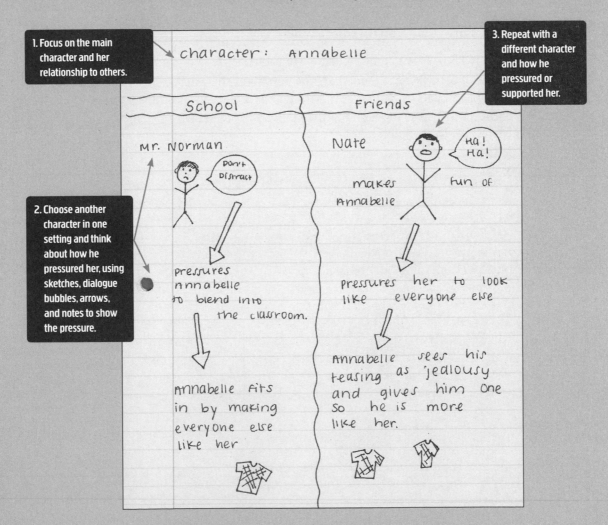

Pressure Graph Example

In this example, I focused on two main characters and how they impacted each other. I used the example that people sometimes have one-sided or two-sided relationships, and this can change over time. Pressure is not always good or bad, positive or negative, but is one major way characters change and grow. My steps for modeling this entry included the following:

1. Sketch and label each character as headings.
2. List the chapters on the side to set it up like a graph.
3. After each chapter, stop and think who was mostly impacting the other and who was mostly pressuring the other. Draw a line to show the direction of the pressure. If it is equal, the arrow can be on both sides showing they both impacted each other equally.

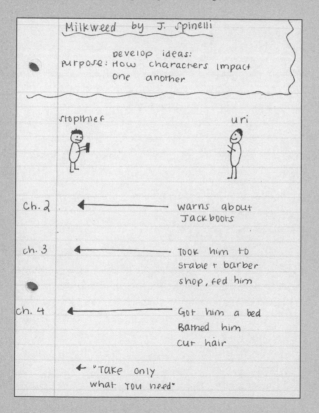

4. After creating the relationship pressure graph, you can model how you read the graph and make a new entry about the characters' roles. Look for patterns to see if one character is more influential on the other and why you might think that is.

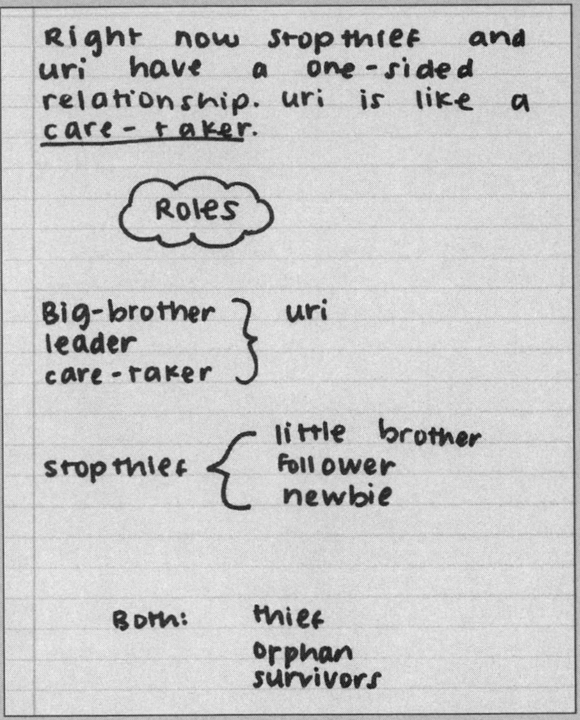

Right now stop thief and uri have a one-sided relationship. uri is like a care-taker.

Roles

Big-brother
leader   } uri
care-taker

stopthief { little brother
             follower
             newbie

Both: thief
        orphan
        survivors

This was a second entry—a **Character Roles Chart**—created after looking over the pressure graph. After a few chapters, readers can reflect and add to this roles chart.

A Few Tips:

- Students might not understand what we mean by the terms *relationship*, *pressure*, and *support*, so you can teach them what these terms mean. It can help to relate them to real-life examples or back to a read aloud text that students know well.

- Taking a comparison entry and acting it out with a reading partner helps some students really understand how characters are similar and different. Partners each act like a character, and then they pause to notice what they say, how they say it, and how their body language is different depending on the character they are acting like.

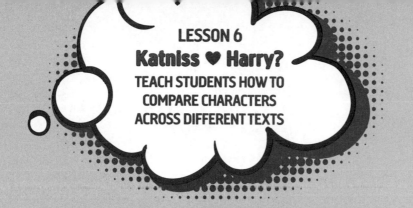

LESSON 6
Katniss ♥ Harry?
TEACH STUDENTS HOW TO COMPARE CHARACTERS ACROSS DIFFERENT TEXTS

In this lesson, we show students how to study characters from different short stories or books and then think about how they are similar and different. Because this requires them to read more than one text, we tend to teach this after we have done a few fiction read alouds that the class knows well that we can refer back to when we model.

Decide to Teach This Tomorrow if Your Students

- Already know how to independently study characters in one book
- Can already compare characters in one book
- Are starting to notice that characters face similar conflicts and learn similar lessons in different books

What You Need:

- Two familiar read aloud fiction books with characters with something in common
- Your own reading notebook

Explain Why: Tell students that even though the characters, setting, and plot are different in different books, there are often typical types of characters, conflicts, and lessons that characters learn. When we look across more than one text at characters, we can learn bigger lessons about people in general that we can take with us in our lives.

Show How:

- Show two familiar read aloud fiction texts and remind students about the important characters.
- Make a T-chart and give each side a heading with a character from each of the two different texts.
- Show how you think about what the characters say, do, and think in each book.

(Continued)

- Think aloud as you compare what the characters say, do, and think across the two books and columns.
- Make a sticky note that shows a larger idea about the two characters in the two books that is common to both. Place that on the T-chart.

This is an example I modeled using two familiar picture books, Bernard Waber's (1972) *When Ira Sleeps Over* and Kevin Henkes's (1991) *Chrysanthemum*.

Ira	Chrysanthemum
says: "But Reggie will laugh. He'll say I'm a baby." p. 12	says: "School is no place for me. My name is too long. It scarrely fits on my name tag. And I'm named after a flower!'"
thinks: p. 10 thinks about not being able to sleep without Teddy Bear	thinks: She did not think her name was absolutely perfect. She thought it was dreadful.
does: p. 25 decides not to take his Teddy Bear to the sleepover	does: took the longest possible route to school

Now I think kids sometimes make decisions because of how other kids treat them – like Ira and Chrysanthemum.

A Few Tips:

- Using a simpler text for complex and new thinking can be a more accessible starting-off point for many students. You can always use a more complex text later when you model a second time.
- As students begin to try this thinking in their own independent reading books, it can be helpful to first have them compare a character in their book to a character in a familiar class read aloud. Once they have had success with this, they can use two of their own independent reading books.
- The final part of this lesson leads to students thinking about themes. Looking across texts can blur the line between character study and themes. Chapter 6 will dive much more deeply into theme.

Harnessing the Power of Partnerships and Book Clubs

Throughout this chapter, we have shown examples from students' reading notebook entries that are either about whole class read alouds, book club books, partner books, or independent books. It can be extremely helpful for students to have at least one person who is reading the same book to talk to while studying characters. This can be a form of support because someone else is able to dive deeper into the book with them. Partners and book clubs can work together in the following ways:

- *All Together:* Each partner or club member reads the same part and studies the same character so both partners or all members of the book club can discuss what they are thinking about the same characters and parts.

- *Divide and Discuss:* Each partner or club member reads the same part but chooses a different character upon which to focus. This means students can begin to compare characters in the conversation together.

- *Parallel Thinking:* Each partner or club member reads a different book in the same series or by the same author, and then they meet to talk about what is similar or different across the books.

Each of these three types of partner and club work has its benefits and drawbacks. Use what you notice about each of your groups to decide which might work best for them or provide them as options and let your students make the choice.

UNDERSTANDING CHARACTERS: AN ACTION PLAN

Even though as teachers of reading it can feel like we have a million decisions to make, we can use the three-decision framework to help us stay focused on what to teach next. After thin-slicing student notebook entries and conversations, we can decide to reinforce what the students are already doing well, to teach a new type of thinking, or coach students to apply a type of thinking they already do to a different part or text. Remember that none of these choices is wrong and all can help students. When you are deciding what to teach next, pick one of these three options and show students what they can do.

As you get started teaching students how to study characters in fiction texts, keep the three types of thinking in mind—Right-Now, Over-Time, and Refining Thinking. Model each one for students in whole class read aloud lessons and then meet with students in conferences or small groups to thin-slice and determine the type of thinking they tend to do. Use the information you gather from these conferences to decide what to teach next.

TYPES OF THINKING READERS USE WHEN UNDERSTANDING CHARACTERS	THREE TEACHING CHOICES WE CAN MAKE
★ Right-Now Thinking ★ Over-Time Thinking ★ Refining Thinking	1. Name and reinforce a type of thinking readers are already using. 2. Show readers a different type of thinking and model how to use it. 3. Coach readers to apply a currently used type of thinking in other sections or books.

GETTING STARTED WITH UNDERSTANDING CHARACTERS

☐ Introduce character lessons to students (see pages 157 and 161).

☐ Show students different ways to record their thinking about characters in notebook entries (see page 164).

☐ Confer with students and look for the types of thinking they tend to do. Use the chart on page 169 that shows the types of thinking.

☐ Make a choice about what to teach next. The three choices are shown above.

☐ Remember there is no such thing as a wrong choice if it is based on what you notice students doing.

Videos and viewing guide may also be accessed at
http://resources.corwin.com/GoldbergHouser-Fiction

 Read Aloud to Explore Characters: The Goal

Video 5.1

 Read Aloud to Explore Characters: The Lesson

Video 5.2

 Read Aloud to Explore Characters: Deciding What to Teach Next

Video 5.3

 Small Group Practice Studying Characters: The Goal

Video 5.4

 Small Group Practice Studying Characters: The Lesson

Video 5.5

 The Decision-Making Process

Video 5.6

© Andrew Levine

Decisions About Interpreting Themes

6

"A NOVEL IS NOT A SUMMARY OF ITS PLOT BUT A COLLECTION OF INSTANCES, OF LUMINOUS SPECIFIC DETAILS THAT TAKE US IN THE DIRECTION OF THE UNSAID AND UNSEEN."

(Charles Baxter)

I sometimes think of a theme as something that permeates the air around me when I'm lost in a story. What exactly am I enveloped by? How would I articulate it? In nifty phrases like "conquering fear," "rooting for the underdog," "survival," or "sibling rivalry"? Not quite, but here's an attempt to capture the *process* of accruing themes from a narrative: When we read stories, we journey through the plot alongside the characters, whom the author constructed in order to have us consider ideas about the human experience that have caught the author's attention. So as we read, we journey and build a relationship with the author, as this writer's words compel us to consider perspectives about the story—and also about the world around us. But here's where it gets interesting and messy: The journey isn't like a trip to, say, Paris, where reader and author see and take snapshots of the same exact view. The author is like a tour guide; he may lead the reader to the Eiffel Tower, but the reader is going to see the scene through his own lens and take a picture of the Eiffel Tower from his unique vantage point. Yep, even novelists can't control every shot. So, essentially, themes are messages and lessons we as readers interpret based on the experiences of the characters and their journeys *combined with ours*. Here are a few common questions that arise, and distinctions to keep in mind, when teaching students about themes.

Is it a subject, topic, or theme?

When we're reading a novel, we often begin filtering scenes and interactions into topics or subject matter that seems apt—maybe envy, loss, or love. These aren't themes per se, but thinking about these topics can lead us to do the deeper work of interpreting themes. For example: love. Love alone is a subject or topic that is written about a lot. However, it is not a theme. When we ask what the author thinks about love or what the characters are experiencing with love, it is through our own answers and thought processes that we move closer to knowing a "theme." **That is, it's helpful to understand a theme as two words—*interpreting theme*—for it's a collection of what the writer put forth and our own experiences of something.** For example, it's not "love" but some take on love that a story offers up like the ocean offers up shells and other gifts from its depths: *Losing love teaches us to appreciate love.* As we read about characters dealing with the topic of love, we use our own experiences to interpret each instance—each "luminous specific detail" (Baxter, 2007, p. 36)—to lift a message, idea, or lesson from the text as a theme.

True enough, students in elementary and middle school are early in their journey of life experiences that they can bring to stories to help them interpret themes, but if we explicitly distinguish topics from themes, continue discussing stories with these distinctions in mind, and encourage our students to bring their own ideas into the process of interpreting themes, they will grow in their sophistication in ways that astound us.

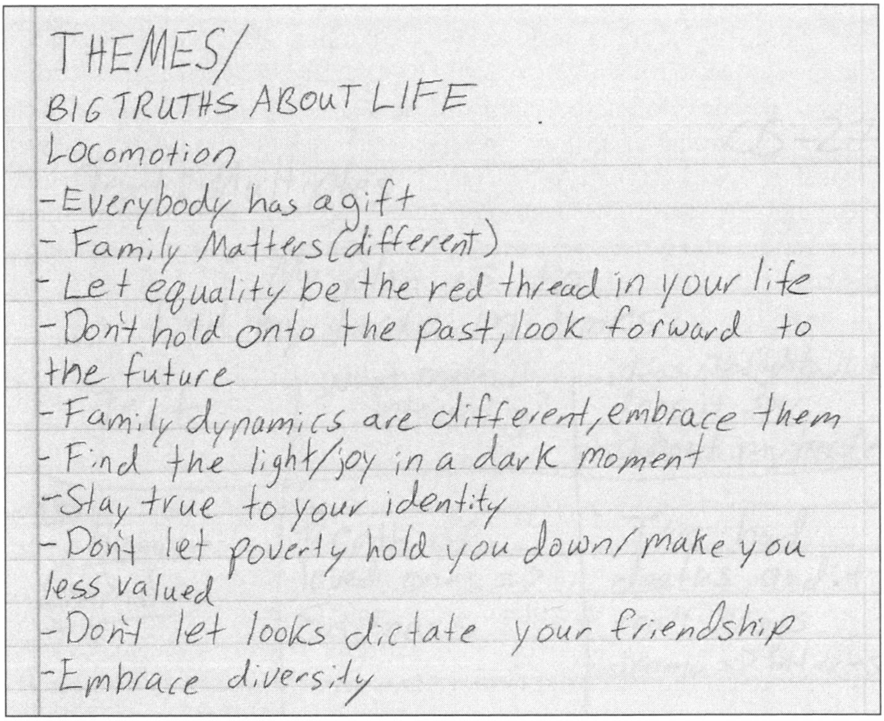

> THEMES/
> BIG TRUTHS ABOUT LIFE
> Locomotion
> - Everybody has a gift
> - Family Matters (different)
> - Let equality be the red thread in your life
> - Don't hold onto the past, look forward to the future
> - Family dynamics are different, embrace them
> - Find the light/joy in a dark moment
> - Stay true to your identity
> - Don't let poverty hold you down/make you less valued
> - Don't let looks dictate your friendship
> - Embrace diversity

Notice how this student knows she can interpret multiple themes in a text. She develops many ideas about one book.

Is it thematic teaching or teaching theme?

It can be confusing to see the difference between thematic teaching and teaching students to interpret themes. In this chapter, we suggest you teach students how to think deeply about themes, which entails studying characters and our own experiences in order to develop larger ideas about the human experience. Thematic teaching, on the other hand, begins with telling students a theme that will come up in a set of texts and spending most of the time teaching students about the content of the theme. The following chart illustrates a few examples of the differences between these two types of teaching.

THEMATIC TEACHING	TEACHING THEME
• Focuses on the topic and content of the text • Often entails listing and labeling parts of a text that match the topic	• Focuses on the thinking you do about possible themes in a text • Entails tracking your thinking and forming bigger ideas about a text you can take into your life

Example
 	
Question:
 	
    What is a hero?
 	
Possible Answer:
 	
    A hero is someone who helps others and rescues them.
	Example
	
	Question:
	
	    What am I thinking about this character who is acting as the hero?
	
	Possible Answer:
	
	    This character is acting like a hero because he sticks up for his friends. I guess friends are like supports for one another.

Example
 	
Question:
 	
    What is friendship?
 	
Possible Answer:
 	
    Friendship is when two people like to spend time with one another and do fun things together.
	Example
	
	Question:
	
	    What are the characters learning about friendship? What lessons can I take away about what it means to be a friend?
	
	Possible Answer:
	
	    Friends help you when things are good and bad. Friends help you be a better version of yourself.

Are themes abstract and universal or specific to a text?

All of the above! Generally speaking, the education field may have overemphasized the idea of expressing a book's idea as a "universal" theme to the point that the quirky particulars of a story's themes get undervalued or glossed over. We think a more useful way to think about themes with your students is that they are applicable to everyone. Think of reading fiction as understanding that books help us think about big ideas. We are using the specific setting, characters, and plot of specific books to think of big ideas and topics that apply universally to everyone. It's in the application that the book's resonant ideas become universal. For example, in *Extra Yarn* by Mac Barnett (2012), Annabelle (a specific character) discovers a magical box of yarn and decides to knit colorful items (a specific event) for everyone in the town (a specific setting). This summary is *specific* to the text *Extra Yarn*. Then, when we move from the specific to the universal, we think about the application for people, places, and events outside of the book *Extra Yarn*. For example, we can learn from Annabelle that *sometimes in life we are given unexpected opportunities to share our talents.* This idea or theme can be applied universally to many books, movies, works of art, and people.

This student shows an understanding of interpreting themes from studying a character. He thought about the specific journey Lonnie took in *Locomotion* by Jacqueline Woodson (2003) and interpreted it universally in a message we can all think about.

> ## My Takeaways From Locomotion
>
> After reading Locomotion, I realized a few vital things. First, appriciate everything, because you never know when time might run out. I think this because in the text, it showed me how Lonnie really doesn't have much! However, Lonnie shows so much optimism...towards everything! In addition, in the preview of the sequal it shared how Lonnie knew he was a poet, but he tried not to be. So, embrace it! No matter what you are, embrace how special you are.

Who decides on themes, the reader or the author?

As the reader, you own the meaning of the themes you deem as long as you don't stray too far from the actual details of the text. There are multiple themes in a well-crafted text that the author either consciously or unconsciously imparts in the narrative, but their prominence, power, and contours are subjective to the reader. And as mentioned earlier, a novel may seem to address the *topic* of love and entice a reader to start by wondering, "Hmmm, what does the author think about this topic?" and this pondering gives way to thinking about the author's themes as the narrative unfolds. Ultimately, however, in a sense the power shifts because the reader interprets or "decides" the universal themes, synthesizing multiple parts of the book along with his own life experiences. This subjectivity is part of what contributes to the complexity of our conversations around themes. Several readers reading the same text might interpret completely different themes. Conversations open the door to seeing possibilities of other ideas based on the observations and life experiences of other readers.

© Daryl Getman, DAG Photography

Interpreting themes is both a literary and a life skill than can enrich all our lives. We get wiser by reading about and reflecting upon characters' experiences.

Why Interpreting Themes Is Important

The texts we read provide a literary model of the world we live in today. This model affords us the opportunity to try on a variety of thinking patterns, ideas, and mind-sets within the "safety" of the text. We become part of the world of the story and journey alongside the heroes, the villains, the underdogs, and the sidekicks, and maybe we get to rehearse how to be resilient in the face of a sibling who seems to eclipse us, a troubled friendship, or the loss of someone we love. When challenges crop up in our everyday lives, we have the comfort and confidence of knowing we are not alone in the difficult circumstances and decisions we must make.

As we write this, the 2016 Olympics were taking place in Rio. To jocks like us, there is something magical about the entire world coming together, and with athletics in the mix, we are in heaven! Throughout my viewing, I noticed a pattern in many of the advertisements and commercials throughout the games. One brand created a commercial that I loved watching every single time it aired. It shared "that's gold" moments and "taste the feeling" images and video clips of athletes in moments of losing, winning, working hard, and celebrating. The music, the words, and the images all resonated with the athlete in me who thrives being someone's teammate and working together as a team. I wasn't physically at the 2016 Rio Olympic Games, but every time I experienced the commercial, I was there mentally and emotionally right beside all the athletes— sharing my "that's gold" moments together with them. It made me think about the part of us that values connection with others. Think about times you've felt a kindred connection with someone. It's often a connection linked to universal ideas, morals, lessons, and themes. These connections with other people often help us learn empathy for others and why we think it's important to teach students to think about themes in their reading of fiction texts.

WHY INTERPRETING THEMES IS IMPORTANT

★ Reminds us of the importance of connecting with others
★ Teaches us empathy
★ Prepares us for the future
★ Opens us to the possibility of new thinking

What Other Reading Skills Fit With Interpreting Themes?

It seems like just about every reading skill connects in some way back to interpreting themes. Some of the specific reading skills involved in interpreting themes include understanding cause and effect. When we look at what causes a character's learning and lessons, we are looking at the effects of the character's actions. Synthesizing events and reactions is also a key skill involved in interpreting themes. As readers, we need to see how one character's choices and motivation along with her reactions and the other characters' reactions all go together. We put each event together and then look at the larger whole that emerges. In many ways, the act of interpreting themes is the process of seeing the big picture—not just the small parts of a person's life, a period of time, and particular settings. One of our favorite quotes that addresses this multiskilled envisioning is from Janet Burroway, a novelist and fiction scholar: "If character is the foreground of fiction, setting is the background, and as in a painting's composition, the foreground may be in harmony or conflict with the background" (Burroway, Stuckey-French, & Stuckey-French, 2006, p. 177).

To interpret themes, our minds and hearts sweep across the entire canvas of text and world, and that's why we dedicated this entire chapter to it. If you worry you need to teach students every reading skill that exists, rest assured that when students interpret themes, they are also doing so much more.

In this section, we offer you a handful of essential practices for deciding what to teach next. The following chart highlights what you will find.

In this chapter, you will learn

In this chapter, we will examine how readers learn strategies for interpreting themes in texts.

- We provide a snapshot of classroom exercises for introducing interpreting themes.

- We offer key lessons, charts, and examples for teaching about themes.

- We show student examples of conversations and notebook entries in order to show you the three main types of thinking about themes.

- We provide a thin-slicing cheat sheet to use when making next step decisions.

THE DAILY PRACTICES

- Introduce interpreting themes in whole class lessons (see page 208).
- Confer with students and look for the types of thinking they tend to do. Use the chart on page 228 that shows the types of thinking.
- Make a choice about what to teach next. The three choices are discussed beginning on page 238.

LESSON 1
Dog-Eared Pages

TEACH STUDENTS HOW TO INTRODUCE THE STAYING POWER OF THEMES

In this lesson, the goal is to introduce the concept of a theme as an idea that resonates. If your students are brand new to reading and thinking about themes or they are approximating their understanding, consider teaching this introductory lesson.

thin slice

Decide to Teach This Tomorrow if Your Students

- Are new to the concept of identifying and thinking about themes
- Demonstrate difficulty in understanding themes
- Tend to focus more on decoding and fluency than comprehension
- Need support moving beyond literal recall of their reading

What You Need:

- A familiar story, movie, song, or piece of artwork—for example, *The Kissing Hand* (Penn, 1993), *Love You Forever* (Munsch, 1986), or *Days With Frog and Toad* (Lobel, 1979)
- Chart paper

Tell Why: When first introducing themes to students, it's helpful to use a story from their childhood. You'll explain to students that themes are big ideas or lessons we learn from the characters and the events of the story. You'll convey that often the *reason* favorite books are so memorable is because their themes were so powerful and right for us at that time, and because the stories tapped into the mysteries of the human quest. Let them know the course of study over the next several days will be exploring strategies to think about interpreting themes in our stories.

Show How:

- Think aloud as you recall the events of the plot from a familiar story. Jot on a chart:
  - Step 1: What is going on?
- Continue to think aloud as you demonstrate your process by thinking aloud the following steps. Show students how you think about the answers to these questions and jot down your thinking. It can be helpful to list these four steps on chart paper to refer back to.
  - Step 2: What's *really* going on?
  - Step 3: What can I learn about what is really going on?
  - Step 4: How did the author create all of this?

Practice How:

- Show students a second familiar text.
- Give them time to think through these same four questions on the chart.
- Offer students time to discuss their ideas, going through the same four steps you just modeled.
- Listen and name back the themes you hear them say.

A Few Tips:

- Instead of a story, use an image, song lyrics, or perhaps a short digital video clip.
- Consider turning Step 4 (or any of the steps) into a separate lesson if your students need help with one at a time.
- Create a chart to record themes from common stories, songs, and images. This chart can grow over time and serve as an anchor for your lessons.

TEXT	THEMES

LESSON 2
DIY Best-Seller List

BOOKS WE LOVE AND
WHY WE LOVE THEM

This lesson is designed to build on the momentum of student engagement and interest connected to the texts they read. In addition, it helps students to start the process of considering bigger ideas, themes, or issues in texts that might be the result of patterns in our reading choices. These patterns are often linked to themes we gravitate toward and result in an interesting discussion that can lead to future decisions in selecting books to read.

thin slice

Decide to Teach This Tomorrow if Your Students

- Need further explanation and experience with the concept of themes
- Have a basic understanding of themes
- Oversimplify themes as (only) what makes the story "interesting" or "exciting"
- Think of themes as subjects or topics rather than ideas

What You Need:

- Chart paper
- Familiar texts with eminent likable characters such as *Extra Yarn* (Barnett, 2012) or *Naked Mole Rat Gets Dressed* (Willems, 2009)

Tell Why: Explain to students that this lesson is going to extend their thinking about themes beyond "Books are exciting!" by encouraging them to think about *why* books are exciting. When we think books are exciting, it's worth thinking about what the author has done to create an exciting story.

Explore How:

- Refer to two or three books you have previously read aloud to the class such as *Extra Yarn* or *Naked Mole Rat Gets Dressed* (see Chapter 2). Remind students of the emotions they experienced while reading these books and what they were thinking along the way.

- Ask students to reread any notebook entries they created when they first read the text and look back at any charts you created as a class about the characters and plot of the books.

- Lead a discussion about what characteristics made these books so exciting and engaging. You might create a chart like the one that follows that lists some common characteristics.

CHARACTERISTICS OF ENGAGING FICTION BOOKS

★ Characters and Character Relationships

- ○ Offer something new to think about
- ○ Are similar to our own lives
- ○ Are different from our own lives

★ Journey of the Character

- ○ Brings up new or unfamiliar emotions
- ○ Connects us to a familiar experience
- ○ Shows the author's style and choices

- See an example below of a chart that was created with a class as a tool to organize and track students' thinking.

WHAT WE THINK ABOUT IN STORIES WE READ	EXAMPLES OF TEXTS WE'VE READ TOGETHER	WHY WE LOVE THEM
Characters	*The Tiger Rising* (DiCamillo, 2005)	Rob is a kid like a lot of us.
Character Relationships		Rob and Sistine are unlikely friends but end up being the best of friends.
Character Journeys		
Author's Craft		The symbolism of the tiger's cage and Rob's suitcase pushes us to think about limitations and fears in our lives.

- As the class conversation continues, start to connect elements we think about to reasons why we love texts. Angle the conversation toward the idea that studying particular elements of fiction can lead us to thinking about themes or big ideas in texts that carry from one text to another and perhaps to our everyday lives.

A Few Tips:

- Ask students to draw or sketch their favorite book titles and have the same conversation as mentioned in the lesson above. Often the visual cue helps to remind students of the initial lure of the book.

- Ask students to collect their favorite books, take a photo (aka "shelfie") of the covers, and share them with their partner or the whole class. Next, lead a discussion that guides students through a reflection process of book choice, ideas, and reading identity.

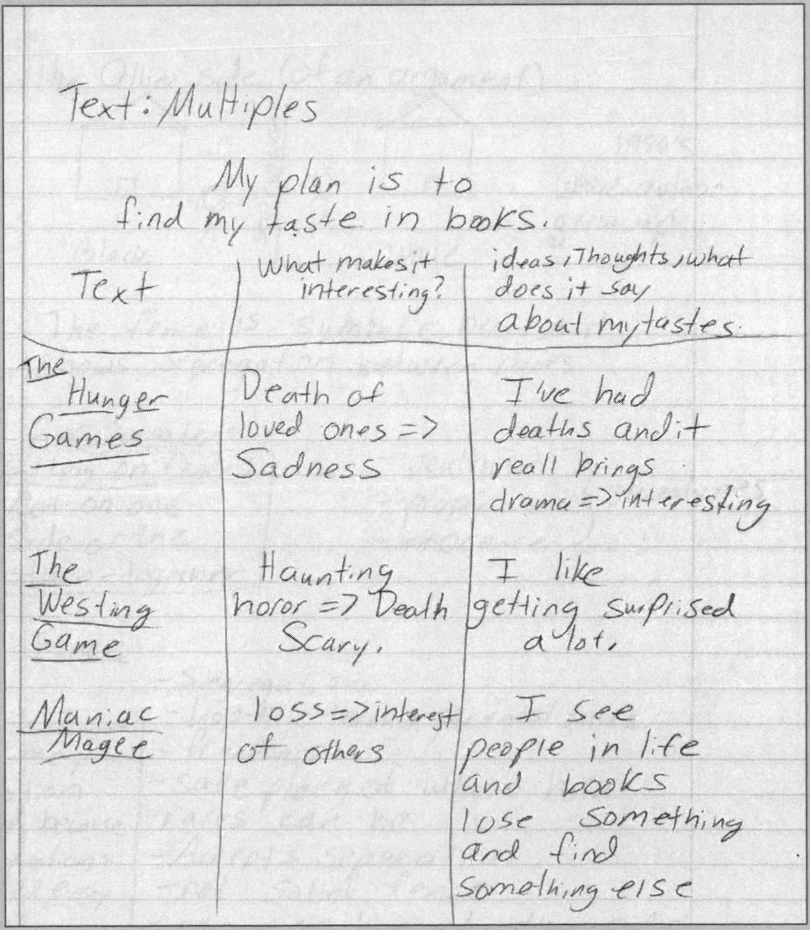

This reader explores her reading interests as a stepping-stone to understanding themes that draw her into her independent book choice and patterns of thinking.

Text: Multiples

My plan is to find my taste in books.

Text	What makes it interesting?	ideas, Thoughts, what does it say about my tastes.
The Hunger Games	Death of loved ones => Sadness	I've had deaths and it reall brings drama => interesting
The Westing Game	Haunting horor => Death Scary.	I like getting surprised a lot.
Maniac Magee	loss=>interest of others	I see people in life and books lose something and find something else

LESSON 3
The Gasp Factor
TEACH STUDENTS HOW TO BE OPEN TO A TEXT'S REALITY

In this lesson, the goal is for students to experience and think about the shock (or surprise) value stories yield as a way of exploring why we are drawn to (or avoid) a particular type of story. There are many reasons why a reader gasps or is shocked or surprised midway through a text. This lesson helps students connect their emotional reactions to themes.

Decide to Teach This Tomorrow if Your Students

- Need support moving beyond the literal meaning of texts
- Are reading without emotional reactions
- Need support with being open to or considering texts that might change their thinking or emotions

thin
slice

What You Need:

- An emotionally charged scene such as "The Fight" from *First French Kiss and Other Traumas* by Adam Bagdasarian (2003), listed in our favorite reads in Chapter 2 (This book is appropriate for older students. For younger students, consider the flying scene from *Let's Go, Hugo!* written and illustrated by Angela Dominguez [2013].)

Tell Why: Remind students there are many reasons why we read stories. We're often drawn to stories or parts of stories that cause us to lose our breath, or "gasp," from an emotional response. When we consider all the gasp moments, there is often a theme or big idea that connects them all together, and when we read with an awareness toward themes, it provides additional layers of the text to study and multiple opportunities to think about its bigger meaning.

(Continued)

Show How:

- Reread a scene(s) from a familiar class read aloud that is likely to evoke strong emotional reactions or, in other words, draw *gasps* from the students.

- Be sure you've prepared ahead of time the places in the text where you'll dramatize your reading in an effort to highlight the compelling scene. Be ready to demonstrate the first gasp (for example, shock or surprise)!

- Continue reading, and as students join you in *gasping*, support them by analyzing the parts of the text that were gasp worthy.

- Make a chart (see the sample on the next page) to help organize and make visible their learning.

- Give students time to participate in partnership, small group, or whole class conversations prompted by these gasp-worthy moments of the story as a strategy.

- Connect these moments to scenes that inspire thinking about possible themes the author has pushed us to think about.

A Few Tips:

- Use the chart on the next page as a guide. Study the chart and the thinking from the students in your class, then select (or create new) categories from the chart that support the thinking the students need additional support with. For more support in teaching the parts of a text worth stopping to read closely, we recommend reading *Notice & Note* by Kylene Beers and Robert E. Probst (2012).

- Introduce categories from the chart a few at a time based on areas of support students need.

- Use an image or short video clip instead of a read aloud excerpt as a starting point for your teaching and then move into written texts.

GASP-WORTHY SCENES THAT REQUIRE US TO STOP AND THINK				
GASP!	EXAMPLE TEXT	OUR REACTIONS	IDEAS OR QUESTIONS	POSSIBLE THEMES
A pattern is broken				
The character(s) have a strong emotional reaction				
You (the reader) have a strong emotional reaction				
The character(s) act out of the ordinary				
There is an unexpected twist of the plot				
The setting changes abruptly				
An object appears to be symbolic				
The character(s) experience conflict(s)				

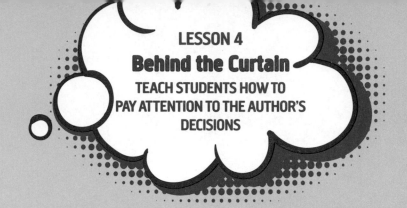

LESSON 4
Behind the Curtain
TEACH STUDENTS HOW TO PAY ATTENTION TO THE AUTHOR'S DECISIONS

I remember when I first saw *The Wizard of Oz* movie as a young girl. My fall from innocence to experience might have been when terrier Toto pulls the curtain back to expose that "The Great and Powerful Oz" was an ordinary human being orchestrating effects. I was shocked. When I think of novelists, I often regard them as doing the same kind of lever-pulling from behind the scenes—literally, behind the scenes. In this lesson, the goal is for students to first raise their awareness of the author behind the curtain, and then analyze the author's writing decisions as a means to interpret themes.

thin slice

Decide to Teach This Tomorrow if Your Students

- Need support moving beyond a literal recall or literal understanding of the text
- Need support in utilizing more than one skill set to think about themes
- Will benefit from examining reading and writing connections

What You Need:

- A familiar text, such as *The Tiger Rising* by Kate DiCamillo (2005) or others listed in Chapter 2, or texts that have well-written scenes that allow readers to envision the setting, the characters, and the events (In text selection considerations, think about the craft decisions made by the author. How does the author use syntax, word choice, tone, pace, and mood? Select a text that has multiple opportunities for discussion in a short scene.)
- Chart paper and markers

Tell Why: Help students understand that authors make intentional decisions in their writing so that we as readers have opportunities to imagine the scene and create ideas about the characters that, when added up, lead to bigger ideas and opportunities to think about and interpret themes.

Show How:

- Remind students of or reread an excerpt from a familiar text.
- Think aloud about your reactions to decisions the author made in the text. Show students that these are the author's deliberate decisions.
- Model thinking about the connections. For example, say, "What does the author want me to think about . . . ?"
- Think aloud about how you form an idea about themes based on the author's craft decisions.
- Create a chart to help students see and understand the thinking process. The chart that follows is one possible example.

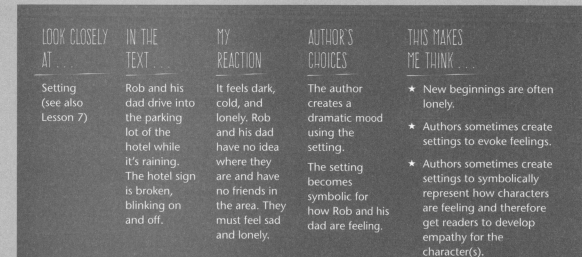

LOOK CLOSELY AT . . .	IN THE TEXT . . .	MY REACTION	AUTHOR'S CHOICES	THIS MAKES ME THINK . . .
Setting (see also Lesson 7)	Rob and his dad drive into the parking lot of the hotel while it's raining. The hotel sign is broken, blinking on and off.	It feels dark, cold, and lonely. Rob and his dad have no idea where they are and have no friends in the area. They must feel sad and lonely.	The author creates a dramatic mood using the setting. The setting becomes symbolic for how Rob and his dad are feeling.	★ New beginnings are often lonely. ★ Authors sometimes create settings to evoke feelings. ★ Authors sometimes create settings to symbolically represent how characters are feeling and therefore get readers to develop empathy for the character(s).

A Few Tips:

- If students need additional support, prepare an alternative experience for them to rehearse the strategy. For example, play an upbeat, fast-tempo piece of music followed by a slower-tempo piece of music and start a conversation about the reactions, feelings, and ideas experienced during each piece of music. Link this to intentional decisions made by the composer.
- Try the above lesson with two pieces of artwork. Perhaps try contrasting color schemes and allow time for students to discuss in partnerships and then as a whole class their reactions, feelings, and ideas compelled by the images.
- Ask students to perform a character's monologue from a well-written scene in their partnerships or for the whole class. Many students can benefit from the dramatization and performance aspect by "seeing" the character.

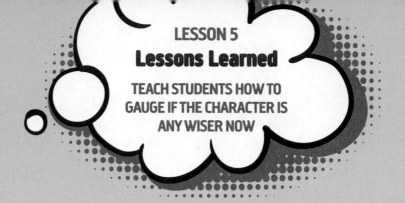

LESSON 5
Lessons Learned
TEACH STUDENTS HOW TO GAUGE IF THE CHARACTER IS ANY WISER NOW

In this lesson, the goal is for students to think about themes in the text by looking closely at the characters and the lessons they learn from their mistakes as possible themes to consider.

thin slice

Decide to Teach This Tomorrow if Your Students

- Are glossing over the conflict characters are facing as an ordinary event
- Can recall the events of the plot and need support in reacting to and interpreting these events as opportunities to think about lessons and themes

What You Need:

- A familiar text with strong characters where a clear lesson is learned from a mistake (For example, Frog and Toad often face roadblocks or make some type of mistake in their decisions and in the end learn a lesson that we can benefit from too.)
- Your own reading notebook to model
- Chart paper

Tell Why: Explain to students that sometimes "I told you so" shows up in our reading. Thinking about the mistakes of others often leads to themes.

Show How:

1. Choose a familiar read aloud text.

2. Show how you use a chart as a way to organize your thinking.

3. Jot down each event that you consider a mistake.

4. Model your interpretations of the mistakes by thinking through your reactions and opinions.

5. Model combining mistakes from the text and your opinions to interpret themes.

Text: Maniac Magee by Jerry Spinell:

RW: My reading work today will be to think about character mistakes and what it means.

Mistake	Wish instead	What it means...
Running away from the Beales	He could've stayed and faced the racism and maybe trusted the grown ups to handle it.	We sometimes take the easy way out. Maniac tells himself he's helping the Beales, but he's really just scared He didn't know how to deal with all the conflict. We have to be strong and face our fears.
Bringing Mars Bar to the McNab's party	He should've brought Hester and Lester	We need to be careful when we want to change things and really think it through. We can't just sacrifice other people for our beliefs. Maybe we need to ask them to be on our side, rather than trick them. Good intentions aren't enough... we need a good plan.

A Few Tips:

- Create a chart such as the one pictured here created by Lori, a fourth-grade teacher. Students often benefit from teaching that is broken into easily replicated steps.

- Be clear in the verbiage you use to teach this lesson. Be sure that the teaching language refers to *mistakes* as *learning opportunities* rather than problems. We all encounter problems, and we all learn from them; therefore, we see them as opportunities to grow. This helps model our own growth mindset.

IF ONLY...

1. Identify a character "mistake."

2. Think, "What do I wish the character did instead?"

3. Write long to think what it means.
   - critique   - theme
   - life lesson

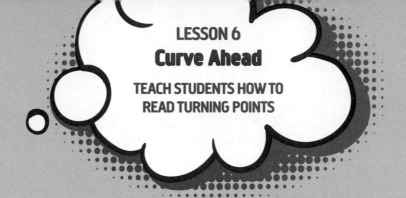

LESSON 6
Curve Ahead

TEACH STUDENTS HOW TO READ TURNING POINTS

In this lesson, the goal is for students to think about the importance of turning points in the plot. Turning points often follow the tension of the plot. A turning point occurs when readers learn whether the characters get what they want or don't. It's in this pivot of yes or no that the characters learn information about themselves and, therefore, the reader learns information, too. The falling action is when the information from the turning point begins to settle in with the character. Many readers begin to "connect the dots" in this final phase of the plot. Authors use this archetypal structure to craft their stories in ways that set us up to interpret themes from these turns of the plot.

thin slice

Decide to Teach This Tomorrow if Your Students

- Are thinking about texts with simple, literal, or cliché ideas
- Need support in reacting to texts
- Gloss over the falling action to get to the end

What You Need:

- A scene from a familiar text that has a clear turning point (For example, in *Rules* by Cynthia Lord [2006], there are several scenes between Catherine and Jason that take unexpected turns. *Naked Mole Rat Gets Dressed* by Mo Willems [2009] has a revealing turning point near the end of the story.)
- Chart paper

Tell Why: Define for students turning points as important parts of the plot that serve as opportunities for readers to think about big ideas and themes. Remind students of examples of turning points in familiar texts and even from pop culture (movies and TV shows). Turning points in books are like turning points on a road. You get to a point where the road sharply curves or you have to choose to go left or right and either choice will set you on a new course. In books, it is when the story line takes a turn due to a *big* event that causes the character to form a realization that brings about a change in the character.

Show How:

- Find a place in the text where a character is facing a turning point. Read that part aloud and stop and think about what this might be revealing about a larger theme.
- Create a chart of helpful language that students might use when they encounter these turning points. An example chart follows.

HELPFUL LANGUAGE FOR THINKING ABOUT TURNING POINTS AND THEMES

Turning Points

(something *big* that has caused a change in the character)

- Wait . . . what?
- The character lost . . .
- The character gained . . .
- The character now realizes . . .

Thinking About Ideas and Themes

- All of this is adding up to . . .
- I'm beginning to realize . . .
- This isn't about . . . but instead it's about . . .
- This is *really* about . . .
- At first I was thinking . . . and now I'm thinking something very different because . . .

Practice How:

- Choose another story students know well, such as "Cookies" from *Frog and Toad Together* (Lobel, 1971).
- Read aloud a section of the text where Frog and Toad are facing a turning point. For example, in "Cookies," Frog and Toad determine they need willpower to stop eating all the cookies. Frog unsuccessfully hides the cookies in several places. They face a turning point in whether or not they will eat the cookies or practice willpower.
- Give students time to discuss their thinking at this turning point event.
- Continue reading the short story until you get to the end.
- Give students time to think about what they learned from studying turning points. Students often realize that turning points serve as a bridge to interpreting themes.

A Few Tips:

- Before introducing this lesson using a text, find "dramatic" headlines from social media, newspapers, or magazines with the latest social gossip or controversial subject that will employ student interest. Try the lesson using these headlines and then move to texts.

- If students need additional support, you might use your own life as an example before looking at a headline or examining characters in a text.

- Sometimes having students write their own stories with turning points helps them think about them in their reading.

LESSON 7
All-Terrain Vehicles

SPOTTING THE SYMBOLIC IN VARIOUS SETTINGS

In this lesson, the goal is for students to consider setting (and other elements of fiction). Many students can benefit from knowing that some settings are symbolic and can lead to thinking about ideas and themes.

Decide to Teach This Tomorrow if Your Students

- Are consistent in their interpretations of themes based on character analysis and are ready for more opportunities to think about themes
- Need support moving beyond cliché themes
- Know what symbols are but don't necessarily think about them as they read

What You Need:

- A familiar text with a skillfully crafted setting such as *The Tiger Rising* by Kate DiCamillo (2005) where she often refers to dark and light scenes, rain, and sun that can be thought about as symbolic representations of themes
- Chart paper
- A prop of your choice to illustrate the concept of symbolism

Tell Why: Explain to students that a symbol is something that stands for something beyond itself. We are surrounded by symbols. The interpretation of these symbols creates symbolism. For example, the American flag symbolizes the United States of America. Perhaps a piece of jewelry you wear symbolizes your belief system. When we think about this as readers, we discover symbols written by authors, and our job is to interpret them and think about what they symbolize for the characters or perhaps for the reader. The symbolic aspects of texts are often connected to themes.

(Continued)

Explain How:

- Show students the prop you've chosen to explain symbolism.
- Give students a few minutes to brainstorm and list familiar symbolic objects and their meanings.
- Frame the importance of looking for symbols in our reading as stepping-stones to interpreting themes.

Show How:

- Select an excerpt of a text to reread and model your understanding of how author's craft decisions in creating setting often contain symbolic meaning that can lead to thinking about themes.
- Create a chart of tips that help students study the crafting decisions made by the author.

Practice How:

- Give students time to identify where authors create symbols and then discuss with their partners the ideas or questions they have as a result of studying symbolic settings.

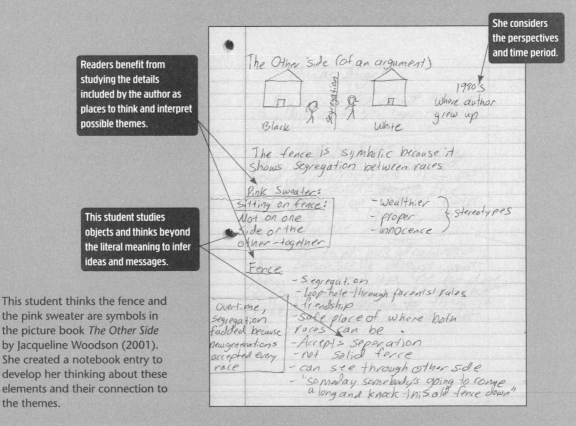

She considers the perspectives and time period.

Readers benefit from studying the details included by the author as places to think and interpret possible themes.

This student studies objects and thinks beyond the literal meaning to infer ideas and messages.

This student thinks the fence and the pink sweater are symbols in the picture book *The Other Side* by Jacqueline Woodson (2001). She created a notebook entry to develop her thinking about these elements and their connection to the themes.

TIPS FOR INTERPRETING SYMBOLIC SETTINGS

★ Study the weather
  ○ Rainy, gray, soggy = lonely, melancholy
  ○ Thunderstorm = frustration, anger, heartbreak
  ○ Sunny = cheerful

★ Pay attention to shades of color
  ○ Bright blue sky = jubilant

★ Look closely at light
  ○ Color of clothing, hair, eyes (sparkle)

★ Consider architecture
  ○ Old house and buildings—restored or in disrepair?
  ○ Ultramodern cityscape or rural town?

★ Notice names of locations
  ○ Hogwarts
  ○ Oz

★ Note time of day
  ○ Late in the evening
  ○ Earlier that day

★ Notice nature
  ○ Are animals tame or wild?
  ○ Are fields barren or lush?
  ○ Are forests dark or light?

★ Study clothing, language, and transportation

A Few Tips:

- Plan for a series of lessons that examine how authors use symbolism to guide our thinking. Each day could lead to a different investigation: setting, colors, and so on.

- Create a chart to support conversations with sentence starters that help guide thinking.
  ○ Could this be . . . ?
  ○ At first I thought . . . but now I think . . .
  ○ This could really mean more . . .
  ○ It might be more about . . .
  ○ Why would the author decide to . . . ?

thin
slice

What to Look for When Students Interpret Themes

We'll continue with the concept of thin-slicing in this section by sharing the trends and patterns we've found in students' thinking about themes. Remember that thin-slicing is *thin*. It's a close look at *part* of a student's work with the idea that every time you take a thin slice of a student's work, those slices are adding up to the bigger picture of this student as a reader and member of the community. Trust your instincts in your ability to thin-slice, and over time you'll see patterns not only in your students, but also in your ability to analyze students' thinking as the driving force of your teaching decisions.

The following categories (or slices) of themes will help guide your decision making. These thinking patterns fluctuate before, during, and after reading as part of the meaning-making process. From our study of reading with thousands of readers, we found there are three main categories or ways that students tend to interpret themes—frames, patterns, and lessons learned.

Frames: In fiction reading, a frame is a way of zooming in and looking closely at a particular aspect of the story. Readers who interpret themes tend to study patterns through a specific frame, or you could say the reader has framed her reading in a way she is able to study patterns and then interpret those patterns to discover themes. There are many ways a reader can frame a text. These decisions will inevitably change based on a variety of factors. For example, perhaps a reader has a new baby sister at home and is now acutely aware of sibling relationships. Life events are just one of the many reasons why readers select particular frames through which to read and think about a text.

Patterns: Authors of fiction carefully and intentionally weave together the stories they write with deliberate craft moves in a way that creates an experience for the reader. Therefore, it's our job as readers of fiction to pay attention to these craft decisions and use them in our journey to make meaning and discover themes. When we access a text knowing that our job is to think about the intentional decisions made by the author, it's as if we are reading with a secret decoder like the ones found at the bottom of cereal boxes. You've been looking at the back of the box all week unable to decipher the secret code without the decoder. Finally, with the decoder in hand, you see the message! As readers, looking for patterns becomes our very own secret decoder tool that helps us unlock big ideas in the texts we read.

Lessons Learned: In fiction stories, readers are often drawn to the drama. Maybe we live in the same drama—or secretly wish we did—or we are preparing just in case we are ever in a similar circumstance. Regardless, when we study characters, we are afforded the opportunity to learn lessons from the dramatic scenes created throughout the plot. By teaching students to consider the lessons characters are taught, we are essentially helping students to think about when a character develops awareness or a realization as a true learning experience. Conflict often illuminates aspects of life that we aren't aware of and again creates genuine learning experiences or lessons learned. When characters encounter conflicts in the stories we read, our job is to think through the everyday application outside of the book. In essence, the lessons happening in the book also impact the lessons happening out of the book.

Now that we've looked at three categories of interpreting themes, we'll look at student reading notebooks and conservations so we can practice thin-slicing with them in mind and more deeply understand what they look like in action. While looking and listening, we will first look for what a student *is doing* and identify that strength before deciding what to teach next.

Let's step into classrooms. In the following examples, the students are from classrooms where teachers conduct daily read alouds to model ways of thinking and using their own reading notebooks. These classrooms also have daily lessons that teachers create to explicitly teach skills based on their ongoing assessments of what students need next. Students in these classrooms select their own independent reading books where the common practice is to transfer the work from class lessons to independent reading experiences.

thin slice

INTERPETING THEMES

Here is a thin-slicing "cheat sheet" for you to experiment with in your classroom to make your own clipboard notes. You can use this chart when looking at your students' reading notebook entries and listening to what your students say in conversations.

INTERPRETING THEMES IN FICTION TEXTS		
FRAMES	PATTERNS	LESSONS LEARNED
What to look for: Lenses you focus on such as personal and intrapersonal relationships, societal issues, global issues, historical contexts, economic issues, gender issues, technological issues, etc.	What to look for: Story elements, author's craft, word choice, your own reader reactions, repetition of character's choices, etc.	What to look for: Turning points, changes in characters, morals, inner dialogue that reveals a bigger message, places where you are giving the characters advice, etc.
What a reader might say: *When I read this text thinking about . . . I notice . . .* *The author is framing . . . in this way . . .* *The author's framing of . . . makes me think . . .*	What a reader might say: *This is coming up again . . .* *A pattern I am noticing is . . .* *The pattern seems to be changing because . . .* *This pattern makes me think . . .*	What a reader might say: *The character seems to be learning . . .* *Based on the character's experiences, I am learning . . .* *A bigger lesson I am thinking about is . . .* *This story seems to really be about . . .*

Thin-Slicing Olivia's Thinking About Themes: Frames

She is framing her reading by thinking about what is "normal" in fairy tales.

She is connecting this frame of what is normal to larger issues and another frame—gender.

She is beginning to interpret themes.

Paper Bag Princess

What would normally happen	What actually happened	Connection to the social issue of gender roles
"Dragons carries off the princess	"Dragon carried off the prince	The princess is usually in distress
The prince goes finds the princess	The princess goes to find the prince	Showing that women can do things men can
Princess wears fancy clothes	Princess puts on a paperbag	Women defy stereotypes
Dragons would eat people	The dragon talks with the princess	Shows that she will stand up for the prince
Princess would be scared when the Dragon blew fire	Using her intelligence to tire out the Dragon (encouraged him)	Showing that princesses are can be smart and very brave.
Would thank the other for saving them	Told her to come back when she wasn't a mess	Shows unappreciation for everything Elizabeth went thro
The Prince and The Princess would end up happy and married.	She called him a Toad (after complimenting him) and don't get married.	She saw through his attire and knew she he wasn't worth it.

Olivia is using her notebook to think through her reading of Robert Munsch's *The Paper Bag Princess* (1980). She's chosen to frame her reading through the lens of gender and what is "normal" in fairy tales. She organized a chart to compare a typical fairy tale with the craft of Munsch's work in the twists and turns Princess Elizabeth faces in her interactions with Prince Ronald and the dragon. Through this comparison chart, she's able to collect her thinking around a few bigger ideas and themes that exist not only in this text but also across texts and in various aspects of our everyday lives. In this case, the combination of a powerful text, a well-organized reading notebook entry, and a frame enables Olivia to push beyond a literal understanding of the text. She takes on bigger ideas that, when combined, become themes we often see in texts.

thin slice

1. WE LOOK AND LISTEN TO STUDENTS.	2. WE NAME WHAT THEY ARE DOING.	3. WE IDENTIFY THE CURRENT TYPE OF THINKING.
What the Reader Said/Wrote	**What We Notice**	**Type of Thinking**
Olivia created a chart in her reading notebook with these categories: • What would normally happen • What actually happened • Connection to the social issue of gender roles She wrote: • "Women defy stereotypes." • "Women can do things men can."	Olivia has a plan for reading, and her notebook organization supports it. Olivia is comparing the archetypal structure of a fairy tale to Munsch's crafted tale. Through her comparisons of typical and actual, she begins to think through interpretations of Elizabeth's actions in outwitting the dragon and confronting Ronald with his lack of appreciation for her efforts in saving him. Her thought process takes her from in-the-book analysis of characters to themes we experience out of the book such as gender stereotypes.	Frames

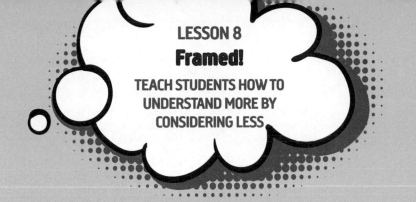

LESSON 8
Framed!
TEACH STUDENTS HOW TO UNDERSTAND MORE BY CONSIDERING LESS

When readers are not yet thinking like Olivia and are having a hard time interpreting messages in a fictional text, it is helpful to create an interpretive frame. While it is inevitable that readers will bring their entire history and beliefs to the text, choosing one aspect to frame in a text can often help them focus and ultimately consider ideas and themes.

Decide to Decide to Teach This Tomorrow if Your Students

- Oversimplify themes as subjects or topics
- Need support moving beyond cliché themes
- Often read with the same frame and are ready to try others

thin slice

What You Need:

- A familiar story such as *Naked Mole Rat Gets Dressed* by Mo Willems (2009) (Using this story, you can select several frames from which to read and understand the story such as the role of government, individuality, or fitting in.)
- Chart paper and a picture frame

Tell Why: Explain to students that having a specific lens through which to read and reread texts often helps us think about the text in meaningful ways. We will call this a frame.

Show How:

- Show students a photograph without a frame and then the same photograph with a frame.
- Explain that the purpose of a frame is to accentuate the image being framed. You might even choose a frame that is smaller than the entire photograph and show how where you put the frame

(Continued)

allows you to focus on that one area and not the rest. Move the frame around a bit to show you can focus on whatever you want by simply deciding to frame a different part.

- Connect the idea of framing a photograph to framing our reading to accentuate various aspects of the text in order to push our thinking about themes.

- Model thinking through different frames with different outcomes. For example, your thinking might stay the same with one frame, while other frames might propel you in a different direction and open up more possible places to interpret different ideas and themes. For example, if you frame your reading around gender, you might notice things you never did when you framed your reading of the same text around family.

- Make a list of possible frames through which to read a text. You can start with the ones listed in the sample notebook entry below and ask students to contribute more.

Practice How:

- Give students two to three minutes to practice with a partner trying on different frames using familiar texts that have been read aloud to the class.

- Support students by coaching them to notice what happens with their thinking with particular frames. For example, say, "It sounded like you had a lot more ideas with that frame. What happened in your thinking that was different with that frame?"

A Few Tips:

- Add to the list of additional frames as an ongoing ritual. You might include family, money, or relationships.

- Consider students' personalities, affinities, and book choice. Organize the students in small groups based on these factors and have them practice various frames using their own texts with support from you and a conversation with a few peers. If the students are reading in book clubs, they can use the familiar content of the text to practice framing. If they are reading different books, they can work to find common ideas across the different texts to study how themes transfer from one text to another.

Thin-Slicing Miguel's Thinking About Themes: Patterns

Miguel has grown in his reading and is starting to tackle higher-level texts with more complicated characters as a result of his teacher strategically designing a yearlong curriculum plan that connects both reading and writing units of study. Miguel's class has a daily interactive read aloud where his teacher models her thinking through conversations and her own reading notebook entries. Miguel also participates in a daily explicit lesson followed by time to implement the variety of strategies he's learned while reading a book of his own choice. Below, we see a sample from Miguel's reading notebook. He's exploring his thinking about the novel *Maniac Magee* (Spinelli, 1990). As we thin-slice his thinking, we focus on the ways he is interpreting themes and try to identify the type of thinking he is using—frames, patterns, or lessons learned. Let's take a look.

> Maniac Magee
>
> My big, I deg about manjac is why he keeps running away.
>
> I think he keeps running away because he wants to avoid any problems that he has but, there's none the only people that could help him was his parents so the but, they are dead.
>
> I think he's drawn to them because he doesn't want them to end up like he did so thats why I think that I think. He's drawn to them is to help them with things that are bad.

The reader generates a question that prompts his thinking.

He identifies a pattern in the character's behaviors and choices.

He forms ideas based on the patterns and uses them to think about how the character's motivation ties to a larger lesson about the character.

After looking at Miguel's notebook entry from his thinking about *Maniac Magee*, we notice the following:

- Miguel generates questions about character motivation as he reads.

- He formed an opinion about what explains Maniac's behaviors. He based his opinion on a consistent pattern throughout the text.

- He's ready for support in how to turn the specific patterns in the book he notices into more universal themes.

1. WE LOOK AND LISTEN TO STUDENTS.	2. WE NAME WHAT THEY ARE DOING.	3. WE IDENTIFY THE CURRENT TYPE OF THINKING.
What the Reader Said/Wrote	**What We Notice**	**Type of Thinking**
"My big idea about Maniac is why he keeps running away." "I think he keeps running away because he wants to avoid any problems that he has but the only people that could help him was his parents but they are dead."	Miguel asks a probing question about the character's motivation. He observes Maniac's behaviors and the situations that cause them. He uses this to form opinions.	Patterns

Thin-Slicing Kai's Thinking About Themes: Lessons Learned

Kai is a member of a classroom community that spent time learning how to use reading notebooks to deepen students' interpretations. In particular, the students are working on creating entries that *grow* across reading texts rather than creating daily entries that run the risk of being mere tasks to complete. Kai and her classmates design their own entries and are encouraged to return to them as they read in order to capture the thinking that evolves across a text. On the next page is an example of an entry from Kai's notebook that demonstrates her thinking about multiple themes in the book *Three Little Words* (Rhodes-Courter, 2008). We can see right away that Kai is able to think about universal themes and has developed her own way to rank the themes based on what she thinks is most important. Let's thin-slice her entry and identify the type of thinking she is using when interpreting themes.

Kai has collected themes over time in this entry. This was created as she read the whole book, not at the end.

Several lessons are examples of more universal themes and applicable to multiple texts and life.

Kai has created a personal ranking system that weighs lessons differently according to her ideas. She considers what is major and what is less important.

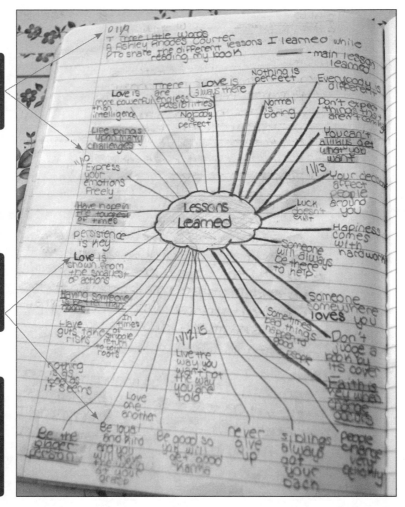

1. WE LOOK AND LISTEN TO STUDENTS.	2. WE NAME WHAT THEY ARE DOING.	3. WE IDENTIFY THE CURRENT TYPE OF THINKING.
What the Reader Said/Wrote	**What We Notice**	**Type of Thinking**
Kai collected her thinking in one entry with multiple lessons listed from across the book.	Kai has worked on themes in this text across several days, which shows she is working to combine multiple aspects of the text in finding themes.	Lessons Learned

(Continued)

What the Reader Said/Wrote	What We Notice	Type of Thinking
There is a coding system—highlighted parts show the main lessons learned. She writes: "Be the bigger person." "Have hope in the toughest of times." "You can't always get what you want."	Kai thinks about what is more and less important in the text and the messages. Kai understands that themes are universal. She is ready for us to support her in digging a bit deeper to move beyond cliché themes.	

If your students are not quite where Kai is just yet, and in need of more support with using patterns to interpret themes, the following chart can help them get started.

Using Patterns to Interpret Themes

I DISCOVERED A PATTERN IN THE BOOK ABOUT . . .	I CAN THINK MORE ABOUT . . .	I CAN MAKE IT UNIVERSAL BY STATING . . .
Characters	The character ❏ Why did you . . . ? ❏ What were you thinking when . . . ? ❏ How did you feel when . . . ?	Sometimes in life . . . It's important to . . . Let's remember that . . . We can all learn to . . .
Author's Craft	The author ★ How do you feel about . . . ★ I can't believe you created . . . ★ Did you create this so we would think about . . .	
Myself	Myself ⇨ I was surprised at the way I felt when . . . ⇨ Maybe this is something to think about in my life because . . . ⇨ I think I might have . . . differently because . . . ⇨ I wonder why . . .	

thin slice

CLIPBOARD NOTES: TYPES OF THINKING ABOUT INTERPRETING THEMES

As you spend time looking at students' reading notebook entries and listening to their conversations, see if you can identify the type of thinking they are doing. You can use a chart like this one or create your own. Take a few days to sit with individual students to find out what type of thinking each is doing. Remember it could be more than one type.

WHAT THE READER SAID/WROTE	WHAT I NOTICE	TYPE OF THINKING
Name: Date:		❏ Frames ❏ Patterns ❏ Lessons Learned

Decide What to Teach Next

Once we thin-slice readers' thinking and identify what our students are already doing, we can begin the next phase of the decision-making process. We can decide what to teach next. If a reader needs support in thinking of themes and is not reading with frames, patterns, or lessons learned, we can teach her to try this. These types of thinking guide the types of choices we might make. They narrow the choices down so we don't feel we need to teach everything or that we have nothing to teach at all. As improvisers, we use these three types of thinking as rules or tenets to follow when thin-slicing and making in-the-moment decisions.

Choice 1: Name and Reinforce a Type of Thinking

Let's step into a classroom where Ashley is reading *Percy Jackson and the Lightning Thief* (Riordan, 2005). We get a chance to thin-slice her notebook entry and a conference with her teacher.

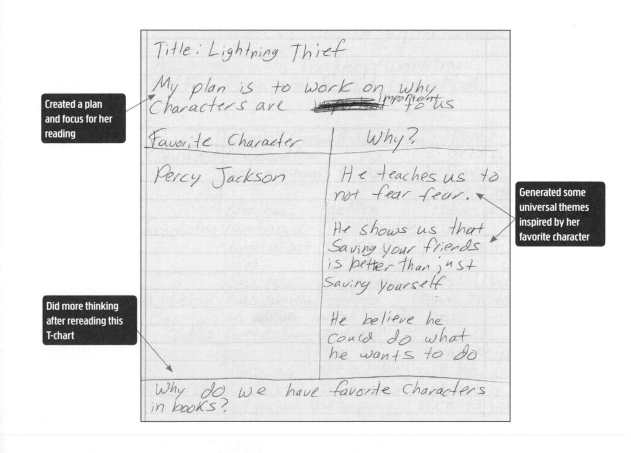

Created a plan and focus for her reading

Generated some universal themes inspired by her favorite character

Did more thinking after rereading this T-chart

Title: Lightning Thief

My plan is to work on why Characters are ~~important~~ to us

Favorite Character	Why?
Percy Jackson	He teaches us to not fear fear.
	He shows us that Saving your friends is better than just Saving yourself
	He believe he could do what he wants to do

Why do we have favorite Characters in books?

Ashley:	[Reads her notebook entries.]	
Teacher:	What are you thinking about as you read these entries?	

Ashley: This notebook entry helped me a lot. I put that Percy is my favorite character. And then I put he teaches us not to fear fear because he went to the underworld and he was, like, feeling too much fear but then he tried to stop it, and then what happened was that he left the underworld and found the lightning bolt. Percy got really scared until that girl hit him and [he] got knocked down for a second and then he relaxed and he didn't fear fear anymore. I also like him because he shows us that saving your friends is better than just saving yourself because when he went to the casino he didn't just leave his friends; instead, he said, "Hey! Don't eat those cookies anymore! They're going to make you stay longer." It's kinda showing he's a great person. But it falls under the category of he's not just great. He's a person that fears fear. Sometimes, controls fear, loves family and friends, likes to save people . . . he's kinda like the hero in the story.

> Uses her notebook in a conference to help her conversation get started

> Explains a possible theme—"not to fear fear"

> Explains her thinking with details from the text

> Notes topics that can be turned into themes

Teacher: Wow! That's a lot of powerful thinking, Ashley. Can you tell me more about how this chart helped you in this thinking?

Ashley: When I was reading, I found out when I wrote down the things . . . sometimes I don't remember, but when I wrote down these things, I was like, wow! Percy Jackson is not only a person who fears fear. I thought of this question: Why do we have favorite characters in books?

> Rereads entry and thinks more deeply about themes

Teacher: Did you come up with an answer?

> The teacher gives time and space for the student to identify, reflect on, and explain her thinking.

Ashley: I've been thinking about favorite characters and maybe they have something in common with you or maybe sometimes you feel the way they feel too.

Teacher: Do you think having things in common with the characters helps you think about the big ideas and themes in the books?

Ashley: I don't know. Maybe.

Teacher: OK. Well, Ashley, you are doing a lot of thinking in your reading! When you described your favorite character Percy Jackson [looking back at notes], you said, "He shows us." Is that a phrase that might help us think about why authors create characters? Because they show us and teach us big ideas to think about? Can you think more about that? You might stop reading and ask, "What is this character showing me? What is this character teaching me?"

> The teacher names the thinking the student is doing.

Ashley: [Nods in agreement.]

Teacher: Great! I look forward to the next time we get a chance to meet. Thanks!

What do we teach Ashley next?

We see from this conference and her notebook entry that Ashley understands the text she is reading. She gives small summaries of the plot and can paraphrase quotes from the text to back up her theories and opinions. Ashley thinks in big ideas. She notices that Percy is a character who doesn't fear fear. Also, she naturally feels comfortable making connections with characters. She is able to separate the emotions a character feels from the specific setting of a book and lift them into her life. This is seen when she says, "I've felt alone before. I've missed my mom, too." As a result of this type of thinking, Ashley has the ability to read with empathy and truly understands characters and the lessons they learn.

thin slice

1. WE LOOK AND LISTEN TO STUDENTS.	2. WE NAME WHAT THEY ARE DOING.	3. WE IDENTIFY THE CURRENT TYPE OF THINKING.	4. WE DECIDE WHAT TO TEACH NEXT.
What the Reader Said/Wrote	**What We Notice**	**Type of Thinking**	**What to Teach Next**
"He [Percy] teaches us to not fear fear." "He shows us that saving your friends is better than just saving yourself." "Why do we have favorite characters in books? . . . [M]aybe they have something in common with you [the reader]."	Ashley examines the conflicts and journeys the character Percy has taken and combines these with her own experiences to think about themes focused on the topics of fear and friendships. Ashley instinctively knows that studying characters is a lot like studying people, and when we look closely, there are big ideas to explore.	Patterns Lessons Learned	*Name and Reinforce a Type of Thinking:* We decided to reinforce Ashley's thinking and encourage her to continue. We named the phrases she uses to discuss her ideas so that she is able to transfer this type of thinking into the next text she reads. • This is showing me . . . • This is teaching me . . .

We made the decision to reinforce Ashley's thinking and encourage her to continue to recognize patterns and use them to think of ways the characters' patterns teach us lessons we can live in our everyday lives. First, we explained to Ashley what she was already doing by naming the kind of thinking she was doing—studying patterns and thinking about lessons learned by the character. We specifically gave her examples from what she said in the conference so that she had concrete examples of what we mean by patterns and lessons learned. In this way, her own work becomes a reminder of the kind of thinking she can use in other books too. We also mirrored back some of her own language: "Ashley, when you told us that Percy Jackson fears fear, it seems as though you studied the patterns of Percy's behaviors. Studying patterns is a very helpful strategy that leads to thinking about big ideas and themes." We also pointed out how she specifically recalled the scenes where Percy warned his friends to stop eating the cookies in the casino, thus helping him learn a lesson. When we mirror back the steps readers took, it can help them become more metacognitive and aware of their process. This awareness often leads to more transfer from one text to another. By reinforcing Ashley's thinking about patterns and lessons learned, we are reinforcing work she is already doing so that she gains confidence and understands when and why to use this same thinking again.

Choice 2: Show a Different Type of Thinking

Let's step into a middle school classroom where students have spent several years utilizing reading notebooks as part of their reading practice and meet Dyanna. Below is an entry from her reading notebook that we use to thin-slice and decide what to teach her. We'll quickly identify her current type of thinking and use it to decide where to go next.

Sets a goal and focus for her reading

Summarizes the relationship between characters

Frames her thinking with the lens of friendship, which has the potential to generate several themes

Shows work over several days so her thinking could evolve over time

Uses a direct quote from the text to support her thinking

What do we teach Dyanna next?

Dyanna's notebook entry reflects her intention to deepen her thinking about this text (*Gallows Hill* by Lois Duncan, 1997). The multiple dates in the margin indicate the evolution of her thinking across days and the concept that building thinking in a notebook entry takes time. Dyanna begins the notebook entry with her interpretation of the relationship between the characters with a brief summary angled toward the topic of friendship. However, the majority of the entry is built from direct quotes of the text. We decide to utilize Dyanna's visual talents and her inclination toward patterns of collecting text quotes to teach her how to envision scenes between the characters in a way that will help her to look closely for patterns the author has created. In less complex texts, the characters often reveal themes by something they say (or think) during a turning point in the plot. However, in more complex texts such as this, the patterns might be subtle, and students might need our support to identify and utilize patterns the author creates to explore themes at first.

thin slice

1. WE LOOK AND LISTEN TO STUDENTS.	2. WE NAME WHAT THEY ARE DOING.	3. WE IDENTIFY THE CURRENT TYPE OF THINKING.	4. WE DECIDE WHAT TO TEACH NEXT.
What the Reader Said/Wrote	**What We Notice**	**Type of Thinking**	**What to Teach Next**
Dyanna wrote her goal with this entry was to "deepen my thinking" (when Charlie and Sarah got close).	Independently initiated goal		*Show a Different Type of Thinking:* We decided to show Dyanna a different type of thinking because she demonstrates collecting quotes around the friendship frame. We can teach her how to look across the quotes she's collected and look for patterns that might lead her to think about bigger ideas about friendships.
Dyanna writes about Charlie and Sarah's friendship that includes topics: Trust Exploration Acceptance Honesty	Summary sketch of the characters Direct quotes from the text	Frames: Friendships, rite of passage	

When we thin-slice Dyanna's notebook entry, we see her thinking about her reading is mostly literal because the majority of her notebook entry contains quotes lifted directly from the text. We see potential in this because the quotes that Dyanna selected were chosen for a reason—we might say she's *framed* her reading in quotes. Our job as teachers is to find out why Dyanna selected these quotes, teach her this is called framing a text, and then link those specific scenes to possible bigger ideas. We can start by teaching her a *different kind of thinking*. For example, instead of (only) recalling specific scenes from the story, we can teach her to react to those scenes within a frame of friendship, gender, or identity. She'll most likely be able to link the quote she wrote in her notebook to a frame(s), which will help her think about bigger ideas inspired by the specific quotes. Once

Dyanna learns how to take what she is doing and read it through a frame, she can then start to use such frames to think about ideas and themes. Many students like Dyanna have intuition about their ideas, and they need our support to help them identify and shape it into bigger thinking. This process of thinking can be transferred to other fiction books Dyanna reads.

Choice 3: Coach Readers to Apply a Currently Used Type of Thinking in Other Sections or Books

In this section, we join a classroom where we meet Jeanette. Jeanette is reading *The Fences Between Us* (Larson, 2010) from the Dear America series. Below is an entry from her reading notebook. We'll use it to thin-slice her thinking and then decide what to teach her next.

Text: Diary of Piper Davis

My plan is to keep working on the Book and Read to find out.

Frames this thinking by focusing on family

Creates a three-column chart to help her examine multiple parts of the text

Purposefully looks for patterns in order to form an idea

Begins to develop another theme

Begins to develop a theme

Makes a specific observation about one character

Conflict	Piper's Brother Leaves and Piper gets emotional	Mr. Lindstrom v.s Piper	Piper gets a Diary
Resolution	She has move on and forget about him	getting in trouble cause Mr. Lindstrom.	She could now write about herself.
Pattern/ Big Idea	She now has something to write about.	Mr. Lindstrom needs to mind his Own busin	Miss Wyatt gave it to her
Message	life can be difficult but you just have to move on	Piper is not a little girl anymore but her parents treat her like one.	Some people will be extremely nice to you

What do we teach Jeanette tomorrow?

As we thin-slice Jeanette's notebook entry, we notice she is trying out many types of thinking. Jeanette is *framing* her reading through family dynamics. With this frame, she is able to understand several big ideas in the text; however, they are a bit overused and general such as "Life can be difficult, but you just have to move on." We decided to teach her how to stick with a frame across a text. Then she can read forward in the text, thinking about the same frame, going deeper, and developing more specific and nuanced interpretations.

We chose to teach Jeanette to stay with her thinking about frames rather than teaching her a different skill because she seems to be approximating and just getting started. Helping Jeanette to put her thinking together at different parts of the text will allow her to synthesize these parts and go a little deeper. If we were to move on and teach her something new and different, we'd run the risk of missing this "teachable moment." Donald Bear, co-author of the *Words Their Way* series, suggests we teach what students are "using but confusing"—in other words, what they are sort of doing or starting to do—and help them do it even better. This will be especially helpful for Jeanette since she is reading complex texts that require her to think across them in order to interpret themes. Many students grow in confidence due to repeated practice and more teaching in the same focus area for a bit, rather than feeling rushed to always move on.

thin
slice

1. WE LOOK AND LISTEN TO STUDENTS.	2. WE NAME WHAT THEY ARE DOING.	3. WE IDENTIFY THE CURRENT TYPE OF THINKING.	4. WE DECIDE WHAT TO TEACH NEXT.
What the Reader Said/Wrote	**What We Notice**	**Type of Thinking**	**What to Teach Next**
Row 1, columns 1 and 2: "Conflict—Piper's brother leaves and Piper gets emotional."	Jeanette thinks about the dynamics between characters.	Frame: Siblings and family dynamics	*Coach Readers to Apply a Currently Used Type of Thinking in Other Sections or Books:* We decided to show Jeanette how to carry the frame (siblings) across the text to think about it in various places throughout the text as a way to develop more complex ideas and sophisticate her thinking.
Row 4, column 2: "Life can be difficult but you just have to move on."	She generates a theme based on Piper's emotional reaction to her brother leaving.		
Row 4, column 3: "Piper is not a little girl anymore but her parents treat her like one."	She generates another theme with a text-specific example; however, this is connected to the frame she's already reading through: family dynamics.		

Interpreting Themes in Multiple Texts

As students gain confidence in interpreting themes in their own books, they'll naturally start to synthesize these ideas and discover cross-text themes. You'll start to hear conversations like "Hey! That's just like in the last story we read when . . ." Design a series of read aloud lessons by collecting a set of stories with similar topics—for example, stories about family dynamics, overcoming fears, sibling rivalry, and so on. Even though the specifics of the story are different, the opportunity to interpret similar themes is connected by the subject matter of the plot. For example, you might read aloud *Extra Yarn* by Mac Barnett (2012) and *Naked Mole Rat Gets Dressed* by Mo Willems (2009). These books have two completely different plot lines and different characters; however, there is a common opportunity to think about individuality and coming together as a community.

An important conversation to facilitate along with these lessons is a discussion around why we think authors tend to write about the same themes. What is it about losing a parent? Or being the new kid? Or defying the odds? Is it that we've all experienced these ideas to some degree in our own lives and we are looking to connect with others who have too? Guide students to think about how closely themes in books relate to our everyday lives. We're essentially given a gift by the author to have the chance to witness characters facing adversity so that we can learn from their choices and actions.

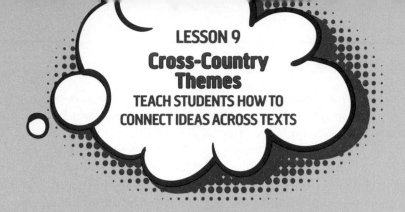

For students like Dyanna and Jeanette, the goal of this lesson is to consider themes across multiple texts. They might do this to

- Check to see that they are thinking about a true universal theme rather than topics or subjects
- Help them think in more complex ways about more than one text

This lesson teaches students to look back at their thinking (in notebook entries and conversations) across several books, to explore the possibility of connecting themes in multiple texts. This type of thinking requires students to synthesize several details across books.

thin slice

Decide to Teach This Tomorrow if Your Students

- Are ready to think beyond an initial understanding of the text
- Can interpret themes in one text and are ready to transfer that thinking across more than one text

What You Need:

- Multiple texts that share the possibility of common themes (Start with two texts and build to others if necessary. For example, you could excerpt scenes from *El Deafo* [Bell, 2014], *Rules* [Lord, 2006], and *Out of My Mind* [Draper, 2012] or choose two different short stories from the same collection. See Chapter 2 for more of our favorite teaching texts.)
- Your reading notebook
- Chart paper

Tell Why: Reminds students that themes are universal. When an idea is universal, it relates to more than one thing. Themes relate to multiple texts, people, movies, songs, and works of art. Explain that studying multiple texts benefits our reading because of the opportunity it affords us to think about texts in more ways than our initial thoughts or ideas.

(Continued)

Show How:

- Design a chart to track your thinking in your reading notebook. See the example below.

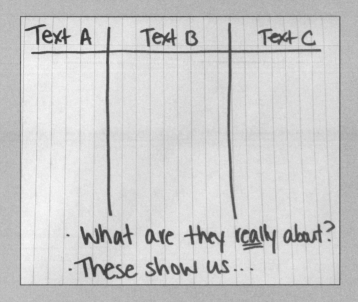

- Model your thinking through a few of these questions:
  - What's common about these characters?
  - What's common about the journey of the characters?
  - What's common about the adversity the characters face?
  - What's common in the reaction of the characters during moments of conflict?
- Demonstrate using your notebook entry as a system for organizing your thinking.

A Tip:

- An alternative version of this lesson is to teach students to begin cross-text thinking by thinking about themes and then looking for texts that match the theme. For example, a reader might be thinking about exploring the topic of fear and the theme that *fear can serve as motivation during certain times of our lives*. With this theme at the forefront of their thinking, we can teach readers to ask, "What other characters teach us this? In what stories is this a key part of the plot?"

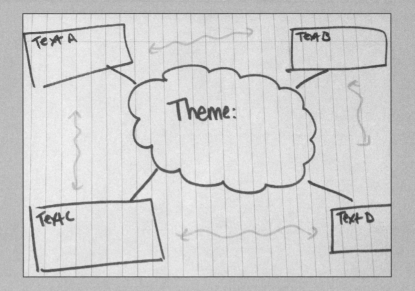

Friendship is when 2 or more people enjoy each others company, support each other, and are able to say and act natural around each other.

☆ As long as we are together By Judy Blume Is a book about 2 girls who are friends when a new girl comes to the neighborhood, 1 of the 2 girls really likes the new girl, and the other feels left out.

☆ My little pony is a tv show about 6 ponies who are best friends, but are opposites, which means sometimes they argue and annoy each other.

☆ Count on me By Bruno Mars is a song about how Bruno is there for his best friend and supporting him/her.

Simone's reading notebook entry reflects cross-text thinking about common topics that lead to themes in texts, media, and songs. She intentionally looked to make these connections.

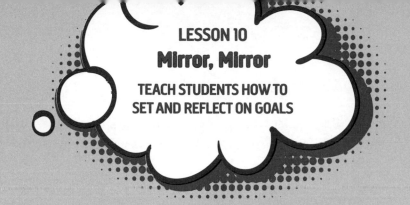

LESSON 10
Mirror, Mirror
TEACH STUDENTS HOW TO SET AND REFLECT ON GOALS

This lesson is designed to remind students like Simone of the importance of setting goals and reflecting on them. It's important to plan for teaching and time for students to think about what they are doing as readers and why they are doing it. Otherwise, students will robotically go through the motions of trying out strategies only because you've asked them to, resulting in a classroom full of dependent students. It's important to start the routine of reflection early so that students have time to practice and benefit from setting their own goals, working toward them, and accomplishing them.

Decide to Teach This Tomorrow if Your Students

- Think through interpretations of the text only when you ask them to
- Need an opportunity to think about their process, have a proud moment, and set goals
- Are wrapping up a unit of study that focuses on interpreting themes

thin slice

What You Need:

- Your reading notebook
- Chart paper

Tell Why: Recap all you have done together and highlight the growth students are making as individuals, partners, and a whole class. Remind students of the importance of looking back at our reading so that we can look forward in setting new goals. They have likely already done this when studying characters and can look back at those entries as a reminder.

(Continued)

Invite Reflection:

- Write a few reflective questions on chart paper.
  - What is your reading process for interpreting texts?
  - What strategies help you to interpret texts?
  - How does interpreting texts help you understand the world better?
- Ask students to reflect by writing some of their answers to the questions in their reading notebooks. Then give them time to have conversations about their reflections with their partners.
- Invite students to share excerpts of their reflections with the whole class.
- Give a few minutes for students to articulate their new goals either in writing or in a conversation with their partner. They might also ask their partner for support in meeting the goals.

A Tip:

- Remind everyone (students and teachers) of the importance of the process of goal setting and reflection. The word *yet* is powerful. We love this inspiring video from *Sesame Street* when Janelle Monáe sings about the power of *yet* (see https://youtu.be/XLeUvZvuvAs).

When students begin to make connections between interpreting themes and understanding people in their lives, they begin to recognize that reading work is life work.

> Interpreting themes help me by understanding the reason why a character will do it's actions. And also it will help me by knowing what is going on with the characters emotions. It also helps me in life by knowing how other people think and their stratigies to feel the emotions there feeling and how they will feel about my actions, either helping them or trying to help them. Like in my class

INTERPRETING THEMES: AN ACTION PLAN

As you continue to implement the thin-slicing protocol into your daily practice, you'll notice patterns in your students' thinking. We also hope you are learning to trust your instincts even more as you hone your ability to analyze students' thinking about themes. Give yourself permission to experiment and explore this decision-making process, knowing that it takes time to make something new your own.

Keep in mind the three types of thinking—frames, patterns, and lessons learned—as you prepare to teach students how to interpret themes in fiction texts. Meet with students in conferences or small groups to thin-slice and determine the type of thinking they tend to do. Use the information you gather from these conferences to decide what to teach next.

TYPES OF THINKING READERS USE WHEN INTERPRETING THEMES	THREE TEACHING CHOICES WE CAN MAKE
★ Frames ★ Patterns ★ Lessons Learned	1. Name and reinforce a type of thinking readers are already using. 2. Show readers a different type of thinking and model how to use it. 3. Coach readers to apply a currently used type of thinking in other sections or books.

GETTING STARTED WITH INTERPRETING THEMES

☐ Introduce interpreting theme lessons to students (see page 208).

☐ Confer with students and look for the types of thinking they tend to do. Use the clipboard notes on page 228 that shows the types of thinking.

☐ Make a choice about what to teach next. The three choices are shown above.

☐ Remember there is no such thing as a wrong choice if it is based on what you notice students doing.

WATCH!

Videos and viewing guide may also be accessed at
http://resources.corwin.com/GoldbergHouser-Fiction

 Small Group Work on Interpreting Themes: The Goal

Video 6.1

 Small Group Work on Interpreting Themes: The Lesson

Video 6.2

 Small Group Work on Interpreting Themes: Deciding What to Teach Next

Video 6.3

 Introducing Themes: The Goal

Video 6.4

 Introducing Themes With Image and Music: The Whole Group Lesson

Video 6.5

 Introducing Themes With a Familiar Text: A Follow-Up Lesson

Video 6.6

 Introducing Theme With Image, Music, and a Familiar Text: Deciding What to Teach Next

Video 6.7

© Andrew Levine

Becoming Confident and Intentional Decision Makers

"ONE OF THE THINGS I LEARNED FROM IMPROVISING IS THAT ALL OF LIFE IS AN IMPROVISATION, WHETHER YOU LIKE IT OR NOT. SOME OF THE GREATEST SCIENTIFIC DISCOVERIES OF THE 20TH CENTURY CAME OUT OF PEOPLE DROPPING THINGS."

(Alan Arkin)

Let's take one more look at thin-slicing and the power to trust our intuitions in the blink of an eye. Malcolm Gladwell (2005) explains that "the task of figuring out how to combine the best of conscious deliberation and instinctive judgment is one of the great challenges of our time. If you're a teacher and you want to make a decision about how to treat a student, how much do you weigh the results of standardized tests, and how much do you weigh your own judgment about the student's motivation and attitude and prospects?" (p. 269). Put another way, what are you looking for, and how will you find it? It is our hope that this book has helped you reflect on how you currently go about making reading instructional decisions and that you now see the value and power of using thin-slicing. When your students become your compass, there really are no wrong choices.

We created the following chart to help you feel more confident implementing the ideas and lessons from this book. We hope you are embracing the idea of being a thin-slicing improviser who gets cues from students about what to teach next. The first column of this chart can help you self-identify where you are right now, and then the right-hand columns offer some ideas for where to go next. Remember there is no such thing as a wrong decision, so thin-slice your classroom, where you currently are with teaching fiction, and then decide where to go from there. Sometimes our fear of making wrong choices gets in the way of getting us going, and we end up sticking to a script rather than being intentional in the moment. We are reminded of this quote from Nelson Mandela: "May your choices reflect your hopes and not your fears." What do you hope for your students?

thin slice

WHERE I AM TODAY	WHAT I CAN DO TOMORROW	WHAT I MIGHT WANT TO REVISIT
I teach whole class lessons using my school's basal reading program. I want to base more of my teaching on my students' needs, but we use a scripted program.	• Begin modeling how to have conversations about the texts students are reading in the basals. Listen and see if you can identify the types of thinking they are currently doing. • Create some time for students to choose what they want to read and learn about during independent reading. • Consider adding in read aloud experiences to model how you think, write, and talk about fiction texts. • Set aside some time for students to read independently their books of choice.	Revisit Chapter 2 to begin choosing engaging texts your students will love. Revisit Chapter 4 to begin showing students how to have powerful conversations.

(Continued)

(Continued)

WHERE I AM TODAY	WHAT I CAN DO TOMORROW	WHAT I MIGHT WANT TO REVISIT
I use guided reading with my students and meet with them in groups regularly. These groups are based on their instructional reading level. I want to diversify the differentiation in my classroom to more than just guided reading. I want students to have time and choice in their independent reading.	• Use guided reading time to identify your students' current types of thinking and jot down what you notice. Focus on either understanding characters or interpreting themes. • Consider reforming groups based on types of thinking and not just reading levels. Begin small group lessons with students who are ready for the same next step regardless of reading level.	If you are focusing on understanding characters, revisit the types of thinking in Chapter 5. If you are focusing on interpreting themes, revisit the types of thinking in Chapter 6.
I use a reading workshop model and teach minilessons based on my district's curriculum. I want to plan minilessons based specifically on what my students need.	• During reading conferences, look at student notebook entries and listen to the students discuss their thinking. Take notes on what types of thinking students are using and what you think they need next. • Plan some minilessons based on what you find during the conferences.	Use the lesson ideas in Chapters 5 and 6 to plan your own lessons.
My students use reading notebooks, but they only write when I tell them to write and they do as little as possible. I want students to use writing about reading as an authentic tool to push their thinking, and I want them to have identified when and why to use it independently.	• Look at how you currently talk about and use the notebooks in your classroom. Decide whether your students match the ones from our research in Chapter 3 who admit to only writing because they have to. • Create your own notebook and model how you use it authentically to collect and deepen your thinking. • Invite students to restart their notebooks in new ways after teaching some of the key lessons in Chapter 3.	Try the lessons from Chapter 3. Restart notebooks with students from the beginning if needed to change how they view the role of entries.
I teach whole class texts that everyone reads, and I give students questions and prompts to answer. I want to give students more choice in their reading.	• If your students like to talk, begin modeling how to have conversations about their fiction texts that help with understanding. • Begin offering daily time for students to talk about their thinking. • Use the whole class text as a read aloud, and model how you think and write about your thinking in your own writing notebook. • Consider moving away from assigning questions and moving toward more authentic reading notebook entries.	Revisit Chapter 3 about setting up notebook entries and Chapter 4 on creating classrooms with genuine conversations going on.

APPENDICES

Appendix A. Fiction Book Rating System

★★★ This book is outstanding in this category.

★★ This book does not wow us throughout, but has many standout parts.

★ Although this book has many attributes we love, this is not its strength.

FICTION BOOK RATING SYSTEM

Title _____

Author _____ Text Type _____

CHARACTERISTICS	RATING
Appeal	
Opportunities to Develop Empathy	
Representation	
Accessibility to Readers	

Appendix B. Some Favorite Fiction Texts

IF YOU LIKED	YOU MIGHT ALSO LIKE
Journey by Aaron Becker Page 26	• *Return* by Aaron Becker • *Quest* by Aaron Becker • *Wave* by Suzy Lee • *Tuesday* by David Wiesner • *Flotsam* by David Wiesner • *Zoom* by Istvan Banyai
Naked Mole Rat Gets Dressed Written and Illustrated by Mo Willems Page 28	• *One Green Apple* by Eve Bunting • *The Other Side* by Jacqueline Woodson • *Bedhead* by Margie Palatini • *Sweet Tooth* by Margie Palatini • *The Dot* by Peter H. Reynolds
Extra Yarn Written by Mac Barnett and Illustrated by Jon Klassen Page 30	• *The Uncorker of Ocean Bottles* by Michelle Cuevas • *Sam and Dave Dig a Hole* by Mac Barnett • *The Incredible Book Eating Boy* by Oliver Jeffers • *I Want My Hat Back* by Jon Klassen
Let's Go, Hugo! Written and Illustrated by Angela Dominguez Page 32	• *Not Norman* by Kelly Bennett • *Your Move* by Eve Bunting • *Spoon* by Amy Krouse Rosenthal
Days With Frog and Toad by Arnold Lobel Page 34	• *Henry and Mudge* by Cynthia Rylant • *Mr. Putter and Tabby* by Cynthia Rylant • *Poppleton* by Cynthia Rylant • *Pinky and Rex* by James Howe
Houndsley and Catina by James Howe Page 36	• *Bink and Gollie* by Kate DiCamillo and Alison McGhee • *Mercy Watson* by Kate DiCamillo • *Katie Woo* by Fran Manushkin • *Ivy and Bean* by Annie Barrows
First French Kiss and Other Traumas by Adam Bagdasarian Page 38	• *Every Living Thing* by Cynthia Rylant • *What Do Fish Have to Do With Anything?* by Avi • *America Street* edited by Anne Mazer • *Baseball in April and Other Stories* by Gary Soto • *After (Nineteen Stories of Apocalypse and Dystopia)* by Ellen Datlow and Terri Windling • *Shelf Life: Stories by the Book* by Gary Paulsen

IF YOU LIKED	YOU MIGHT ALSO LIKE
The Breadwinner by Deborah Ellis Page 40	• *Parvana's Journey* by Deborah Ellis • *Mud City* by Deborah Ellis • *Home of the Brave* by Katherine Applegate • *Weasel* by Cynthia DeFelice
Pax Written by Sara Pennypacker and Illustrated by Jon Klassen Page 41	• *The One and Only Ivan* by Katherine Applegate • *Crenshaw* by Katherine Applegate • *Glory Be* by Augusta Scattergood • *Kizzy Ann Stamps* by Jeri Watts
Rules by Cynthia Lord Page 42	• *Slob* by Ellen Potter • *One Crazy Summer* by Rita Williams-Garcia • *The Higher Power of Lucky* by Susan Patron • *How to Speak Dolphin* by Ginny Rorby
The Tiger Rising by Kate DiCamillo Page 43	• *Maniac Magee* by Jerry Spinelli • *Stargirl* by Jerry Spinelli • *Walk Two Moons* by Sharon Creech • *One of the Murphys* by Lynda Mullaly Hunt
Out of My Mind by Sharon Draper Page 44	• *Locomotion* by Jacqueline Woodson • *Wonder* by R. J. Palacio • *Fish in a Tree* by Lynda Mullaly Hunt • *Flipped* by Wendelin Van Draanen
Milkweed by Jerry Spinelli Page 45	• *Number the Stars* by Lois Lowry • *The Watsons Go to Birmingham* by Christopher Paul Curtis • *Freedom on the Menu* by Carole Boston Weatherford • *The Bracelet* by Yoshiko Uchida • *Kira Kira* by Cynthia Kadohata
El Deafo by Cece Bell Page 47	• *Amulet Series* by Kazu Kibuishi • *Fashion Kitty* by Charise Mericle Harper • *Babymouse* by Jennifer Holm
Roller Girl by Victoria Jamieson Page 50	• *Smile* by Raina Telgemeier • *Drama* by Raina Telgemeier • *Sisters* by Raina Telgemeier • *Hamster Princess: Harriet the Invincible* by Ursula Vernon

Appendix C. Clipboard Notes: Reading Notebook Entries

thin slice

NAME AND DATE	OBSERVATIONS
	☐ Writes to remember
	☐ Writes to record thinking
	☐ Shares writing and thinking with others
	☐ Organizes thinking
	☐ Uses writing to discover thinking
	☐ Other
Notes:	
	☐ Writes to remember
	☐ Writes to record thinking
	☐ Shares writing and thinking with others
	☐ Organizes thinking
	☐ Uses writing to discover thinking
	☐ Other
Notes:	

Appendix D. Clipboard Notes: Student Conversations

thin slice

NAME AND DATE	OBSERVATIONS
	Conversational Behaviors ☐ Initiates ☐ Listens ☐ Takes turns ☐ Clarifies ☐ Summarizes
	Conversational Tools ☐ Uses notebook entries ☐ References the text ☐ Uses classroom charts
	Conversations and Thinking ☐ Supports thinking ☐ Challenges thinking ☐ Inspires a plan ☐ Encourages rereading
	Other Notes:

Appendix E. Understanding Characters

thin
slice

UNDERSTANDING CHARACTERS IN FICTION TEXTS		
RIGHT-NOW THINKING	OVER-TIME THINKING	REFINING THINKING
What to look for: Thinking is based on one part of the text.	What to look for: Thinking happens in multiple places in the text. Ideas are based on connecting information from throughout the section or text.	What to look for: Changes in thinking are based on new scenes or events, or the thinking is made more specific from an earlier broad idea.
What a reader might say: *This character action means . . .* *I'm thinking . . . in this one part.* *I think this part shows the character is . . .*	What a reader might say: *Based on this scene and this event, I am thinking . . .* *When I look at this part and this part, I think . . .* *A pattern I am noticing is . . .* *Another example is . . .*	What a reader might say: *I used to think . . . but now I think . . .* *I no longer think this because . . .* *Based on more events, I now think . . .* *To be more specific, I now understand . . .*

Appendix F. Clipboard Notes: Types of Thinking About Understanding Characters

thin slice

WHAT THE READER SAID/WROTE	WHAT I NOTICE	TYPE OF THINKING
Name: Date:		☐ Right-Now Thinking ☐ Over-Time Thinking ☐ Refining Thinking

thin slice

INTERPRETING THEMES IN FICTION TEXTS		
FRAMES	PATTERNS	LESSONS LEARNED
What to look for:	What to look for:	What to look for:
Lessons you focus on such as personal and interpersonal relationships, societal issues, global issues, historical contexts, economic issues, gender issues, technological issues, etc.	Story elements, author's craft, word choice, your own reader reactions, repetition of character's choices, etc.	Turning points, changes in characters, morals, inner dialogue that reveals a bigger message, places where you are giving the characters advice, etc.
What a reader might say:	What a reader might say:	What a reader might say:
When I read this text thinking about . . . *I notice . . .* *The author is framing . . .* *in this way . . .* *The author's framing of . . . makes me think . . .*	*This is coming up again . . .* *A pattern I am noticing is . . .* *The pattern seems to be changing because . . .* *This pattern makes me think . . .*	*The character seems to be learning . . .* *Based on the character's experiences, I am learning . . .* *A bigger lesson I am thinking about is . . .* *This story seems to really be about . . .*

Appendix H. Clipboard Notes: Types of Thinking About Interpreting Themes

thin slice

WHAT THE READER SAID/WROTE	WHAT I NOTICE	TYPE OF THINKING
Name: Date:		☐ Frames ☐ Patterns ☐ Lessons Learned

REFERENCES

Ambady, N., & Rosenthal, R. (1993). Half a minute: Predicting teacher evaluations from thin slices of nonverbal behavior and physical attractiveness. *Journal of Personality and Social Psychology, 64*(3), 431–441.

Angelillo, J. (2003). *Writing about reading: From book talk to literary essays, grades 3–8*. Portsmouth, NH: Heinemann.

Bagdasarian, A. (2003). *First French kiss and other traumas*. London, UK: Walker.

Barnett, M. (2012). *Extra yarn*. New York, NY: HarperCollins.

Barnhouse, D., & Vinton, V. (2012). *What readers really do: Teaching moves and language to match process to instruction*. Portsmouth, NH: Heinemann.

Baxter, C. (2007). *The art of the subtext: Beyond plot*. Minneapolis, MN: Graywolf Press.

Beck, I. L., McKeown, M. G., & Kucan, L. (2002). *Bringing words to life: Robust vocabulary instruction*. New York, NY: Guilford Press.

Becker, A. (2013). *Journey*. Somerville, MA: Candlewick Press.

Beers, K., & Probst, R. E. (2012). *Notice & note: Strategies for close reading*. Portsmouth, NH: Heinemann.

Bell, C. (2014). *El deafo*. New York, NY: Abrams.

Bergen, B. K. (2012). *Louder than words: The new science of how the mind makes meaning*. New York, NY: Basic Books.

Blau, S. (2003). Performative literacy: The habits of mind of highly literate readers. *Voices From the Middle, 10*(3). Retrieved from http://www.northernhighlands.org/cms/lib5/NJ01000179/Centricity/Domain/149/BlauPerfLit.pdf

Borko, H., & Shavelson, R. J. (1990). Teacher decision making. In B. F. Jones & L. Idol (Eds.), *Dimensions of thinking and cognitive instruction* (pp. 311–346). Hillsdale, NJ: Erlbaum.

Bradbury, R. (1992). Zen in the art of writing. In *Zen in the art of writing: Releasing the creative genius within you* (pp. 123–140). New York, NY: Bantam Books.

Brown, B. (2015). *Rising strong*. New York, NY: Spiegel & Grau.

Bunting, E. (2006). *One green apple*. New York, NY: Clarion Books.

Burkins, J. M., & Yaris, K. (2016). *Who's doing the work? How to say less so readers can do more*. Portland, ME: Stenhouse.

Burroway, J., Stuckey-French, E., & Stuckey-French, N. (2006). *Writing fiction: A guide to narrative craft*. New York, NY: Pearson.

Calkins, L. (2001). *The art of teaching reading*. New York, NY: Longman.

Campbell, J., & Moyers, B. D. (1988). *The power of myth*. New York, NY: Doubleday.

Canales, V. (2005). *The tequila worm*. New York, NY: Random House.

Collins, S. (2008). *The hunger games*. New York, NY: Scholastic.

Cook, E. (2011). *Fourth grade fairy*. New York, NY: Aladdin.

Cunningham, K. E. (2015). *Story: Still the heart of literacy learning*. Portland, ME: Stenhouse.

DiCamillo, K. (2005). *The tiger rising*. Cambridge, MA: Candlewick Press.

Dominguez, A. N. (2013). *Let's go, Hugo!* New York, NY: Dial Books for Young Readers.

Draper, S. (2012). *Out of my mind*. New York, NY: Atheneum Books for Young Readers.

Duncan, L. (1997). *Gallows hill*. New York, NY: Bantam Doubleday Dell.

Ellis, D. (2001). *The breadwinner*. Toronto, ON: Groundwood Books.

Emig, J. (1977). Writing as a mode of learning. *College Composition and Communication, 28*(2), 122. doi:10.2307/356095

Ferlazzo, L. (2014, February 22). *Quote of the day: Have you ever wondered how many decisions we teachers need to make each day?* Retrieved from http://larryferlazzo.edublogs.org/2014/02/22/quote-of-the-day-have-you-ever-wondered-how-many-decisions-we-teachers-need-to-make-each-day/

Fisher, D., & Frey, N. (2009). *Background knowledge: The missing piece of the comprehension puzzle.* Portsmouth, NH: Heinemann.

Fisher, D., Frey, N., & Hattie, J. (2016). *Visible learning for literacy.* Thousand Oaks, CA: Corwin.

Fletcher, R. J. (1993). *What a writer needs.* Portsmouth, NH: Heinemann.

Frey, N., & Fisher, D. (2013). *Rigorous reading: 5 access points for comprehending complex texts.* Thousand Oaks, CA: Corwin Literacy.

Gladwell, M. (2005). *Blink: The power of thinking without thinking.* New York, NY: Little, Brown.

Glatshteyn, Y. (2006). *Emil and Karl* (J. Shandler, trans.). New York, NY: Square Fish. (Original work published 1940)

Goldberg, G. (2016). *Mindsets and moves: Strategies that help readers take charge.* Thousand Oaks, CA: Corwin.

Goldberg, G., & Serravallo, J, (2007). *Conferring with readers: Supporting each student's growth and independence.* Portsmouth, NH: Heinemann.

Harper, D. (2016). Study. *Online Etymology Dictionary.* Retrieved from http://www.etymonline.com/index.php?l=s&p=89&allowed_in_frame=

Hattie, J. (2012). *Visible learning for teachers: Maximizing impact on learning.* London, UK: Routledge.

Hattie, J., & Yates, G. C. (2014). *Visible learning and the science of how we learn.* Thousand Oaks, CA: Corwin.

Henkes, K. (1991). *Chrysanthemum.* New York, NY: Greenwillow Books.

Howard, M. (2012). *Good to great teaching: Focusing on the literacy work that matters.* Portsmouth, NH: Heinemann.

Howard, T. C. (2013). *Black male(d): Peril and promise in the education of African American males.* New York, NY: Teachers College Press.

Howe, J. (2006). *Houndsley and Catina.* Cambridge, MA: Candlewick Press.

Howe, J. (Ed.). (2006). *13: Thirteen stories that capture the agony and ecstasy of being thirteen.* New York, NY: Atheneum Books for Young Readers.

Jamieson, V. (2015). *Roller girl.* New York, NY: Penguin Group.

Johnston, P. H. (2012). *Opening minds: Using language to change lives.* Portland, ME: Stenhouse.

Keene, E. O., & Zimmermann, S. (2007). *Mosaic of thought: The power of comprehension strategy instruction.* Portsmouth, NH: Heinemann.

Kidd, D. C., & Costano, E. (2013). Reading literary fiction improves theory of mind. *Science, 342*(6156), 377–380. Retrieved from http://science.sciencemag.org/content/342/6156/377

Kondo, M. (2014). *The life-changing magic of tidying up: The Japanese Art of decluttering and organizing.* Berkeley, CA: Ten Speed Press.

Kondo, M. (2015). *Life-changing magic: Spark joy every day.* New York, NY: Random House.

Larson, K. (2010). *The fences between us: The diary of Piper Davis* [a Dear America series book]. New York, NY: Scholastic.

Lobel, A. (1971). *Frog and Toad together.* New York, NY: HarperCollins.

Lobel, A. (1979). *Days with Frog and Toad.* New York, NY: HarperCollins.

Lord, C. (2006). *Rules.* New York, NY: Scholastic.

Lowry, L. (1993). *The giver.* New York, NY: Houghton Mifflin.

Martinelli, M., & Mraz, K. (2012). *Smarter charts, K–2: Optimizing an instructional staple to create independent readers and writers.* Portsmouth, NH: Heinemann.

McKnight, K. S., & Scruggs, M. (2008). *The Second City guide to improv in the classroom: Using improvisation to teach skills and boost learning.* San Francisco, CA: Jossey-Bass.

Mills, C. W. (2000). *The sociological imagination.* Oxford, UK: Oxford University Press.

Munsch, R. (1980). *The paper bag princess.* Willowdale, ON: Firefly.

Munsch, R. (1986). *Love you forever.* Willowdale, ON: Firefly.

Palacio, R. J. (2012). *Wonder.* New York, NY: Knopf.

Paterson, K. (1977). *Bridge to Terabithia.* New York, NY: HarperCollins.

Penn, A. (1993). *The kissing hand.* Washington, DC: Child Welfare League of America.

Pennypacker, S. (2016). *Pax.* New York, NY: Balzer & Bray.

Pink, D. H. (2010). *Drive: The surprising truth about what motivates us.* Edinburgh, Scotland: Canongate.

Quaglia, R. J., & Lande, L. L. (2016). *Teacher voice: Amplifying success.* Thousand Oaks, CA: Corwin.

Ray, K. W. (1999). *Wondrous words: Writers and writing in the elementary classroom.* Urbana, IL: National Council of Teachers of English.

Ray, K. W. (2010). *In pictures and in words: Teaching the qualities of good writing through illustration study.* Portsmouth, NH: Heinemann.

Rhodes-Courter, A. (2008). *Three little words.* New York, NY: Atheneum Books for Young Readers.

Rief, L. (2007). Writing: Commonsense matters. In G. K. Beers, R. E. Probst, & L. Rief (Eds.), *Adolescent literacy: Turning promise into practice* (pp. 189–208). Portsmouth, NH: Heinemann.

Riordan, R. (2005). *Percy Jackson and the lightning thief.* London, UK: Puffin Books.

Riordan, R. (2009). *The last Olympian.* New York, NY: Hyperion Books.

Roth, V. (2011). *Divergent.* New York, NY: HarperCollins.

Russell, R. R. (2009). *Dork diaries: Tales from a not-so-fabulous life.* New York, NY: Aladdin.

Sinek, S. (2009). *Start with why: How great leaders inspire everyone to take action.* New York, NY: Portfolio.

Soto, G. (1990). *Baseball in April and other stories.* New York, NY: Harcourt Children's Books.

Spinelli, J. (1990). *Maniac Magee.* Boston, MA: Little, Brown.

Spinelli, J. (2005). *Milkweed.* New York, NY: Scholastic.

Stevenson, S. (2014, March 30). Getting to "yes, and." *Slate.* Retrieved from http://www.slate.com/articles/business/crosspollination/2014/03/improv_comedy_and_business_getting_to_yes_and.html

Swinehart, J. (2009). Metacognition: How thinking about their thinking empowers students. In S. Plaut (Ed.), *The right to literacy in secondary schools: Creating a culture of thinking* (pp. 25–35). New York, NY: Teachers College Press.

Turkle, S. (2015). *Reclaiming conversation: The power of talk in a digital age.* New York, NY: Penguin Press.

Waber, B. (1972). *Ira sleeps over.* New York, NY: Houghton Mifflin.

Willems, M. (2009). *Naked mole rat gets dressed.* New York, NY: Hyperion Books for Children.

Winne, P. H., & Hadwin, A. F. (2008). The weave of motivation and self-regulated learning. In D. H. Schunk & B. J. Zimmerman (Eds.), *Motivation and self-regulated learning: Theory, research, and applications* (pp. 297–314). Hillsdale, NJ: Erlbaum.

Woods, B. (2009). The right to think: Giving adolescents the skills to make sense of the world. In S. Plaut (Ed.), *The right to literacy in secondary schools: Creating a culture of thinking* (pp. 13–24). New York, NY: Teachers College Press.

Woodson, J. (2001). *The other side.* New York, NY: Putnam's Sons.

Woodson, J. (2003). *Locomotion.* New York, NY: Putnam's Sons.

INDEX

Telling habit, 13–16
Tequila Worm, The, 117
Thematic teaching, 202–203
Themes, 121–122
    as abstract and universal or specific to texts, 203–204
    action plan, 251
    All-Terrain Vehicles lesson, 223–225
    Behind the Curtain lesson, 216–217
    clipboard notes, 264
    coaching readers to apply currently used type of thinking in other sections or books, 243–244
    Cross-Country Themes lesson, 246–248
    Curve Ahead lesson, 220–222
    decided by authors or readers, 204–205
    deciding what to teach next about, 238–239
    DIY Best-Seller List lesson, 210–212
    Dog-Eared Pages lesson, 208–209
    Framed! lesson, 231–232
    frames, 226, 229–232, 264
    Gasp Factor lesson, 213–215
    importance of studying, 206
    interpreting, 201
    lessons learned, 226, 234–236, 264
    Lessons Learned lesson, 218–219
    Mirror, Mirror lesson, 249–250
    in multiple texts, interpreting, 245
    patterns, 226, 233–234, 264
    reading skills that fit into interpreting, 206–207
    reinforcing type of thinking about, 238–241
    showing a different type of thinking about, 241–243, 265
    subject, topic, or, 201–202
    thematic teaching or teaching, 202–203
    using patterns to interpret, 236–237
    what to look for when students interpret, 226–228
Think It, Write It! lesson, 80–81
Thin-slicing, 1
    character study, 168–175
    fiction texts, 24–25
    helping decision making, 4–5
    student conversations, 118–119, 134
    theme interpretation, 228

13: Thirteen Stories That Capture the Agony and Ecstasy of Being Thirteen, 33
Three Little Words, 234
Three-phase model of learning, 7–8
Tiger Rising, The, 43, 121, 135, 216, 223
Top Dog and Underdog lesson, 191
Transfer, 7
Turkle, S., 154
Turning points, 220–222

Universal themes, 203–204
U-Turn lesson, 92–94

Video resources
    character study, 199
    read alouds, 54
    reading notebooks, 109
    student conversations, 150
    teacher decision-making practices, 21
    themes, 252
Vinton, V., 12
Visible Learning for Literacy, 7, 76

Waber, B., 196
"What next" question, 5–8
When Ira Sleeps Over, 196
Whose Line Is It Anyway?, 2
Willems, M., 28–29, 231, 245
Winne, P. H., 19
Woods, B., 18
Wordless books. *See* Picture books and wordless books
Working World, The, lesson 67–68
Worksheets, 99–102
Writing
    about reading, reasons for, 61–62
    lessons that wake up, 63–72
    notebooks (*See* Notebooks, writing)
    teacher-assigned written responses, 102–105
    as tool for understanding, 58–61
    what to let go of when asking students for, 99–107
Writing About Reading, 106

Yaris, K., 23
Yates, G., 5
You Got This! lesson, 66

NOTES

NOTES

NOTES

NOTES

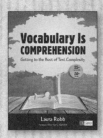

BECAUSE ALL TEACHERS ARE LEADERS

Gravity Goldberg, EdD, holds a doctorate in education from Teachers College, Columbia University, in New York City. She is a former staff developer at Teachers College Reading and Writing Project and was an assistant professor at Iona College's graduate education program. She leads a team of literacy consultants and is a sought-after professional development resource.

LEARNING OUTCOMES

Participants will
- Leave with specific ideas (and strategies to implement) on how to ensure their teaching leads to reader ownership and greater student independence
- Learn how to help every student find his or her niche and restructure lessons to support meaningful student engagement
- Discover how to use authentic assessment techniques that help teachers know where each student is and understand what steps to take next to improve his or her reading

POPULAR WORKSHOPS (Other Workshops Available)

Supporting Student Independence: Creating Classrooms Where Students Take Charge

Drawing on the research on mindset, Gravity helps participants look at what gets in the way of student independence, as well as how to apply the research on motivation and engagement each and every day with a framework called the 4 Ms. Teachers of all subject areas will leave with concrete ideas for what they can do (and possibly stop doing) so students can take charge of their own learning process.

Tweaking the Gradual Release Model to Support Ownership and Independence

Gravity clarifies what the gradual release model is and breaks down each part of the model into manageable and easy-to-replicate steps. Teachers will learn how to use the gradual release model of instruction dynamically so that it brings about amazing learning results in the reading and writing classroom.

Cultivating Growth Mindsets With Readers

Gravity explains the concept of mindset and the relevant research about how it impacts student readers. Teachers then learn the moves they can make to identify students' mindsets and, if needed, help shift them toward greater growth.

Teacher Decision Making

Gravity helps teachers develop confidence in their decisions by streamlining their process and offering a framework for using students as the guides. Teachers learn to "thin slice" student work and conversations to decide what each reader needs next.

To bring Gravity Goldberg to your school/district, call 800-831-6640

CORWIN HAS ONE MISSION: to enhance education through intentional professional learning.

We build long-term relationships with our authors, educators, clients, and associations who partner with us to develop and continuously improve the best evidence-based practices that establish and support lifelong learning.